Issues in Public Sector Accounting

Edited by
ANTHONY HOPWOOD
Professor of Accounting, London Business School

and
CYRIL TOMKINS
Professor of Accounting, University of Bath

Philip Allan

First published 1984 by

Philip Allan Publishers Limited
Market Place
Deddington
Oxford OX5 4SE

British Library Cataloguing in Publication Data

Issues in public sector accounting.
1. Finance. Public — Great Britain —
Accounting
I. Hopwood, Tony   II. Tomkins, Cyril R.
657.835′ 00941   HJ9925.G

ISBN 0-86003-523-9
ISBN 0-86003-622-7 Pbk

Typeset by Typesetters Birmingham Ltd,
Smethwick, West Midlands
Printed and bound in Great Britain by
Billing and Sons Ltd, Worcester

CONTENTS

v

Part 2   Financial Planning and Control

Part 3   Value for Money and Performance Review

vii

CONTRIBUTORS

I. Colville	Lecturer in Management Control, University of Bath
J. Fielden	Consultant, Peat, Marwick, Mitchell & Company
N. Hepworth	Director, The Chartered Institute of Public Finance and Accountancy
C. Holtham	Director of Finance, London Borough of Hammersmith and Fulham
A. Hopwood	Professor of Accounting and Financial Reporting, London Business School
S. Jönsson	Professor of Accounting, University of Gothenburg
P. Kimmance	Member of the Audit Commission for Local Authorities in England and Wales; formerly Chief Inspector of Audit, Department of the Environment
A. Likierman	Senior Lecturer in Accounting, London Business School
L. Metcalfe	Civil Service College, London
J. Perrin	Director, Centre for Research in Industry, Business and Administration, University of Warwick
S. Richards	Civil Service College, London
J. Stewart	Professor and Director of the Institute of Local Government Studies, University of Birmingham
C. Tomkins	Professor of Accounting and Finance, University of Bath
P. Vass	Assistant Secretary, The Chartered Institute of Public Finance and Accountancy

1
Introduction

ANTHONY HOPWOOD and
CYRIL TOMKINS

In a very short period of time, accounting in the public sector has become a major topic for both debate and action. Today much more attention is given to the accountings made by central and local government agencies, nationalised industries and the mass of other bodies that constitute the public sector than previously. Greater demands are being made for regular reviews of the financial performance of public sector bodies. The mechanisms for government audit and efficiency and value-for-money assessments have been both discussed and reformed. Within the machinery of government itself more attention is now being given to the adequacy of financial management practices. Consideration is being given to the changes that need to be made to management accounting systems, approaches to financial planning and the appraisal of the financial implications of new policy initiatives. Indeed, wherever one looks in the public sector, accounting topics have become the subject of very active debate and reform in the last few years.

The sources of this upsurge of interest are diverse. A period of major economic restraint has put pressure on existing instruments of financial management, and the resulting resource constraints have placed a premium on the efficient use of public sector resources, both actual and prospective. Greater demands have also been made for improvements in the financial accountability of public sector bodies. More and more requests are being made to observe, question and appraise the financial management of those in positions of responsibility. Equally, changing conceptions of the role of the state have served to emphasise the need to analyse and question the economic activities and consequences of public sector organisations. How efficient are they? Are their actions in line with the original plans and policies? Just how can the imperatives of economic efficiency be pursued within the machinery of government?

The raising of such questions has already resulted in quite major changes within the public sector. Existing mechanisms for financial planning, budgeting and control have come under serious review. Through the Financial Management Initiative, attention is now being given to the design of more comprehensive and more management-orientated financial information systems. Comparable exercises are underway in many local government, health and water authorities and in the nationalised industries. Serious attention has also been given to improving the ways in which the Treasury can monitor, influence and control the financial consequences of public sector activities. In addition, more assessments of the adequacy of public sector performance have been made not only by the newly reorganised National Audit Office, but also by the Cabinet Office, the Monopolies and Mergers Commission and a host of other agencies and external parties scattered throughout the public sector.

In these and other ways, much more emphasis is now being placed on the economic costs and consequences of public sector activities. As a result, accounting has very quickly become more generally recognised as a skill relevant and useful to the management of public affairs.

Indeed, the speed of these developments is such that they are straining both the human and the intellectual resources available for their implementation. Public sector accounting was once the specialised activity of a relatively small number of professionals. Now, however, it is in the process of becoming a much more substantive and significant area of accounting endeavour. As a result, accountants with little or no experience of the conduct of activity in the public sector are being called upon to contribute to its accounting. Equally, relatively little consideration has been given to many of the conceptual and practical problems raised by public sector accounting developments. Action has been demanded; thought has often been considered a luxury. There is, for instance, very little tradition of public sector accounting research and very few accounting academics have been concerned with public sector questions. However, the nature of current pressures for change is such that many quite fundamental and practically significant questions are being, and should be, raised.

How can accounting systems be designed to relate to the competing demands of both public and management accountability? Can they complement, rather than merely confront, the very different styles of organisation and management that prevail in the public sector today? And are methods developed in the private sector likely to be appropriate? If not, can they be adapted to account for the more contested domain of the public sector, and with what effects? Just how will greater investments in accounting affect other aspects of organisational and public life? These and a host of more detailed questions abound in all areas of the public sector. In health care, the social services, water supply, and all other agencies of both central and local government, questions arise about the nature of their interest in accounting, the relationships it might have to both the management of the organisation and the existing distribution of power and influence, and its ability to map the aims, tasks and outcomes of particular organisations both accurately and sympathetically; for, in every specific area of public sector activity, it can quite legitimately be asked how the general aims of the accounting endeavour will intersect with the particular operations in which it is embedded. Just how are these often complex and uncertain activities to be accounted for? What parts of the organisation will feature in the accounts? Who will see the resultant information, and how will it be taken up in ongoing organisational processes? What decisions are likely to be made on the basis of it? And with what effects?

Rather than focusing on either the more general aims of the accounting mission, or the technical practice of accounting, in isolation from the contexts in which it operates, most such questions focus on how specific accountings operate in specific contexts with specific effects; for it is these questions which need to be considered before accounting can be effectively mobilised in the public sector and before any real understanding can be gained of its likely achievements and consequences. Yet, it is precisely this knowledge of the organisational, institutional and social nature of accounting practice that is weakest at the present time. To date, accounting in the public sector has been advanced in the name of its general aims, and what accounting treatises exist tend to focus on the technical nature of accounting practice. The domain of the organisational practice of accounting, which lies between the general and the technical, has been relatively ignored despite the fact that this is where many of the more problematic issues associated with the practice of accounting in the public sector arise.

Many of the contributions collected in the present volume are designed to address issues in the intermediate area between the general potential and the specific technical practice of public sector accounting. Consideration is given to some of the significant factors lying behind the current interest in the area, some of the important policy debates and the ways in which accounting intersects with other organisational processes in the public domain.

Some Issues for Debate

The contributions are organised into three sections. First, consideration is given to questions of external reporting and accountability. Thereafter, aspects of internal accounting are discussed, emphasising the roles which accounting and accountants play in financial planning and control in public sector organisations. Finally, attention is devoted to performance monitoring and review, with particular consideration being given to the practice of efficiency and value-for-money assessments.

External Reporting and Accountability

In Chapter 2, Stewart considers the wider concern with accountability which gives rise to an interest in accounting. He discusses the pressures which are resulting in greater demands for public sector accountability and some of the institutional developments which are occurring, as well as some which are not, in response to these demands. The management of public information flows, including those provided by accounting, is seen by Stewart as just one of these institutional developments, albeit an important one. Information, however, is not an end in itself in the public arena. Stewart makes it quite clear that information constitutes only the basis for judgement and action, and that accounting, as a source of information, provides, as yet, only a part of the information required for an effective basis for the informed exercise of accountability in the public domain.

The agenda which Stewart provides for those interested in public sector accounting is a challenging and provocative one. Can accounting, he wonders, provide the information that is necessary for the review of policy as well as management accountability? Is it possible for it to make adequate and useful assessments in terms other than the financial? And can accounting be made to map the growing complexity of governmental organisations and activities? Perhaps more controversially, he asks whether accounting can be made to facilitate more actively the political processes surrounding public decision making. Is it possible, he wonders, for accountants to recognise the interested nature of the accounts that they provide? Can accountants even aim to provide accountings from the diverse perspectives of those who are active in the political arena?

Discussing the roles which accounting standards can serve in the public sector, Hepworth and Vass emphasise in Chapter 3 the political and institutional grounding of interests in public sector accounting. In their discussion of the seemingly technical problems of accounting standardisation, they reflect repeatedly on the ways in which organisational and political factors influence the nature of accounting practice.

Interests in particular accounting standards emerge because of the effects that they are seen to have. The accounts provided by public sector organisations are seen as reflecting both their different institutional traditions and their location in the network of other public organisations. Debates also take place over the appropriate institutional location for the standardisation of public sector accounting. Even such central bodies as the government and Parliament are seen to have conflicting interests over the achievement of the enhanced organisational comparability that more standardised accounting practices might provide.

Thus, however desirable accounting standardisation might be, and Hepworth and Vass have no doubts on this, progress towards this goal cannot be seen in purely technical terms. Standardisation increases the ability of some to examine and compare the activities and performance of others. Equally, it increases the probability that those others will themselves be examined and compared. Particular standards will have a particular impact on the activities and performance that are reflected in the accounts. For reasons such as these, accounting standardisation is inextricably enmeshed in an institutional context which results in the need to consider organisational and political, as well as technical, questions.

By focusing on one specific area of accounting practice, namely accounting for public sector assets, Perrin usefully demonstrates in Chapter 4 how technical accounting questions and options arise in the context of policy discussions, planning processes and the monitoring, evaluation and review of the performance of organisations in the public sector. He shows how discussion of such questions as the alternative use of public sector resources, their equitable pricing, distribution and financing, and the adequacy of financial return, results in a need to critically assess the state of current accounting practice in the public sector. Once again, therefore, it is shown how technical issues in public sector accounting come to be grounded in the social, economic and political debates which shape the contexts in which accounting operates.

Financial Planning and Control

The organisational bases of accounting practice are explicitly discussed by Tomkins and Colville in Chapter 5. In contrast to traditional normative approaches to the roles which accounting should have in the public sector, they emphasise how the specific contexts in which accounting systems operate influence how the information they provide is actually used. Basing their discussion on two contrasting departments in a local government authority, Tomkins and Colville illustrate how organisational structures, the nature of tasks, organisational climates and traditions, and intra-organisational networks of power and influence have a profound effect on the significance which is attached to accounting, the roles which it is required and allowed to serve, and the consequences which it has for both organisational functioning and performance.

In Chapter 6, Holtham emphasises both the economic and the political contexts of the current interest in improved financial planning and control in the public sector, and goes on to provide a useful review of the main technical developments that have taken place in the area in recent years. Giving particular consideration to developments in local government, he discusses organisational planning, approaches to the appraisal of capital projects, budgetary control, and some of the impacts which developments in information technology are likely to have. Throughout the discussion Holtham also emphasises the need to relate technical accounting practices to the context of the organisations in which they operate. If this is not done, he warns, the technical developments may have little, or even a negative, effect on organisational efficiency.

A contrasting but complementary discussion of the impact of economic restraint and political change is provided by Jönsson in Chapter 7. Although clearly aware of the technical innovations that are introduced to facilitate financial planning and budgeting in the midst of environmental uncertainty and political debate, Jönsson nevertheless emphasises the continuities in the organisational processes which shape how the new and seemingly more rational practices of budgeting are used, and the effects which they have. The discussion emphasises the complexities of financial decision making in a political context, the consequences of both task and political uncertainty, and the rationalities inherent in the organisational processes of bargaining and commitment generation and maintenance which confront the very different rationalities on which the technical practices of accounting are usually designed.

The struggles of the British central government with the dilemmas analysed by Jönsson provide the basis for Likierman's discussion (in Chapter 8) of recent developments in financial planning and control. Economic, political and institutional change and uncertainty provide the backcloth for a review of the emergence and functioning of cash planning, the imposition of cash limits, and developments in both internal financial control and the mechanisms for the enhancement of parliamentary control. Likierman's discussion makes it clear that in none of these areas have we witnessed an unfolding of the technically obvious. In all cases, technical innovations have emerged from the flux of political and administrative practice. Rather than being well designed and articulated, the use of the technically new has been associated with uncertainty, vigorous debate and frequent revision and change.

Value for Money and Performance Review

Recent years have witnessed the emergence of a major new emphasis on government efficiency and the achievement of 'value for money' in the public sector. In Chapter 9, Hopwood discusses both the pressures for this change and some of the consequences which might result.

Emphasising the ways in which many of the new interests in the roles which accounting might serve in the public sector have emerged from political rhetoric, Hopwood notes the gap which frequently exists between the missions which are created for accounting and the specific accounting practices to which these give rise. The specific accountings can often have a large measure of autonomy from the rationales which gave rise to them. They can still have quite significant organisational and social consequences however, frequently including ones that were not part of their original justification. Hopwood discusses how accounting has the potential to change patterns of organisational visibility, influence and legitimacy, and, over time, to shape that which is regarded as significant, problematic, desirable and possible.

A detailed study of one recent attempt to increase the efficiency of government operations is provided by Metcalf and Richards in Chapter 10. Based on the experiences of the Rayner initiative, an analysis is provided of the ways in which the concept and practices of efficiency function in public organisations. Once again, the organisational prerequisites of change are emphasised. Consideration is given to the mobilisation of a will to change, the securing and maintenance of commitment, and the strategies which might be associated with more radical and lasting reform.

More general discussions of the role of review and audit in the achievement of efficiency and accountability are provided in Chapters 11 and 12 by Fielden and Kimmance respectively. After charting the diversity of present practices, Fielden discusses the arguments and debates which have taken place in recent years over the nature, role, location and affiliation of public audits. Many of the same issues are addressed by Kimmance, though in a different way and from a different perspective. Attempting to ground present controversies in the debates and changes which have taken place over several decades, Kimmance stresses that neither the roles expected of auditing, nor the practices by which we try to realise them, are static. Not only do public expectations change but, in addition, many of the problems that auditors of efficiency and effectiveness face reach to the very heart of the political process; and here, however helpful the new technical approaches and organisational arrangements may be, the policy choices which have both been made and remain to be made must ultimately be confronted. This suggests, if nothing else, that the debate on public sector auditing is likely to remain an open one.

Conclusion

Taken together the contributions to this volume do not provide a conventional text. That, however, has not been our aim. As both the discussion of the problems which we seek to address and the review of the arguments to follow should have made clear, public sector accounting is an area that is still subject to debate and change. Moreover, many of the important debates in the area cannot, and should not, be divorced from those political and organisational processes which give rise to the significance of the accounting issues and shape the consequences which accounting developments can have. All of the contributions to this volume make this clear. By doing so in the context of a wide range of different aspects of public sector accounting, they provide, together, a rich, fruitful and realistic basis for considering the forces which shape accounting in the public domain, the roles which it is, and should be, asked to serve, and the possibilities, both technical and organisational, which exist to secure the improvement of its practice.

Part 1
External Reporting and Accountability

2

The Role of Information in Public Accountability

J. D. STEWART

In our society the exercise of governmental powers is legitimated by the requirements of public accountability. Those who exercise the power of government have to be publicly accountable for their action. It is on that basis that the very substantial powers of government are accepted. It is public accountability that is relied upon to transform arbitrary action into the legitimate exercise of governmental power.

Public accountability, like accountability itself, is not a simple concept. The requirement that those who exercise public power should be accountable for that exercise may appear simple and clear, but the application of that requirement to the complexity of government and to the variety of forms taken by governmental organisation is by no means straightforward.

Public accountability has been defined by Normanton as

> consisting in a statutory obligation to provide for independent and impartial observers holding the right of reporting their findings at the highest level in the state any available information about financial administration which they request. (Normanton, 1966)

Normanton appears, however, to be defining an intermediate stage in public accountability, namely, public audit, which is a commonly found component in public accountability, but does not by itself constitute public accountability. After all, when audit is complete, accountability has still to be applied. In fact, the need for a wider concept of public accountability is recognised by Normanton in his later work: 'Public accountability is a pheno-menon associated with the Western-type states. It calls for openly declared facts and open debate of them by laymen and their elected representatives' (Normanton, 1971, p. 312). He goes on to describe public accountability in wider terms than would be used for other forms of accountability. 'There is no clear master–servant relation-ship; public accountability means reporting to persons other than to one's own superiors who have the power to make open criticism' (Normanton, 1971, p. 313). The stress here is upon information and upon debate and discussion about the information.

Jackson has argued that,

> Basically, accountability involves explaining or justifying what has been done, what is currently being done and what has been planned. Accountability arises from a set of established procedures and relation-ships of varying formality. Thus, one party is accountable to another in the sense that one of the parties has the right to call upon the other to give an account of his activities. Accountability involves, therefore, the giving of information. (Jackson, 1982)

This is a restricted concept of accountability limited to the provi-sion of information. Dunsire (1978), on the other hand, goes further, arguing that

> Being accountable may mean as is now said about ministerial responsi-bility, no more than having to answer questions about what has happened or is happening within one's jurisdiction . . . But most usages require an additional implication: the answer when given, or the account, when rendered, is to be evaluated by the superior or superior body, measured against some standard or some expectation, and the difference noted; and then praise or blame are to be meted out or sanctions applied. It is the coupling of information with its evaluation and application of sanctions that gives 'accountability' or 'answerability' or 'responsibility' their full sense in ordinary organisational usage.

Dunsire has recognised that the common usage of accountability involves information (and not merely financial information), and also evaluation of that information, and that it is then that praise or blame is applied.

Accountability has also been seen as an element within the concept of responsibility (Jones, 1977). Accountability

> is the liability to give an account to another of what one has done or not. done. It is the antithesis of autonomy, where accountability is to oneself alone. Responsibility as accountability implies a liability to

explain to someone else, who has authority to assess the account, and allocate praise or censure. (Jones, 1977)

Or again,

> In governmental terms, . . . a responsible person or institution is one on whom is laid a task, function or role to perform, together with the capability to carry it out. There is also conferred some discretion and the liability to account for the performance of the duty, which should induce the person or institution to act with concern for the consequences of the decisions made and, in so deciding, to act in conformity with the wishes and needs of those who conferred the authority and receive the account. Accounting should also provide information for the controllers to assess performance. If they are dissatisfied they can withdraw their conferment, and by dismissal break the relationship of responsibility. (Jones, 1977)

Forming a Framework for Analysis

There are two strands present in this discussion:

(1) The need for information, including the right to question and debate that information as a basis for forming judgements, which we shall call the element of account. Accounts have to be given in a form that is understood. Moreover, accounts can be given in different languages, depending on what has to be expressed and to whom. The language of the financial account is not the language of the legal account, and it need not be the same as the language of the policy account. Many languages are needed for a full account.

(2) The judgement, and the action taken on the basis of that judgement—which is an exercise of power—we shall call the element of holding to account. Holding to account involves both evaluation and consequence. It can involve approval or blame which, in turn, can involve reward or penalty. It can involve dismissal or renewal of confidence. It may involve only inaction, but clearly there must be a capacity for action.

Analysis of accountability has to recognise that both the elements of accounts and holding to acounts are involved. The full concept of accountability involves both rendering and judging as a basis for action. Whereas the giving of an account is necessary to the holding to account, giving an account can stand on its own right. However, if it does stand on its own, then it is not a full expression of public accountability. Accountability also requires the capacity for the exercise of power.

The government's accountability to Parliament involves this

capacity for power. It involves the potential for withdrawal of confidence as well as the renewal of confidence. Accountability to the electors of Parliament or council, of MP or councillor, involves the possibility of non-election as well as of re-election. In all these instances there is both the element of the account—albeit the often imperfect account given in political debates or in an election campaign—and the element of holding to account.

There is a danger that public accountability is seen in too narrow terms. Much that is advocated in the improvement of account-ability concentrates on the account, as we shall do in the latter part of this chapter. The account is important, but it is not the totality of accountability.

The relationship of accountability, involving both the account and the holding to account, can be analysed as a bond linking the one who accounts and is held to account, to the one who holds to account. That bond can be defined by reference to the persons or institutions who are accountable and those to whom they are accountable. For accountability to be clear and enforceable, the bond must be clear. The relationship expressed in the bond is a relationship of power. It is a bond of accountability; only the person to whom the account is given has the power to hold to account the person who gives the account.

There will be relationships which fall short of the bond of accountability in that accounts are given, but there is no power to hold to account. These will be called 'links of account', and have an important role to play in supporting accountability, but do not in themselves constitute a bond of accountability.

To define a bond of accountability it is not sufficient to define the person or institution which accounts and the person or institution which holds to account; the activities covered by the bond of accountability, which we will call the 'field of accountability', must also be defined. A person who accounts may be subject to different bonds for different activities.

Within any field of accountability the bases of accountability must be defined. In relation to the activities for which accounts have to be given, the purpose of the account and hence the base of accountability can vary.

Accountability for probity is concerned with the avoidance of malfeasance. It ensures that funds are used properly and in the manner authorised. Accountability for legality is concerned with ensuring that the powers given by the law are not exceeded. Accountability for efficiency is designed to ensure that there is no waste in the use of resources. Accountability for good administration is designed to ensure that there has been no maladministration and, in particular, maladministration leading to injustice. These are all different bases of accountability.

These bases of accountability represent necessary standards that have to be met by public bodies. That is, however, not the whole of public accountability. There is a wider sense of performance accountability concerned with whether a performance achieved meets required standards, and one of programme accountability, which is designed to establish whether a particular agency is meeting its objectives.

Robinson (1971) distinguishes three bases of accountability. First, programme accountability, which is concerned 'with the work carried on and whether or not it has met the goals set for it.' Second, process accountability, which is concerned 'with whether the procedures used to perform the research were adequate, say in terms of the time and effort spent on the work and whether experiments were carried out as promised'. Finally, fiscal accountability, which is concerned 'with whether the funds were expended as stated and whether items purchased were used for the project'.

Programme accountability is the more difficult to enforce precisely because goals may be difficult to define with any degree of precision. Yet accountability may still be required when goals have not been defined. Indeed, it could be argued that such bases of accountability are only appropriate to subordinate parts of government for which such standards can be set, or goals laid down. For government itself — both central and local — there can be no set standards used in the formulation of policy. In one sense it is the setting of policy and of standards for which government is accountable to the electorate, yet it is the government's accountability to the electorate that is most crucial. It is accountable for both the policies it has pursued and those it has failed to pursue. It is accountable for its budget, for expenditure approved and taxes raised. Policy accountability is at the heart of electoral accountability.

These alternative bases can be set out as a ladder of accountability:

Accountability for probity and legality

Process accountability
Performance accountability
Programme accountability
Policy accountability

It is a ladder that leads from accountability by standards to accountability by judgement.

The elements that we have used in building a framework for the analysis of public accountability are, first, *the account* and, second, *the holding to account*. These elements are expressed in a *bond of accountability* which is a relationship of power between the point of account and the point, which we shall call the focal point of the bond, to which the account is given and which can hold to account. Where there is no bond of accountability, but only an obligation or custom to account, we shall define as *a link of account*.

A bond of accountability is for a *field of accountability*, that is, activities for which the account is given and which have *bases* that can be set out on a *ladder of accountability* according to the purposes for which the bond is constituted.

This framework has been constructed for the analysis of public accountability, but can be used for other forms of accountability, such as managerial accountability and commercial accountability. Managerial accountability is the accountability of a subordinate to a superior in an organisation and can, of course, be found in the public sector as well as outside. Commercial accountability is the accountability of a firm to its owners and, once again, can be found inside the public sector as well as outside. Public accountability, in the sense of the accountability of a government or council for activities undertaken in the public sector, can depend on the existence of managerial accountability within the departments of government, or commercial accountability for a publicly owned firm.

Public accountability, however, ranges more widely than managerial or commercial accountability. As Johnson has argued:

> This brings us to the broadest political sense of accountability. There are many occasions when we want to go beyond the specific grievance and the possibility of redress. We wish to pass judgment on the general performance or conduct of those exercising public authority. If they can be said to be 'accountable', then it follows that they can, in a political sense, be praised or blamed for their actions. In the extreme case, sanctions can be imposed and traditionally this has meant the withdrawal of their right to continue in office. At this stage a very obvious

point needs to be stressed. Accountability in this sense can really apply only to those holding elected political office. So long as we stick to the notion of a permanent bureaucracy, subordinate to elected representatives, then its members cannot, without some contradiction, be held accountable in a way which involves public censure and their removal from office. This in turn underlines one of the inherent difficulties in reading accountability in the public sector: we need different modes of accountability depending on whether we are concerned with the opportunities for passing judgment on those who are politically responsible, or with the need to apply certain checks and controls to those who, by reason of the terms on which they operate in the political and administrative structure, enjoy virtually complete security of tenure. (Johnson, 1974)

The distinctive feature of public accountability, as opposed to other forms of accountability, may be that it involves bases of accountability higher up the ladder of accountability. Managerial accountability will involve programme and performance accountability rather than policy accountability. For commercial accountability the market can provide standards. The dilemma for public accountability at the highest point of the ladder is that there are no predetermined standards.

Public accountability may also appear to be distinguished by the variety of bonds of accountability. The head teacher of a school has an apparent bond of accountability to his board of governors, the local authority, his pupils' parents and perhaps the community at large, his profession and himself. There is not the apparent clarity of managerial accountability. Many of those bonds, however, are imperfectly defined. Indeed, many of them are links of account only, rather than bonds of accountability. The head teacher has to explain himself in many languages, to many different audiences. These audiences cannot hold him directly to account. That requires a bond of accountability. Nevertheless, the links of account are wide-ranging.

The Changing Patterns of Public Accountability

In one sense the bonds of public accountability are well established in our system of government. Ministers' responsibility for the actions of their departments, and collective cabinet responsibility, are enforced by accountability to Parliament and through Parliament to the electorate. The officers of a council are accountable to the committees of the council and through the full council to the electorate. These bonds are supported by accounts in both financial and non-financial terms. For other public agencies the bonds of accountability will normally be laid down in the Acts creating them, but may involve, directly or indirectly, a bond of accountability to a minister on defined bases.

The present period, however, is marked by proposals for change in the pattern of accountability to meet demands for the greater accountability of public bodies. Issues of police accountability, demands for greater accountability of schools to the local community, interest in community control, concern for the rights of redress for aggrieved persons and demands for a stronger system of audit, are all part of a wider demand for greater accountability in government.

The reasons for the demands for greater public accountability lie in the changing nature of government in our society. There are general forces at work. On the one hand, the increased scale and complexity of government has weakened traditional modes of accountability; on the other, the increased impact of government has heightened the demand for accountability. Expectations generated by government have not been met in many instances and dissatisfactions have grown with perceived failures by government. In a period of economic difficulty, dissatisfaction has grown as the means of meeting those expectations has lessened.

The scale of government has robbed certain bonds of public accountability of much of their force. The doctrine of ministerial responsibility for the acts of officials within a department loses much of its meaning when the department contains many thousands of civil servants. A 'minister will not now be held blameworthy if one of his officials acts (a) illegally (b) in defiance of an instruction or (c) in a manner which the Minister could not have known or which if he had known, he would have disapproved' (Dunsire, 1978, p. 42). Such changes mean that ministerial responsibility can no longer be regarded as providing public accountability for many of the actions of civil servants. Nevertheless, the myth of ministerial responsibility is still important. As has been said, 'The constitutional structure of public accountability is still a necessary myth and to that extent a reality. "Untune that string" and we are without guidance as to our proper political allegiance' (Hague, MacKenzie and Barker, 1975, p. 21). What is being demanded are new bonds to supplement or reinforce ministerial accountability. One approach has been found in the role of the ombudsman, giving a means of redress to the citizen who has a complaint about maladministration.

The growing complexity of government has made it more difficult to identify who is accountable for what. The fragmentation of urban government, symbolised by the division of the county borough's powers in the 1974 re-organisation between county, district, health and water authorities, has made the fields of accountability for closely interrelated activities difficult to identify. For example, accountability for the care of the elderly is divided between the health authority, the social services department and the housing department, the latter two being in separate authorities in the shire areas.

The growing dependence of local authorities on central government grants confuses accountability for local government expenditure and hence the issue of where accountability for that expenditure lies. The Layfield Committee highlighted the weakening of local accountability brought about by the combination of two features of the present arrangements: 'the tendency for government grants to grow as compared with the contribution from local taxation, and the natural concern of the government with the total of local government expenditure' (Layfield, 1976, p. 72). It is no longer clear whether the bond of accountability for local government expenditure lies between central government and its electorate or between local government and its electorate.

The growth of quangos and the merging of public action and private contract can raise questions about the base of accountability when the dilemma is how to reconcile a perceived need for independence and initiative, with public control. At issue is 'how the government can hold these organisations accountable without losing the essentials of ingenuity, creativity, and initiative which we have associated throughout our history with independent groups in our society' (Staats, 1975).

As the scale and complexity of government has grown so has its impact. The lives of all of us are affected at a myriad of points by the actions of government. The formal bonds of accountability, based on Parliament and local council through the electoral process, must inevitably seem remote from the activities which impinge on the public. Those actions, be they the actions of a policeman, a civil servant in a social security office, or a rent collector, are the actions of the apparently unaccountable, rather than of the accountable. Those with least access will inevitably come to regard the actions of government as coming from 'them', and not 'us'. Formal doctrines of public accountability can seem remote from the reality of life in the inner city. Demands for greater accountability are expressed in demands for community control.

Demands for greater public accountability are also expressions of deeper dissatisfaction. Government has generated expectations that it has not been able to meet. Economic difficulty and restraint in public expenditure have resulted in a reduction in the capacity of government to meet problems with services.

There is, in addition, a wider decline in acceptance of government, which is reinforced by economic problems, but has separate origins and an independent impact. It derives, in part, from the apparent failure of the solutions on which there was consensus in the 1950s and 1960s. It can be illustrated by the dilemmas of the city. The accepted solutions of the early 1960s — high flats; large-scale redevelopment; urban motorways; and the removal of non-conforming uses (or small businesses) from inner areas — represent the consensus of the past. No new consensus has replaced the urban consensus of the past, based as that was on the authority of the accepted professional solution (Stewart, 1983). It is possible that given economic growth a new consensus could have been found. Without it, the challenge to the modes through which government has expressed itself has grown. The particular actions of government, be they the building of a new motorway or nuclear-based power station, are more sharply challenged. Dissatisfactions lead to demands for greater accountability and to demands for new bonds of accountability. Some seek through privatisation the accountability of market forces. Others seek through decentralisation bonds of community control. Each ideology seeks to replace the hierarchical control dependent on ministerial responsibility or council accountability by more direct bonds.

A wide variety of steps have been taken to add to the structure of accountability:

(1)   the institution of select committees|of the House of Commons to scrutinise fields of departmental responsibility;

(2)   the creation of ombudsmen to investigate complaints of mal-administration;

(3)   the opening up of the meetings of certain public bodies to the public;

(4)   the requirements on local authorities to publish annual reports;

(5)   the creation of Community Health Councils to review the activities of health authorities;

(6)   the implementation of the Taylor reports on the government of schools;

(7)   the creation of the Audit Commission for local government.

The new forms of public accountability have been marked by certain key characteristics.

(1)   They have been increasingly directed at local authorities and agencies separate from central government. Thus, the movement towards the publication of information, the opening up of public meetings, the establishment of community health councils and of the new Audit Commission, are not parallelled by changes of the same significance in central government.

(2)   The changes that have taken place in relation to central government have been limited (with the possible exception of the institution of the ombudsman) to attempts to restore some of the impact of Parliament on the workings of central government.

(3)   None of the changes involved major adjustments to the working of the institutions of government.

In other words, most of the changes designed to achieve greater accountability developed within the existing structure of government. Indeed, some of the changes introduced were probably designed more to secure central government policy aims than to introduce new forms of accountability as such. Thus, the requirements on local authorities to publish more information was part of a general strategy of the Government to put pressure on local authorities to reduce expenditure. The significant point is that, whatever the motivation, the actions taken were related to the demand for greater public accountability, which indicates, at least, the high visibility of that demand. These demands require a further response. In so far as they are created by real problems, the response may have to go further than existing changes. The problems, however, vary in their nature.

The weakening of formal accountability caused by the increasing scale of government is a weakening in both the account (due to a lessening in the capacity to appreciate what is happening in the machinery of government) and in the capacity to hold to account (as the responsibility of minister and council become remote from the actions of public servants). The weakening of formal accountability caused by the increasing complexity of government is due to confusion about the bonds of accountability, and the fields covered by the bonds and their base. The demand for greater accountability caused by increasing impact and growing dissatisfaction can be regarded as a demand for multiple bonds of accountability.

The different causes of the apparent weakening of traditional modes of accountability, and of the new demands for greater accountability, suggest different approaches. The increased scale of government may suggest the need for new supports for existing bonds of accountability, both to obtain accounts and assist the holding to account. Many of the reforms set out above are attempts to strengthen existing bonds.

The confusion of bonds of accountability caused by growing complexity may demand a restructuring of government. Thus, the confusion over local government expenditure led the Layfield Committee to recommend a fundamental change in the method of financing that expenditure as a means of clarifying accountability. 'The system should be based on accountability; whoever is responsible for spending money should also be responsible for raising it, so that the amount of expenditure is subject to democratic control' (Layfield, 1976, p. 283). In other contexts the confusion in accountability caused by the fragmentation of urban government has led us to put forward proposals for a new restructuring (Jones and Stewart, 1983).

The suggested clarification of the bonds of accountability may, however, run counter to demands for multiple bonds of accountability caused by the dissatisfactions already plotted. There certainly are multiple demands for accountability. The industrial ratepayer demands accountability from the local authority as do community groups. The head teachers, as we have seen, face multiple demands for accountability. If all these demands are met, accountability will not be increased because multiple bonds for the same field confuse rather than clarify. If accountability is to be effective, the bonds of accountability must be clear and strong.

The dilemma of accountability is how to reconcile the demands for multiple accountability with a clear and effective bond of accountability. A distinction has been drawn between accounts and the holding to account. Multiple demands for accountability can be met by multiple links of account without weakening the bond of accountability. Multiple links of account can be created, and government can respond to the links. This is responsiveness in

government. The holding to account within the bond of accountability is required not for responsiveness, but for responsibility in
government. As Jones has argued:

> connections of control and responsibility are different from linkages of
> responsiveness; officials and civil servants, ministers and MPs may be
> responsive to a variety of forces in society— trades unions, employees,
> consumers, pressure groups of various kinds, but they are not
> responsible to them. A prudent concern for the views of such groups,
> arising out of an appreciation of their political influence, leads those
> holding responsible positions in government to pay them attention. But
> this relationship does not involve responsibility. Responsibility certainly
> entails responsiveness, but responsiveness does not entail responsibility.
> (Jones, 1977, p. 5)

A link of account can be a recognition of responsiveness in
government. The bond of accountability is a recognition of responsibility. Multiple links of account should not be allowed to create
multiple bonds of accountability because that will defuse responsibility. Multiple links of account can strengthen a clear existing
bond of accountability. The understanding spread more widely by
multiple links of account can inform the bond of accountability.
Multiple links may be necessary for understanding. The bond of
accountability is a lever for action in the holding to account. Action
will be the more ensured by clarity of the bond of accountability.
Wider understanding can inform that leverage of power.

A three-part strategy for strengthening public accountability may
involve:

(1) a strengthening of traditional modes of accountability against the
     scale of government, which may involve both a strengthening of
     account and of the holding to account;
(2) a restructuring of government to combat complexity and clarify
     the bonds of accountability;
(3) a widening of the links of account to meet multiple demands for
     accountability.

The Role of Information in Public Accountability

Public accountancy is concerned first and foremost with the
account element in public accountability. It provides the financial
information which is the basis of one form of that account. Public
accountancy is treated here as an important, though not the sole,

component in the build up of the account element. It is one component of the wider universe of information, and provides one language for the expression of that information.

The role of information within the wider concept of accountability lies in forming the raw material for the account. This means that while information is of critical importance, it does not constitute the whole of accountability. Information expressed in the account is the basis for both judgement and action in the holding to account. Without that basis judgement must be inadequate and action misguided. But information, though the basis for judgement and action, is not in itself the holding to account – more is required!

This has to be clearly stated because from this point on, the chapter concentrates upon information. It does so to establish the place of public accountancy, but in doing so, it concentrates on the account rather than the holding to account, within the overall concept of accountability. This is because the direct contribution of public accountancy lies more in the element of account than the holding to account.

The formal structure of public accountability and the potential to hold public officials and institutions to account would be, and often is, a mere form because there is inadequate information to make a judgement or to make that judgement effective.

The account is in part determined by the institution rendering the account, for the information in it is provided by the institution. This is not an adequate basis for accountability. Information is a source of power, and as such, is guarded by the institution. In giving information the institution would be giving up power. For this reason, rules may be laid down in legislation as to the form in which the account – and not merely the financial account – is to be given. Thus, the Local Government Planning and Land Act laid on local authorities a series of obligations to publish information:

> The Secretary of State may issue . . . a code of recommended practice as to the publication of information . . . about the discharge of their functions and other matters (including forecasts) which . . . [the Secretary of State] considers to be related. (Local Government Planning and Land Act, 1980, S.2 (2))

On failure to carry out the code, the Secretary of State may make regulations requiring adherence to the code. (Ibid., S2).

The aforementioned Act also contains provisions specifying the form in which accounts for direct labour organisations should be kept (Ibid., S.10 to 14), thus adding to existing legislation governing the accounts of land authorities. In addition, the Act gives the Secretary of State the power to prepare a register of the land holdings of particular local authorities and certain other public bodies. The register will be sent to local authorities who must make it available for public inspection (Ibid., S.93 to 100).

These are recent examples of the vast body of legislation governing local authorities and other public bodies. Nationalised industries are also required to publish annual reports and accounts. In certain instances central government or Parliament is the focal point for the bond of accountability, as in the case of nationalised industries; and it is, in effect, laying down the nature of the account required — an account that has often been judged inadequate because it does not permit a proper assessment of the policy, or even the performance, of nationalised industries. In other instances, central government or Parliament are not the focal point of the bond of accountability. The bond of accountability lies between local authorities and their local electorate and not between Parliament and local authorities. In these instances, central government and Parliament specify the form of account for the bond between local authorities and their electorate.

It is, however, not merely a matter of specifying the information to be provided. The conditions cover not only the form of information, but also the way in which it is published, and the right of access. It is not sufficient merely to have an account: that account has to be distributed or, at the very least, the public has to be given access to it. However, having access to information is not, in itself, sufficient. For, if the total responsibility for the account is laid on the accountable body, then too much may have to be taken on trust.

There can be various means of providing information that is not entirely under the control of the accountable body. One method is greater openness in government. Thus, the Public Bodies (Admission to Meetings) Act 1960, introduced the provision that council meetings and education committee meetings (and the meetings of certain other public bodies) should be open to the public and the press — a provision extended by S.100 of the Local Government Act 1972, to cover all committee meetings. Public access and access by the press provide direct information. The provision of such direct access can be frustrated to a degree by the authority, which can remove decision making to other settings. Nevertheless, these provisions secure a greater openness than, for example, in central government, and that openness provides information in forms not entirely predetermined by the local authority.

The other approach adopted to avoid the over-dependence of the account on the accountable body, is to give an external person or institution the right of scrutiny into the account and beyond. This is the role of public audit. The strength of public audit is an important support in public accountability, but it is not itself public accountability, as perhaps the quotation from Normanton suggested. Public audit is a means of checking the account that has been given by the accountable body. It can add to that account information not contained in the account. Public audit is not public accountability, because the need of governmental organisations to give an account, and the need of those to whom the account is given, to hold to account on the basis of their judgement of the account, stands in its own right apart from public audit. Public audit can assist that judgement. At lower points on the ladder of accountability, public audit can even apply rules about probity and the legality of action, because those rules enforce judgements already made. But, as one ascends the ladder of accountability towards policy accountability, the role of public audit becomes more restricted.

The need for an account to be rendered and judged requires one who accounts and one who holds to account. That is the bond of accountability. Public audit does not constitute a bond, but a means of improving the effectiveness of the bond.

Public audit does not stand alone. Other institutions can be set up with similar rights of scrutiny, though for different purposes. For example, Inspectorates of education or of the police can aid performance accountability. The courts can scrutinise to establish a 'correct' account or the facts when enforcing legal accountability. In addition, the ombudsman has the right to scrutinise in order to establish a 'correct' account that does not rest solely on the accounts of the complainant or of the institution about which the complaint has been lodged.

Scrutiny must go beyond the collection of information: explanation is necessary. The

mystique of accounts is a hindrance, not a help to public accountability in this sense. The accounts themselves are no more than the basic guide for the investigation, the outline may be of the whole financial territory. The outline must be filled in by systematic exploration; by obtaining explorations and documentation about all unusual features encountered. (Normanton, 1966, p. 2)

But even such scrutiny is not itself accountability. Public audit must remain a support of public accountability and not supplant it.

The Information Requirements of Public Accountability

The information requirements vary with the bases of account. As the ladder of public accountability is mounted, the information requirements become more difficult to define precisely because the ladder is defined as a movement from accountability by reference to standards, to accountability by judgement. It is a ladder that moves, therefore, from greater use of external bodies, not merely to collect information but to appraise it. At the highest level of accountability there is danger in the use of such bodies for anything other than information collection. There is only information and judgement on that information, and judgement can only be carried out by those at the focal point of the bond of accountability. Auditing and the ombudsman cannot be substituted for the electorate.

The information requirements of accountability for financial probity and legality can be defined with precision. The information required for process accountability can, if narrowly conceived, be defined. Programme and performance accountability imply stated goals which may not always be available. Policy accountability cannot be confined within pre-set standards. Yet, as demands grow for accountability, or at least for accounts, it is for policy accounts — precisely because the information of account is often inadequate.

It is because public accountability extends to policy accountability, which cannot be contained within predetermined standards, that the information requirements extend beyond those required for commercial or managerial accountability.

It is significant in this context to note that where public bodies are regarded as subject to commercial accountability, it is regarded as a reason for lessening access to information. Thus, whereas local authorities and health authorities have to admit the public to meetings, this is not required of nationalised industries. Com-

mercial accountability, with its narrower information requirements, is regarded as sufficient.

Managerial accountability, which can itself be set within a framework of public accountability, has more limited information
requirements than public accountability. This is precisely because
the bond of accountability involves the simpler relationship of
superior and subordinate, rather than the infinitely more complex
relationship between electorate and government, or even between
Parliament and government.

Policy accountability cannot be kept within set bounds. If new
demands for greater public accountability are to lead to a range of
accounts, they will have to meet the widening demands of those
requiring accounts.

'In giving an account, its form and substance depend upon the
values, beliefs and perceptions of the person giving the account'
(Jackson, 1982, p. 221). To be meaningful the account must also
recognise the values, beliefs and perceptions of those to whom the
account is given.

The Place of Financial Information

It is the job of an accountant to prepare an account. Marshall has
written:

> we are concerned with accounting's place in accountable management.
> How does it help the council to 'account' to the public, the chief officer
> to account to the committee, the foreman to account to the engineer?
> . . . We shall view accounting as a technique seeking to help in laying
> down what is to be done, what resources should be used, and in
> monitoring operations, individually and in the aggregate. We shall
> approach it from the layman's point of view, regarding it as embracing
> not only the records' cost in financial terms, but those having financial
> overtones or consisting of statistical information to be used in conjunc-
> tion with the financial facts. So conceived, accounting will cover a vast
> range of information, generated and assembled in many departments by
> persons having different degrees of skills, arrived at by different
> processes, and demanding varying standards of precision according to
> the use to be made of it. (Marshall, 1974, p. 155)

Within the framework of public accountability the accountant
has a special role to play in the preparation of the account. He is
one who deals almost exclusively in information. The financial

account is a necessary account, but the financial account is only one account, using but one language. The accountant has an important role in describing the different processes in the organisation in a common language. As the ladder of accountability is mounted, the financial account becomes less adequate by itself. Accounts must still encompass the language of the accountant, but other languages are also required. In accounting for financial probity the language of the accountant is sufficient, but for other bases of accountability, other languages are required. For performance accountability output data must be added to financial data; for programme accountability the language of objectives becomes critical; and for policy accountability, a range of languages becomes important. In all bases of accountability financial information, as a measure of the use of resources, must remain. The accountant's language is important to public accountability, but if it is the only language used, the bases of accountability will be limited.

There is a challenge to public accountants to meet more fully the information requirements of performance and programme accountability and, above all, of policy accountability. As the links of account grow, new skills will be required from the accountant if these demands are to be met by accounts able to meet the requirements of those making the demands. The accountant himself cannot meet these demands by supplying merely what he considers necessary for professional accounting. New demands for accountability will place new requirements on the. accountant. The accountant will have to work increasingly with other accountants who use different languages and will have to learn a sufficient number of those languages to translate into them from his own.

Both performance and programme accounts require accounts that relate financial inputs to achieved outputs (i.e. goods or services provided) or outcomes (i.e. effect or impact of goods or services provided). The need is widely recognised by public sector accountants, though the difficulties of obtaining adequate measures of output, and even more of outcomes, on the systematic basis required to match financial data are also great.

The requirements of policy accounts are less recognised, precisely because those requirements are not normally stated in language seen as meaningful by accountants. The public sector accountancy profession has laid down its own definition of the account. In most forms of account it is the dominant voice, and it is not accustomed to meeting requirements which are expressed in unfamiliar language and which do not fully accept the public sector accountant's definition of his task.

Some requirements can be more easily met. The new complexity of government has, it has been argued above, confused formal bonds of accountability, and this can best be met by a re-structuring which would reduce or eliminate the confusion. Without such developments there may be a role for public sector accountancy in describing more fully and more carefully the use and allocation of resources across institutions. In a fragmented system of government, there is a challenge to public sector accountancy to develop inter-organisational statements of account (for example, for the care of the elderly) that show the totality of resources used, as well as where the bond of accountability lies. Such a line of advance will, however, create few problems for the public sector accountant. He can still use the accountant's language; however, much of the work involved in preparing policy accounts lies in meeting the new demands for accountability which require the use of new languages along with the accountant's language.

Some of the demands are political, which is hardly surprising given that public accountability in our society is achieved through a political process. It may well be that the public sector accountant has to learn more of the language of politics in order to express his accounts more clearly in the political process. Thus, 'manifesto accounting', both in the sense of cost estimates of manifestos, and records of achievement in relation to manifestos, could be an important line of advance.

Politics can be defined more widely: it can encompass concern for public participation. Professions other than accountancy have encompassed that concern. Planning and social work have, as professions, both responded to demands for greater accountability by processes of participation. They have also moved towards advocacy planning and community work. The accountant remains relatively isolated. Not merely is the neighbourhood accountant comparatively rare, but little in the way of public participation has been allowed to approach the budgetary processes of public bodies which are at the centre of governmental choice.

Many of the demands for greater public accountability come from groups or interests within the wider political community. For example, a minority group may be pressing for special recognition, or those living in a particular area may consider that they have little control over governmental action whether instituted by local or central government or by the proliferating special agencies. Accounts are required which can indicate the resources spent on particular groups or which can show how the resources of government are divided between different areas. A poverty budget can highlight the actions of government in meeting the needs of the deprived in society. Understanding who gains or who loses in financial as well as in other terms may be a necessary part of a developed political process. Public sector accountancy has perhaps been built too readily on the assumption that there is one public, whose interests can be expressed in unitary accounts. Accounting for the variety of interests that make up the public to whom accounts have to be given may require new values from the public sector accountant.

As demands for more responsive management arise, processes may have to develop including the provision of community accounts. Decentralised resource management operating within frameworks set by central or by local government may be required.

All these lines of advance require new approaches from public sector accountancy: they may challenge values written into past professional tradition; the financial information required may lack the precision of the professional account; the financial language of account may lose its separate identity in merging with other languages; and the unitary nature of the account may be lost.

As the ladder of public accountability is mounted, so the language of account must change.

References

Barker, A., Hague, D. C. and MacKenzie, W. J. M. (1974) *Public Policy and Private Interests*, Macmillan.

Dunshire, A. (1978) *Control in a Bureaucracy: The Execution Process*, Martin Robertson.

Hague, D. C., Mackenzie, W. J. and Barker, A. (1975) *Public Policy and Private Interest*, Macmillan.

Jackson, P. M. (1982) *The Political Economy of Bureaucracy*, Philip Allan.

Johnson, N. (1974) 'Defining accountability', *Public Administration*, December, No. 17.

Jones, G. W. (1977) *Responsibility in Government*, London School of Economics.

Jones, G. W. and Stewart, J. D. (1983) *The Case for Local Government*, George Allen and Unwin.

Marshall, A. H. (1974) *Finance Management in Local Government*, George Allen and Unwin.

Normanton, E. L. (1966) *The Accountability and Audit of Government: A Comparative Study*, Manchester University Press.

Normanton, E. L. (1971) 'Public accountability and audit: a reconnaissance', in B. L. R. Smith and D. C. Hague, *The Dilemma of Accountability in Modern Government: Independence versus Control*, Macmillan.

Robinson, D. Z. (1971) 'Government contracting for academic research: accountability in the American experience', in B. L. R. Smith and D. C. Hague, *The Dilemma of Accountability in Modern Government: Independence versus Control*, Macmillan.

Staats, E. B. (1975) 'New problems of accountability for federal problems', in B. L. R. Smith, *The New Political Economy: The Public Use of the Private Sector*, Macmillan.

Stewart, J. D. (1983) *Local Government; the Conditions of Local Choice*, George Allen and Unwin.

Layfield Report (1976) *Report of the Committee on Local Government Finance*, HMSO.

3
Accounting Standards in the Public Sector

N. HEPWORTH and P. VASS

Introduction

The development of accounting standards for the public sector is in a state of transition—from an *ad hoc* past, to a possibly more certain future. We cannot, therefore, set out the definitive standards. The debate is wide open, both on the need for, and the substance of, such standards, as well as on the form that they might take. Not least of the questions that should be debated is the role of the accountancy profession in their formulation.

There is also a political context to this debate. One must beware of a tendency to denigrate the rules and procedures that already exist in the public sector, denying them the substance of standards purely because they lack an accepted name. Critics of public sector accounting have stated that there are no standards in the public sector because the Statements of Standard Accounting Practice (SSAPs) issued by the Accounting Standards Committee are applied only to commercial accounts. This may fit nicely with prejudices against the public sector, but it does no justice to the facts.

The questions that need to be asked about accounting standards for the public sector are not just technical ones. Accounting standards have to be a firm part of the information process which both allows the economic system to operate and influences the direction in which it moves. In the private sector, the required information is fairly clearly defined in the concept of profit, which embodies within it ideas of economy, efficiency and effectiveness, as well as stewardship. In the public sector there is no such clearly defined measure. Profit, for example, has no meaning in economic terms except as a consequence of the market place. There is no market test for many public sector goods, and where a market may appear to exist, that market is almost invariably constrained by political and social pressures. The equity holder is either central or local government, and their concern is, by definition, expressed in political terms. That may provide an argument on economic efficiency grounds for maximising the size of the private sector, but the purpose of this essay is not to enter into that debate, rather it is to take the size of the public sector as given and to examine the relevance of accounting standards to that sector. In so doing, we have no doubt that the public sector record on stewardship in this country is outstandingly good. Of course, there is much to debate about the economy, efficiency and effectiveness with which the public sector operates, but equally there is no doubt that views about these matters are often expressed in political terms, rather than as objective statements based on substantive analysis of the inputs and outputs. Part of the problem, however, is that 'outputs' are difficult to define.

Standards: A New Idea?

Professor Joad, when on the Brains Trust, frequently used to say: 'it all depends on what you mean!' Frustrating as this often was to the questioner, the technique of drawing attention to any ambiguities at the start of a discussion usually left listeners wiser than they were before. The discipline of asking 'what do you mean?' is very relevant to much of the debate which has been taking place in recent years over the role of accounting standards in the public sector.

The Oxford English Dictionary defines 'standard' as either, 'a definite degree of any quality viewed as a prescribed object of endeavour', or as 'an authoritative or recognised exemplar of correctness'. Both are clearly relevant to what are known now as 'Accounting Standards', but it would be a mistake to assume that the present standards are the only ones that have ever existed, even though their form and perceived authority has previously been quite different.

Standards existed in accounting before SSAPs appeared in the early 1970s. All the accounting bodies have promoted standard accounting practices and encouraged the development of those standards, taking into account changing commercial, economic and political requirements, as well as any changes in public expectation. For example, professional training has been designed to instil not only accounting technique, but an appreciation of 'received best practice'. The Companies Acts — and even that of 1981, which significantly extended statutory prescription — recognize this when they refer to 'generally accepted accounting principles'. The Chartered Institute of Public Finance and Accountancy (CIPFA) had issued guidance on proper accounting practices for local authorities for nearly a century (see CIPFA, 1979), and because the overwhelming majority of local authority treasurers are members of CIPFA, these recommendations have been adopted.

However, until the development of the Consultative Committee of Accountancy Bodies, no real attempt was made to formalise these practices for the profession as a whole, and only within the last few years have attempts been made to apply the formal standards to the public sector.

Standards in Context

Establishing the criteria for a standard is one task, but the fact of the matter is that accounting needs to be compatible with economic efficiency; where it is regarded as independent of economic demands, great difficulties can develop. The debate about accounting and inflation has shown this. Yet, standards are also part of the mechanisms of control in our society and this places them firmly in the political arena. 'Authoritativeness' is therefore essential to the achievement of control where statutory provision does not exist. Sanctions have been developed to reinforce that authority, the most important of which are the accountants' disciplinary code and the qualification procedure to audit certificates. However, it is less easy for the professional non-statutory bodies of accountants to exert authority and discipline in the public sector. In addition, in the public sector politicians are impatient of any attempts to constrain

what they see as their flexibility and power. Moreover, the accountability of the public sector to Parliament means that the authority
which the accounting bodies may have over the practices of private
sector accountants cannot be applied in the same way to the public
sector. Authority in these circumstances can only work in the
public sector where it would create more political difficulty for
politicians to go against a professional standard than it would to
support it.

Formal accounting standards in the private sector came from a
public demand for the accountancy profession to put more substance into the 'true and fair view' audit opinion in the financial
statements of companies. The report of the previous chairman of
the Accounting Standards Committee, Tom Watts (ASC 1981),
argues that by 1969 it was apparent that the basic framework in company law needed to be supported by mandatory requirements and
that 'recommendations' issued by accountancy bodies would not, in
themselves, suffice. Elimination of discretion has been one of the
main purposes of Accounting Standards since ASC was asked to
'advance accounting practice by publishing authoritative statements on best accounting practice' (Accounting Standards Committee, 1981).

The purpose of accounting standards is, therefore, most
accurately summed up by the word 'comparability'. Many of the
other reasons we often see adduced in support of standards, such
as consistency and the need for less overall interpretative information to be given with each financial report (because standard
practice is taken for granted), in fact come naturally from the
pursuit of comparability.

Comparability is also the essence of the demand for accounting
standards in the public sector: how does the performance of one
institution compare with another — most obviously, one local
authority with another? However, because the essential difference
between the private and public sectors (and the difference is only
one of degree between the trading and non-trading parts of the
public sector) is the absence of a full market test of efficiency and
effectiveness, namely, market-based profit, comparability, if it is to
have any substance, needs to extend beyond the financial inputs of
resources into the measured outputs of services. That is where the
present developments in accounting standards for the public sector
are most deficient. Such an extension would, of course, take the

accountant well beyond the immediate bounds of his conventional thought.

It is clear, however, that standards which regulate and control will be subject to particularly strong pressures from affected parties. In the preparation of a standard, pressures will exist to either not implement it, dilute it by having options or alternatives within it, or achieve exemptions from it. Even when it is introduced, the game continues in like vein to lawyers who attempt to distinguish their client's case from the unassailable legal precedents put forward by the other party. As with the law, some cases will distinguish legitimately and others will be based purely on semantics, and not every jury—or auditor—will make the right decision as to which is which.

David Solomans (1980) has discussed the political implications of accounting and accounting standard setting, pointing out that it is widely believed that the appointment of the Sandilands Committee, in January 1974, was timed to thwart the issue of a current purchasing power standard by the ASC. This was because the government of the day believed it would lead to a demand for general indexation of wages and other incomes; a prospect it did not relish. In fact, one of the Sandilands Committee's terms of reference was an instruction to take into account 'the need to restrain inflation in the UK'. He cites other cases where pressure has been brought to bear on the ASC to bend its standards to serve special interests, but makes the caveat that 'it is difficult to draw a line between what is a helpful submission to the ASC of a reasonable point of view and the exertion of pressure on it'.

The Public Sector

A development which has both promoted the concept of accounting standards in the public sector, and made the SSAPs appear possibly more relevant to the non-trading part of the public sector, has been the introduction of the 'present fairly' audit opinion. The public sector has always been concerned with stewardship, and the audit certificate reflected this. In local government the auditor has been statutorily obliged to consider whether 'proper accounting practices' have been applied, and in health authorities it was a question of the accounts being certified 'correct'. However, public confidence could be increased if the auditor expressed an opinion on the accounts derived, in spirit, from the concept of 'true and fair'. The Government provided the statutory basis for this in local authorities in the 1982 Local Government Finance Act. In addition, the recommendation of the CIPFA/District Auditors' Society (CIPFA, 1982a) is that the auditor should state his opinion that the relevant financial statements 'present fairly' the income and expenditure and financial position of the authority. The Audit Commission, when Parliament adopted its Audit Code of Practice, followed this recommendation.

The influence of these ideas is being felt throughout the non-trading public sector. Consider the Appropriation Accounts of central government. The Comptroller and Auditor General's Certifcate was, prior to the 1981–82 Accounts, designed to certify that the account was correct, based on accuracy and regularity in relation to Parliamentary authorisations. Recognising that to certify accounts running into billions of pounds as 'correct' was a literal absurdity, and taking account of developments elsewhere, the opportunity was taken to alter the certificate for accounts from 1981–82 to show that 'In my opinion the sums expended have been applied for the purposes authorised by Parliament, and the Account properly presents the expenditure and receipts of class (x) vote (y) for the year ended . . .'. Trading Funds, as constituted under the Trading Funds Act 1973, go further and receive a true and fair certificate consistent with the philosophy that they should operate on commercial lines.

There is, additionally, one argument against accounting standards which, though used to suggest that accounting standards are not necessary for commerce, would clearly not apply to the public sector. The persuasive argument is that accounting standards in the private sector are unnecessary (ASC, 1981, para. 2.4) because an efficient securities market with sophisticated financial analysts will automatically adjust share prices to reflect reality. This argument implies that it is not the accounting principles which matter, but the extent of the disclosure. Unhappily for the supporters of accounting standards, this has not been an easy hypothesis to test, and certainly not to disprove, though in a useful way it sets the scene for the kind of accounting standards which might be appropriate to the public sector. Even if disclosure and a free market would be sufficient to guarantee that all was well in the private sector without accounting standards, it is the absence of a continuing, politically-free market mechanism in the public sector that leaves a clear need for both disclosure and measurement standards to be established there.

The Conceptual Framework: A User Basis

It has been argued that one purpose of accounting standards is served by their being 'authoritative'. Yet, that purpose is still only a means rather than an end. It still leaves us with the question: authoritative for what purpose? The present chairman of ASC, Ian Hay Davison, in an address entitled 'Do accounting principles have any place in the public sector?', said:

> I use the phrase 'accounting principles' to mean the entire corpus of logical thought which provides a framework for our profession of accountancy; 'accounting standards' are the expression of that thought in codified form. (Davison, 1982)

Read literally, this appears to be saying that Accounting Standards are—or at least reflect—a conceptual framework. This view is somewhat at variance with much of the criticism of Accounting Standards, namely that they have been developed *ad hoc* in response to events and without regard to any underlying theoretical basis.

It was, in part, to respond to that criticism that Professor MacVe was asked to research the issue. However, the result has not so much solved the problem as shifted the emphasis. One important conclusion from Professor MacVe's study which bears repeating is as follows:

> The chief implication of the uncertainty about what is useful information, and of the need to reconcile the interests of different parties, is that what is 'good (or better) accounting' is fundamentally a subjective matter . . . The history of the development of accounting suggests that it serves many purposes reasonably well rather than any one purpose very well. It therefore seems unlikely that searching for an agreed conceptual framework of theory in abstraction from individual problems of disclosure and method will be successful. (MacVe, 1982)

Why should it be that accounting standards cannot be validated by reference to theory or principles? Interestingly, the answer to this will probably only emerge from the test of time: when unsatisfactory standards are amended and special pleading becomes recognised for what it is. This seems consistent with the philosophy contained in *The Corporate Report* under the heading 'Our basic philosophy':

> Our basic approach has been that corporate reports should seek to satisfy, as far as possible, the information needs of users: they should be useful. To identify user needs, and thereby arrive at the fundamental objective of corporate reports, it is first necessary to determine who should publish corporate reports and why. (ASC, 1975)

A good analogy to this arose when Lord Denning described justice as what fair-minded people think is right and proper. This appears to beg more questions than it answers, but at the same time it has a revealed truth to it. We know what he means and we think we know justice when we see it. Perhaps the same should be said of accounting standards. If we ask the right questions about which standards are needed for accounting statements to facilitate the development of economic relationships in both the public and private sectors, then we will get the standards we require. Likewise, just as views of what can be described as 'justice' change over time, so views of what purposes accounting standards can be expected to meet can also change over time. In the words of Professor MacVe:

> The role of a 'conceptual framework' is to provide a structure for thinking about what is 'better' accounting and financial reporting . . . a common basis for identifying issues, for asking questions and for carrying out research rather than a package of solutions. (MacVe, 1982)

The Application of SSAPs to the Public Sector

The Foreword to SSAPs

If we accept the authoritative position of SSAPs, then we should consider carefully whether the SSAPs themselves might apply equally to public sector organisations. SSAPs were developed specifically for commercial undertakings. The explanatory foreword to all the SSAPs states that they 'describe methods of accounting approved by the Councils [of CCAB] . . . for application to all financial accounts intended to give a true and fair view of financial position and profit or loss.' Some have chosen to read this negatively, suggesting that SSAPs should not apply outside the limited sphere of 'true and fair', but there is also the forceful argument that because the purpose of many public sector organisations is so fundamentally different from that of commerce, any development of authoritative accounting standards for the public sector should start from the beginning, rather than merely adopt the practices found suitable for commerce. Persuasive though this argument can be, it overlooks the advantages both of achieving a common approach where there are common elements, and of having that expressed in a single authoritative statement. In addition, the borderline between the public and private sectors is constantly shifting, and the disciplines of one may be relevant to the other.

This has been persuasively argued by Peter Bird and Peter Morgan-Jones in their study, *Financial Reporting by Charities* (1981):

> It is our opinion that as far as possible all SSAPs, excluding of course those not relevant, are intended to apply to all enterprises, including charities and other non-profit organisations. This view is supported by the large majority of those with whom we have discussed the matter at a number of seminars we have attended in connection with our research project. Our opinion is also supported by correspondence we had early in 1978 with the then Technical Director of the ICAEW. (Bird and Morgan-Jones, 1981)

Concluding this line of argument they go on to say:

> To those who are in favour of a separate new set of accounting standards for charities we would say surely it is preferable to follow those standards used for business organisations which are familiar both to users and those who prepare charity accounts except where, because of the nature of charities, they require some modification. (Bird and Morgan-Jones, 1981)

The Present Position

We now discuss the progress to date in the application of SSAPs to the various parts of the public sector, with reference to points of interest or problems, in particular on SSAP 16 current cost accounting.

Nationalised Industries   Nationalised industries (including the water industry, which has similar objectives) each have their own statutes, but commonly the provisions of the Nationalisation Acts have given recognition to their predominantly commercial nature by requiring their accounts to follow 'best commercial practice'. (See, for example, Likierman (1981, p.5) who cites Section 46(1) of the Electricity Act 1947, which refers to 'best commercial standards'.)

Accounting Standards apply, therefore, except where government regulations from each industry's sponsoring department state otherwise. An example of this was when, in its first year, British Rail was instructed not to publish a current cost balance sheet, even though it was a requirement of the Standard. Some consistency of approach to the nationalised industries as a whole has been provided by the Treasury's overall responsibilities and by the advisory role of the Nationalised Industries Chairman's Group: the latter, for instance, having published a Code of Practice on the application of SSAP 16.

This notwithstanding, a word of caution should be sounded. Nationalised industries are trading bodies, but as both the Chairman of ASC (Davison, 1982) and Likierman (1981) have shown, their position is peculiar in a number of respects. First, their capital is primarily loan capital from the government (not shareholders' capital) and, more importantly, loan capital which may not need to be repaid. In effect, creditors are guaranteed against loss and the balance sheet (except where it is restructured to pave the way for privatisation) does not have to be viewed in 'break-up' terms. Also important is the fact that certain fixed assets, such as water and sewerage facilities, have very long lives and it may not be appropriate to apply the sort of valuation rules that the private sector uses, particularly if this involved revaluing the entire network on a current cost basis.

Typically SSAPs have not distinguished between the types of industry to which they apply, though they have made distinctions on grounds of size. Consequently, we might not have expected to see particular reference to nationalised industries in any of the SSAPs, for any different treatment required by the government is more properly dealt with by regulation and, if necessary, discussion in Parliament. Paragraph 51 of SSAP 16 states, however, that 'no gearing adjustment should be made in the profit and loss accounts of Nationalised Industries in view of the special nature of their capital structure.'

We need not dwell here on the technical arguments of whether or not this is a correct position, the point of interest is that paragraph 51 was necessary at all in an ASC standard. Certainly, the question of the meaning of the gearing adjustment is not resolved in the minds of the NICG, since their Code requires the calculations to be shown by way of a note to the balance sheet. The view taken on the gearing adjustment may depend on whether the industry is making an historical cost profit or loss (witness the public difference in opinion between British Gas and the water industry); but the trump card has been played by the Treasury in its determination to impose its will on the structure of the standard itself.

Universities Universities receive a substantial proportion of their operating income from government funds. For this reason, we judge them to be within the spirit of the public sector and would hope to see a common accounting approach. The position is, in fact, much less clear than one might suppose, as Hilton (1981) has demonstrated. Their accounts do not need to comply with the Companies Acts and there is a variety of audit certificates, ranging from 'properly prepared in accordance with accounting policies' through 'the said accounts give a true and fair view of the state of affairs' to 'fairly stated'. More importantly, Hilton demonstrates the dramatic variety of accounts, with some universities not even providing a statement of accounting policies. One university was unconcerned that it had 'not complied with the requirements of SSAP 10 in that it has not presented a source and application of fund statement', and the treatment of fixed assets varied between universities. The question of hidden reserves also came in for stringent comment.

Hilton states: 'It is unclear what effect SSAPs would have on university accounts even if universities chose to apply them.' So, why does it matter? Well, clearly it does. The ASC was established to minimise the variability of reporting, but with the purpose of serving user interests. Obviously there can be debate about who users are, but there is no doubt that an important user is the public sector funding source. The issue becomes more significant at a time when the University Grants Committee's resources are limited. If there is to be equity of treatment, then comparable information on the capacity of different universities to cope financially with fluctuations in recurrent income needs to be obtained. The function of accounting standards is not to decide the policy; their function is to facilitate the provision of reliable and useful information to users who have a reasonable right to knowledge (ASC, 1975).

The Committee of Vice-Chancellors and Principals, under some pressure from the University Grants Committee and the ASC, has recognised the force of the argument and has prepared a discussion paper which sets out a recommended statement on accounting and reporting practice. If it gets support from the universities, this could prove to be one of the first areas in which the ASC is asked to provide a specific 'seal of approval' that it accords with good accounting practice. In this way public confidence can be strengthened.

Local Authorities   Local authorities not only produce accounts, but also give considerable information to central government for its own purposes, including the public expenditure survey system and the distribution of grant aid. We discussed earlier the new requirement in the 1982 Act which recognises the concern, expressed for some time, that an 'auditor's opinion' should be given on the accounts. We argued that this clearly brings the local authority accounts a step nearer to the philosophy of 'true and fair', and that the accounts and the supplementary information drawn from them should mean something useful to the users. The question of the application of accounting standards has therefore become more relevant.

Table 3.1 sets out the SSAPs as they have been applied to local authorities and health authorities, though the way in which the SSAPs have been applied in these two sectors is rather different. The Chartered Institute of Public Finance and Accountancy has, with the ASC, drafted a series of guidance notes on the application of SSAPs; these were published for comment. Comments are, of course, received only from those 'contracting in', so the response has to be considered cautiously to ensure that a balanced view is taken. An analysis of the three series issued to date is shown in Table 3.2. Final versions, with reasons for amendments, were published on behalf of the ASC in *Public Finance and Accountancy* (February 1982, March 1983 and April 1983), with supporting commentary (CIPFA/ASC, 1982/3).

SSAP 12 and 16 and Local Authorities   The case for separate public sector standards is particularly clear when we examine the debate which has taken place over a number of years on SSAPs 12 and 16 and their applicability to the non-trading public sector.

Table 3.1 The Application of SSAPs to Local and Health Authorities

Statements of standard accounting practice issued	Local authorities	Health authorities
SSAP Explanatory foreword (Revised May 1975)	under consideration as relevant	
SSAP 1 Accounting for associated companies (Revised April 1982)		×
SSAP 2 Disclosure of accounting policies	√	√ ×
SSAP 3 Earnings per share (Revised Aug. 1974)	×	
SSAP 4 The accounting treatment of government grants	√	×
SSAP 5 Accounting for value added tax	√	√
SSAP 6 Extraordinary items and prior year adjustments (Revised April 1975)	√	
SSAP 8 The treatment of taxation under the imputation system in the accounts of companies (Revised Dec. 1977)	limited applicability	limited applicability
SSAP 9 Stocks and works in progress	× √	×
SSAP 10 Statements of source and application of funds	√	√
SSAP 12 Accounting for depreciation	× √	√
SSAP 13 Accounting for research and development	√ under consideration as relevant	×
SSAP 14 Group accounts	×	limited applicability
SSAP 15 Accounting for deferred taxation	×	×
SSAP 16 Current cost accounting	× √	×
SSAP 17 Accounting for post balance sheet events	√	×
SSAP 18 Accounting for contingencies	√	limited applicability √
SSAP 19 Accounting for investment properties	×	×

Key

√ Relevant or partially relevant

× Not relevant under current form of accounts

Table 3.2 Major Comments on Draft Guidance Notes

SSAPs	Commentators (total)	Expressed general agreement	Major comments on draft guidance note taken into final version
Series I (2, 3, 4)	107	80	*SSAP 2* (i) to make clear that accruing revenue expenditure should not appear to increase local authority expenditure – emphasis on prior year adjustment (see PFA Feb. 1982) *SSAP 4* (ii) to allow matching of grants with the financing period of an asset if less than the life of the asset (see PFA Feb. 1982)
Series II (5, 6, 8, 10, 13, 15)	149	76	*SSAP 6* (i) to make clear that prior year adjustments are made in the current year's accounts and do not involve opening the accounts of previous years. (ii) to clarify the treatment of capital receipts by way of a note to the accounts. *SSAP 10* (iii) to clarify the treatment of funds flows to and from joint bodies (see PFA March 1983).
Series III (1, 9, 14, 17, 18) (*Note:* 1 and 14 were excluded from the final draft)	125	75	No comments were carried through into the definitive version (see PFA April 1983)

Note: All the letters/comments received are available on public display at the ICAEW/ASC library.

Local authorities in particular have been subject to the criticism that comparability between them suffers because capital charges to the revenue accounts are based on financing considerations rather than on physical capital consumption and concepts of capital maintenance. While this accounting basis may be perfectly correct given the different objectives of local authorities (namely, service provision financed in part by tax rather than profit made by sales income), there has, nevertheless, been a persistent feeling that such an important and innovatory standard as SSAP 16 should have some worthwhile lessons to teach local authorities about the form of their accounts.

The argument about the need, both for standardising reported information to allow improved comparability between authorities, and for improving information to service managers on their asset utilisation, has largely been accepted. Both of these improvements would yield benefits by creating pressure to consider alternative uses for assets and more cost-effective ways of producing services. The Secretary of State for the Environment has also added motivation for such information through his interest in ranking authorities by published 'Comparative Statistics'.

The question remains, however, as to the most practicable path. Two reports have been produced which recommend the application of SSAPs 12 and 16 respectively (CIPFA (1975), Woodham (1982)), but the view which is now finding favour is that 'notional asset rents' in service accounts would do the job of giving information about potential efficiency savings without necessarily distorting the tax levy purely to finance an inappropriate concept of capital maintenance (Pearce, 1983).

SSAP 12 and 16 are firmly based on a premise of shareholder and creditor protection, which means that companies should not distribute out of their capital. Other things being equal, a revenue charge should be made which represents the capital consumed in the period. This deducts from profits sufficient money to allow the business to continue at the prevailing level of operation through renewal of assets.

This is the proper neutral position in the private sector. However, such a neutral position does not exist in local authorities, who neither have shareholders nor distribute gains to them. The service potential of the authority is politically determined, as is the rate levy, although the two will be related. One conclusion in

CIPFA's submission of comments on ED18, the draft standard on current cost accounting, referred to this:

> The question of maintenance of an ownership interest is at its most complex in the non-trading parts of the public sector, where the public is both customer, owner and, through democratic representation, manager. To attempt to superimpose an accounting mechanism designed for the private ownership situation on such an environment, where economic behaviour stems from quite different perceptions of interest, must be highly questionable.

There are, of course, arguments for and against maintenance of physical capital (Jones, 1982a). We agree that information on the change in the level of operating capability would be useful, but this is quite different from saying that tax charges should be based on maintaining a particular level. Asset rents, as the CIPFA working party demonstrated (Pearce, 1983), would overcome this and at the same time solve a weakness in SSAP 12, namely, that non-depreciable assets such as land do not generate a user charge; as the working party report states: 'If there are no charges for land holdings, the incentive to make best use of the land is weakened and the demonstration of accountability for efficiency made more difficult.'

Clearly, the accounting systems and standards should be related to the objectives of the organisation.

Health Authorities The different approach taken by health authorities reflects their closer relationship with central government, and at the same time a difference between them and local authorities in reporting to the public. In 1980, when the Association of Health Service Treasurers set its Accounting Committee the task of preparing a report on this issue, it was considering the application of SSAPs to the statutory accounts submitted to the government under Section 98 of the National Health Service Act 1977. These are more akin to the capital and revenue out-turn forms submitted by local authorities to the government than to financial reports and accounts published by an organisation directly to the public—the latter being uncommon in health authorities until very recently.

Not surprisingly, therefore, the Accounting Committee's report (CIPFA, 1982b) was drafted with the help of both the Treasury and the Department of Health and Social Security, since the accounts to which the SSAPs would apply are ultimately a part of the government's Appropriation Accounts. The Government do not accept that this is an area in which the accountancy profession can act independently. If SSAPs were to apply, then they could only be applied by the government using its powers under Section 98.

Two points from this are worth noting. First, in preparing its report, the Committee distanced itself from the concept of applying SSAPs directly, not by preparing guidance notes as CIPFA/ASC did for local authorities, but by preparing separate 'standard accounting practices' which stand alone. These separate standards do, however, clearly draw upon SSAPs or their underlying principles. Second, the ASC involvement has been sought not to represent the accountancy profession in establishing the standards, but simply to endorse or commend the 'standards' as developed bilaterally by the government and health service treasurers. There is some advantage to the government, when promulgating them, to be able to say to the public that its accounting rules are acceptable to the profession.

The sharply negative reaction of the government to the idea of the ASC preparing its own guidance notes on the application of SSAPs to health authorities was one cause of the ASC's re-appraisal of its role in the public sector. Yet, if the trend towards producing locally published annual financial reports in health authorities (CIPFA/AHST, 1982) had been a little further advanced, it might have been that the ASC would have had a legitimate basis for issuing its own advice.

Central Government   The application of SSAPs has not been considered relevant for central government's supply expenditure. The central services of government departments are mainly provided for by supply grants voted yearly by the House of Commons, and accounted for in the annual Appropriation Accounts which set out the actual payments and receipts on the services concerned.

Time has conferred considerable tradition on this approach, which ensures that the money expended has been applied to the purpose or purposes Parliament intended. While we can accept that here the relevance of SSAPs is at best indirect, we suggest that, for public purposes, an accounting statement which makes clearly understandable the purpose of the published accounts and brings in common definitions would be a great step forward.

The Next Steps

The Future Role of the ASC in the Public Sector

We have argued that authoritative standards of accounting constitute a logical step towards the achievement of accountability,
and have described some of the progress attained in applying
SSAPs to the public sector. However, this progress has been limited
and undertaken against a background of support that is less than
wholehearted.

One academic's response to the draft guidance notes for local
authorities was particularly stringent:

> I rationalise the attempt to 'fit' SSAPs as a way of providing more
> credibility to local authority financial reports. In comparative terms, the
> credibility of business accounts has been increased by Accounting
> Standards. Local authorities, *collectively*, desire the same credibility.
> We have already seen reports in the popular accounting press to the
> effect that local authorities have adopted business standards and aren't
> they wonderful. My view is that this is intolerable. . . . My suggestion is
> that the draft guidance notes be set aside. Standards can then be set,
> under the auspices of the ASC, which apply specifically to local
> authorities and which were developed with their clients' needs in mind.
> (Jones, 1982b)

Jones concludes, however, 'of course, the ASC's experience with
extant SSAPs will be valuable in this exercise'. But, in effect, he was
only saying in less temperate terms what the head of the Government Accountancy Service has said both at the ASC and in corre-
spondence with the ASC over the local authority guidance notes
(Sharp, 1981).

The argument on whether it makes better sense to adopt extant
private sector standards or to start from scratch should not,
however, be allowed to disguise the real issue; the development of
public sector standards aimed at ensuring a standard measurement
of performance. Comparability can only have meaning when such
standards have been fully developed: the question is, who will be
responsible for their development?

The ASC is in a difficult position. First, it has a history of setting
accounting standards for the private sector; and the primary
interests of almost all the ASC members are with the private sector.

Second, the ASC has become progressively concerned with trying
to distinguish between what it terms 'measurement issues' as

opposed to 'disclosure requirements'. This is, in part, a political response to the criticism which the ASC has received, since it can be argued that 'measurement' is somewhat more neutral, or scientific, than 'disclosure requirements'. The chairman of ASC took this line when he said:

> The Committee has a second function, that of calling for disclosure of accounting bases when items of account include judgements of value or estimates of future events or uncompleted transactions. In this second respect, we have sometimes shown ourselves to be in danger of overstepping our brief, which is to define terms not to mandate disclosures, the latter being a job for Parliament and the Companies Acts.

We suggest that it is fairly difficult to draw such a line satisfactorily.

Third, and this follows on from the previous point, the UK's membership of the EEC has had a considerable impact on the form of company legislation. In particular, the 1981 Companies Act incorporates the requirements of the EEC's Fourth Directive and brings with it the mainland European tradition of prescribing formats for accounts statutorily, as well as many of the matters previously covered by Accounting Standards. For instance, the Act in Part 1 and schedule 1 writes into the law many of the requirements of SSAP 2 (Accounting Policies), SSAP 9 (Stocks), SSAP 17 (Post balance sheet events), and SSAP 18 (Contingencies) (see Tweedie, 1983).

Fourth, no committee structure existed within the ASC which could consider individual topics in the public sector, but at the same time take a view of the public sector as a whole. The ASC attempted to solve this by establishing a standing Sub-Committee on Public Sector Accounting in 1982. However, in forming this Sub-Committee, two problems were immediately apparent. First, its terms of reference were drawn up on the assumption that its activities would continue in the traditional vein of ASC work, that is, the preparation and publication of work directed by its own working parties. Second, the government representatives – the Treasury and the E. and A.D. – had to declare themselves as nonvoting members since, as they are responsible to their ministers, they could not be in a position to vote on matters which subsequently might be seen to bind ministers in areas for which they had statutory duties and powers. Two meetings provided sufficient evidence that the general disquiet concerning the application of SSAPs *per se*, as well as the discouraging experience of attempting to prepare its own guidance on the health service report referred to earlier, were sufficient for the ASC formally to reconsider its role and its approach to the setting of standards in the public sector. The chairman of the ASC invited the vice-chairman of British Rail (Derek Fowler) to consult and present a report for the November 1982 meeting of ASC (see Fowler, 1982/83).

The Fowler Report

ASC decisions on the Fowler Report were:

(1) To initiate consultation with principal reporting groups and user groups within the public sector, as a basis for formulating a framework for developing accounting standards in the public sector.

(2) To ensure that a statement is issued by authoritative persons within the public sector about the role of the Accounting Standards Committee in this area.

(3) To issue a statement itself about its policies and objectives for facilitating the publication of accounting standards tailored to the requirements of principal divisions within the public sector, including the use of a system of franking.

(4) To formulate a programme of work taking into account that already undertaken by the Public Sector Sub-Committee.

The principle that the ASC should play a role in the setting of public sector standards has been accepted, *nem. con.*, which is a vital decision for the accountancy profession in building up an effective influence in the future. However, equally important is the clear recognition by the ASC in minutes (2) and (3) above, that the way forward is to achieve a publishable consensus, and that the role of the ASC will be to facilitate standard setting in the public sector and 'frank' the results. At the time of writing, we cannot say how this will work out in practice. Consultations are continuing, but we agree that the mechanisms envisaged are an ideal way of resolving conflicts of interest. Emphasis on the objective of 'facilitation' has, in fact, been shown already by the proposal which has been accepted to change the name of the Accounting Sub-Committee to the 'Public Sector Liaison Group of the ASC'.

At its simplest, franking—by whatever words or formal mechanism it finally emerges—will be seen as a commendation, or 'seal of approval', indicating that the accountancy profession accepts the recommendations as being proper professional practice but within the wider context of the objectives and requirements of the public sector body adopting it[1].

The mutual benefit arises, however, because ASC work will be in harmony with the various statutory duties laid on ministers to make certain of the accounting arrangements in their areas of responsibility (e.g. Section 98 of the NHS Act 1977). At the same time the ASC can use its status to be an initiating and co-ordinating force; something at which the Treasury has not been completely successful. For the government, it has the considerable advantage of maintaining the correct constitutional and statutory position while being able to declare publicly, in respect of work so franked, that the accountancy profession commends it. This benefits the government if there is increased public confidence that the rules and procedures operating in the public sector are proper ones, both for the organisations involved and in relation to other sectors.

Which Areas of Work Might be Taken Up First?

We consider that while it is very sensible to apply SSAPs to the public sector, their limited scope means that standards setting in the public sector must be capable of extension into at least the area of reporting standards. A clear example of the need for this is provided by the Third Report from the House of Commons Transport Committee: 'The form of the Nationalised Industries' Reports and Accounts' (26 May 1982). The recommendations of the committee showed particularly that a perfectly proper role existed for the accountancy profession. For example:

> In one area in particular—the lack of standardisation in the use of financial terminology—we believe that present practices are clearly unsatisfactory and that action should be taken as quickly as possible to improve the situation. The fact that so many different meanings can attach to crucial terms such as 'profit' and 'loss', as described in Mr Likierman's paper, is a cause for concern not only because profit and

---

[1]The ASC issued a statement in September 1983 announcing a completely reconstituted Public Sector Liaison Group with new working procedures. Significantly, this was welcomed in the House of Commons by the Chancellor of the Exchequer, Nigel Lawson, in November 1983. The concept of 'franking' was not in the event included because it was judged to conflict with the constitutional prerogatives concerning ministerial responsibility to set accounting standards in the public sector.

loss figures are so widely quoted as indicators of the commercial performance of the industries, but also because it suggests either considerable
confusion in the industry accountant's own handling of the terms and
the facts and figures they purport to describe, or a deliberate
imprecision intended to obscure, rather than illuminate, those facts. In
view of the need not only for consistency in the use of significant
financial terms by each industry, but also for comparability in their use
by other nationalised industries, we hope that this problem will be
seriously examined by the Nationalised Industries Finance Panel, the
accountancy bodies and, in particular, by the Accounting Standards
Committee.

What is particularly significant in this perceptive analysis is that
it shows quite distinctly the different interests of Parliament and
government. Government may wish to circumscribe the role of the
accountancy profession in general (and the ASC in particular) to
set standards for the public sector, but Parliament seems anxious
that the skills of the profession are mobilised to force clearer and
more understandable reporting by public sector organisations. The
mistake the profession could make in these circumstances is to see
the problem in private sector terms. Until recently, it has traditionally done this. The developing public sector role of the ASC should
help to counteract private sector influence, but at some point
tension is bound to develop between the ASC and central government. It may then need to look to Parliament for support.

Clear reporting needs constant and well-regulated definitions.
Two examples will illustrate why tension may arise. First, the term
'subsidy' is not defined consistently throughout the public sector.
Yet different definitions lead to entirely different perceptions of
costs and benefits. Imposed consistency would suit Parliament and
the profession, but not government, because it would destroy an
element of political flexibility. Second, the term 'capital' is not
defined consistently across the public sector. Changes in definition
to suit the political circumstances of the moment are convenient for
government. These issues are more relevant because of the discussions which have recently taken place in Parliament on a Private
Member's Bill (now an Act) to give Parliament direct control over
the Comptroller and Auditor General and his staff, and to give him
a greater duty to investigate public funds wherever they flow.

Another issue which may interest the profession in the future is
the definition of terms which affect financial management in the
public sector. For example, should the profession have a view on

the presentation of the Public Expenditure Survey—say, when the volume series was dropped in favour of cash—or, on the recent revelations concerning the use of 'creative accounting' by local authority treasurers in an attempt to maximise grant entitlements for their authorities. They are both areas in which the accountancy profession, by declaring what reporting standards would be appropriate, would be entering into a political debate, of which they have little experience and with which they may find themselves ill-equipped to deal. But can the profession, in its long-run interest, be allowed to fail to respond? These issues are at the heart of public sector financial management. Is the accounting profession also at the heart of it, or is the interest of the economist and politician absolutely paramount in a democratic society? The answer ought to be that the accountant should at least be the equal of the economist, but unless he thinks in imaginative terms he will lose influence.

Conclusion

The Chairman of the ASC, Ian Hay Davison (1982), has said, in respect of nationalised industries: 'I suspect it would not be unfair to say that private sector accounting standards are tolerated as long as the Treasury and the sponsoring departments do not find them inconvenient.' This could prove to be much truer for the non-trading public sector because of the almost totally political nature of its decision making. At least a recognition of this would reveal the place of accounting standards in the public sector, even if that position were unsatisfactory from the profession's point of view. Meanwhile, pressure for accounting standards must be maintained and, as Ian Hay Davison also said, we '. . . cannot assume the battle will be won until ministers come to realise that breaching an accounting standard is more than an offence to professional discipline (of accountants), it is also inexpedient'.

If we do succeed in this country, the profession will be fore-runners in a development which will be of interest to the rest of the world. We cannot look abroad for inspiration, or advice in detail, on how to develop accounting standards in the public sector. In Europe, for example, the legal tradition has meant that matters which would be dealt with here by self-regulation are dealt with by the law.

Outside Europe, the United States provides an example of a system similar to our own. However, progress there has been slow, even though the idea of a Governmental Accounting Standards Board (GASB) has grown in strength since 1979 (Gregory, 1979). By August 1981, the Financial Accounting Foundation (FAF) had said that a new proposal for setting up a GASB provided a satisfactory basis for moving forward. Among the conditions for FAF's support was that the proposed GASB be modelled after the Financial Accounting Standards Board (FASB), and be under FAF oversight. The new proposal would expand the FAF board to include three governmental representatives and would give the National Council on Governmental Accounting veto power over appointment of the initial GASB chairman, vice-chairman and members. As recently as January 1983, FAF said it had reached a tentative understanding with representatives of state and local government organisations and the accounting profession on the establishment of a GASB under the oversight of FAF, and that FAF 'would be prepared to move forward quickly with implementation of the agreement' once formal confirmation of the understanding was made by the Municipal Finance Officers' Association, the National Association of State Auditors and the American Institute of CPAs. Implementation was also contingent on obtaining sufficient commitments for funding the new body, which will be responsible for setting accounting standards for state and local governments.

It would appear from this that the United Kingdom and the United States are in a similar position.[2] It is not a race and we must learn from one another, but it would be nice to think that the United Kingdom profession had 'squared the circle', and found a way to match self-regulation and professional standards with the statutory and constitutional position as seen from government. The

---

[2]Canada has also made significant progress in the last year, the Public Sector Accounting and Auditing Committee of the Canadian Institute of Chartered Accountants (CICA) having just published its first pronouncements: 'Introduction to Public Sector Accounting and Auditing Recommendations' and 'Accounting Statement 1 – Disclosure of Accounting Policies'. The close professional association with the Government over the development of standards and reporting practice is described in their booklet 'Accounting for Government Spending – A Framework for the Future' ((c) CICA 1983). Australia has also set up a similar Committee under the Australian Accounting Research Foundation.

answer, of course, lies with identifying the user and his needs. If, in the end, this fails and more authoritative public sector accounting standards do not emerge, the result will be an inevitable drift towards further central prescription. The effect is that of a ratchet; once the centre has entered the field, it will never retract and the ratchet effect will cause central government over time to become more involved in public sector accounting standards, building on the experience gained in the private sector. So the time left to square the circle may be short![3]

References

Bird, P. A. and Jones, M. J. (1981) *Financial Reporting by Charities*, ICAEW.

Davison, I. H. (1982) *Do Accounting Principles have any place in the Public Sector?*, CIPFA.

Fowler, D. (1982/83) *Accounting Standards in the Public Sector — Memoranda to ASC, November 1982 and March 1983*, ASC Secretariat.

Gregory, W. R. (1979) 'Statements in quotes — setting accounting standards for local and state governments', *Journal of Accountancy*, November, pp. 82–83.

Hilton, K. (1981) 'Are university accounts any use?', *AUTA REVIEW*, Autumn, Vol. 13, No. 2, pp. 21–32.

Jones, R. (1982a) 'Financial reporting in non-business organisations', *Accounting and Business Research*, Autumn, pp. 287–295.

Jones, R. (1982b) *Accounting Standards for Local Authorities — A Comment on Draft Guidance Notes on the Application of SSAPs*, ICAEW Library.

Likierman, A. (1981) *The Reports and Accounts of Nationalised Industries — A User's Guide*, Civil Service College Handbook, 20, HMSO.

MacVe, R. (1982) *The Possibilities for Developing an Agreed Conceptual Framework for Financial Reporting and Accounting*, ICAEW.

Pearce, N. (1983) *Issues in Public Sector Accounting I — Capital Accounting in Local Authorities*, CIPFA.

Sharp, K. (1981) 'Accounting Standards and central government — against,' *Public Finance and Accountancy*, October, pp. 19–20.

Solomans, D. (1980) *The Political Implications of Accounting and Accounting Standard Setting*, Arthur Young Lecture No. 3, University of Glasgow Press.

Tweedie, D. P. (1983) 'The ASC in chains: whither self-regulation now?', *Accountancy*, March, pp. 112–120.

---

[3]See, for instance, the DoE discussion paper, 'Standardised Statements of Accounts For Local Authorities' (January 1984).

Woodham, J. B. (1983) *Current Cost Accounting in the Non-Trading Services of Local Authorities*, CIPFA.

ASC (1975) *The Corporate Report—A Discussion Paper*.

ASC (1981) *Setting Accounting Standards—Report and Recommendations by the Accounting Standards Committee*.

CIPFA (1975) *Local Authority Accounting Exposure Draft I—Accounting Principles*.

CIPFA (1979) *The Standardisation of Accounts: General Principles*.

CIPFA (1982a) *Standards for the External Audit of Local Authorities and Other Public Bodies Subject to Audit under Part III of the Local Government Finance Act 1982*.

CIPFA (1982b) *Standard Accounting Practices for the National Health Service—Final Report*.

CIPFA/AHST 1982 *Local Accountability—The Need and Scope for Health Authority Published Annual Financial Reports*.

CIPFA/ASC (1982/83) 'Guidance notes on the application of statements of standard accounting practice to local authorities in England and Wales', *Public Finance and Accountancy*, Feb. 1982, March 1983 and April 1983. Also published by ASC/ICAEW.

House of Commons (1982) *Third Report from the Transport Committee Session 1981-82—The Form of the Nationalised Industries' Reports and Accounts*, 26th May, HMSO.

4
Accounting for Public Sector Assets

JOHN PERRIN

Introduction

In Accounting, the term 'assets' includes current assets and investment assets as well as fixed assets (i.e. tangible assets with a useful
life exceeding one year). This chapter is concerned mainly with
fixed assets because the resource ownership of most public sector
organisations is dominated by long-life assets such as houses,
schools, town halls, roads, sewers, dams, water-mains and sewage
treatment works, hospitals, docks, airports, steel mills, coal mines,
and railway lines and rolling stock. Shorter-life fixed assets, such as
motor vehicles, computers, plant and equipment, and furniture and
fittings, together with current assets, make up only a small fraction
of the total value of the stock of public assets.

To place public assets in scale, we may note that government
expenditure plans for 1982/83 envisaged capital expenditure
approaching £7,000 million even in a period of capital expenditure
retrenchment. That figure is the annual *flow* of capital, and can be
measured (though some capital items are paid for out of revenue
funding and are not separately reported). As to the total *stock* of
public sector capital, there is no accurate measurement. Many of
the assets (sewers, hospitals, etc.) are 50 to 100 or more years old
and their historical cost, even if still on record, is totally irrelevant.
However, we have some glimmers of insight from sectors where
replacement-cost valuation has been attempted. The CCA (current
cost accounting) net book valuation for the ten Regional Water

Authorities in England and Wales was estimated for their accounts as of March 31 1982, at a total a little under £24,000 million: gross CCA value may exceed £50,000 million. Rough estimates for capital values in the NHS (National Health Service) suggest a gross figure exceeding £20,000 million at 1983 prices. For the Electricity industry, the most capital intensive of the nationalised industries, a CCA valuation estimate of £21,480 million at 1979 prices was reported by Gibbs and Tailor (1979). For most local authority and central government (for example, defence) fixed assets there are no CCA valuation figures. However, in broad terms it appears nationally that we are dealing with a stock of public assets whose gross replacement cost in 1983 prices may be in the range of £400,000 million to £600,000 million. That is imprecise, but estimates of net current value would be even more imprecise: the realistic length of the useful life of hospitals, town halls, defence establishments and sewers is as difficult to predict as that of steel mills.

The figures in the preceding paragraph may seem regrettably vague. Even where asset registers or equivalent records are kept, they are frequently incomplete. Many of the assets of local, water and health authorities were acquired long ago, before modern accounting concepts: often ownership has shifted several times during the asset lives, from voluntary bodies or small local authorities to larger or different authorities — for example, when the NHS was constituted from hospitals owned separately by local, voluntary and private ownerships in 1948. In most of the non-trading public sector no conventional balance sheets are prepared, no asset valuations or revaluations are disclosed, and depreciation accounting is not practised. And yet matters can change: for example, the water and sewerage services, which as recently as 1974 were largely a subset of local authority activity, have been trans-formed into public corporations charged to use best commercial practice in their accounts, to follow the Accounting Standards and to adopt full current-cost asset valuations and depreciation accounting. Much hard work on identifying, recording and valuing fixed assets had to be done in the Water Industry. But what water authorities have done, local and health authorities, and even central government, could also be required to do.

'Capital' is a wider (or, vaguer) term or concept than 'assets'. Capital signifies a store of value: it can mean the monetary value of ownership rights reflected in the liabilities side of the balance sheet; or sometimes it can mean a store of money or credit not yet committed to real assets; or indeed it can even mean the real assets themselves, measured by some relevant valuation. Assets, typically, are tangible or 'physical'. Capital is intangible and 'financial'. The term, in the accountant's sense perhaps more than the economist's, implies a quantum of wealth or purchasing power which may move through successive and changing combinations of physical assets. In the modern world of rapidly shifting technology, social needs and political wants, it follows that there may arise an increasing demand for information on how far individual public sector organisations are 'maintaining their capital' and using it efficiently and effectively, and on what the alternative uses and benefits (or, opportunity cost values) of existing capital (assets) may be.

The main part of this chapter will be structured around four important questions which managers in public services, or taxpayers or ratepayers, or consumers of the services, or indeed their political representatives, might usefully ask. Following each question will be a discussion of technical accounting or financial topics most relevant to that question. The four questions (with the technical topics shown in brackets) are as follows: (1) Is opportunity value acted upon? (Accounting for capital assets); (2) Is capital expenditure wisely decided and controlled? (Capital appraisal, and financial targets); (3) Is capital stock being maintained? (Capital maintenance and depreciation accounting, and capital accounting with changing prices); (4) Is the cost of maintaining capital stock equitably shared? (Accounting, self-financing and equity; and the capital gearing adjustment).

(1) Is 'Opportunity Value' Acted Upon?

Sometimes public bodies may benefit from selling off particular assets either because they include land or buildings with a marketable value higher than the total cost (i.e. including social costs) of relocating the public facilities elsewhere, or because the assets are inefficient (e.g. a particular school or hospital in terms of layout, or heating or maintenance efficiency) and would best be replaced either by more modern assets or sometimes by a complete change of approach to service – as in the substitution of sheltered care in the community for the elderly, chronic sick and handicapped, in place of old-style long-stay hospitals. Except when under pressure from public spending cuts many managers in public services may avoid redeploying capital resources, as distinct from increasing them, because of the 'aggravation' of negotiating with trade unions and pressure groups over any closure, contraction or relocation. The lack of any cost of capital charge for use of capital assets reduces incentives for change in many non-trading public services, as does the convention, widely followed until quite recently, that all proceeds from the sale of redundant land and buildings should revert to the parent body or Department: this left no local incentive to promote asset redeployment. The likelihood that the opportunity value of capital assets will be systematically considered may partly be a function of the quality of each organisation's capital asset accounting.

Accounting for Capital Assets

The nationalised industries and certain other public corporations, trading funds and water authorities broadly follow the same conventions as in commercial accounting, and account for fixed assets independently from their accounting for the source of funding for those assets: indeed, in general there is a presumption that their fixed assets are financed from the 'common pool' of financial resources derived from operational net cash flows plus any increments in long-term equity or debt financing. For a detailed discussion, see Likierman (1979, 1982, 1983).

Central government, aside from its trading funds such as the Royal Ordnance Factories, does not capitalise fixed assets or depreciate them, nor does it publish any balance sheets or memorandum information on its capital stock valued in accounting terms, as distinct from estimates of capital provision and consumption based on economists' valuation approaches (Griffin, 1975 and 1976). Basically the same situation prevails in the NHS. The government looks on the NHS as an extended arm of central government activity, and the Department of Health and Social Security (DHSS) has never encouraged the individual health authorities which act as its operational agents, to introduce commercial-style accounting. No fixed asset accounts are kept in the books, and indeed asset registers are often incomplete. Major asset investments (mainly hospitals and other buildings and their initial set of plant, equipment and furnishings) are charged to capital funds. Most replacement fixed-assets expenditure (other than items such as ambulance fleets, scanners or X-ray equipment, where there is a desire for higher-level policy control and monitoring) is charged to revenue budgets. It was found (Perrin, 1978) in a survey of a sample of health authorities that most of these kept no record of how much of their revenue funding was expended on fixed assets.

A recent study by NHS Treasurers (CIPFA, 1982) recommends that in addition to statutory accounting reports to the DHSS, there should also be local reporting in a format more intelligible to those accustomed to conventional published accounting reports, and indeed to the public more generally. These local reports would, *inter alia*, include summarised analyses of income and expenditure subdivided between revenue and capital funding. The booklet also states:

> Since, at present, health authorities do not have asset accounts, the statement of balances will only include debtors, creditors, stocks and stores, and cash. However, estimated asset values would also be desirable on a memorandum basis, prior to any further consideration being given to the question of the accounting treatment for capital assets in the health service. (CIPFA, 1982)

An interesting example of a public service which does come close to using full commercial accounting (and even obtains a 'true and fair view' audit), is the British Broadcasting Corporation (BBC). Ignoring the rather specialised accounting arrangements for the External Services which are funded by grants in aid, the BBC's main activity, the Home Service, is accounted for by a balance sheet, income and expenditure account, source and applications of funds schedule, and statement of fixed assets (BBC, 1983). Capital expenditure is written off 100 per cent in the income and expenditure account of the year of spending, but in the balance sheet and statement of fixed assets the fixed assets are notionally capitalised and depreciated on a straight-line basis over the estimated useful life of the assets. The net value of fixed assets is offset in the balance sheet by the Capital Account. The asset values and depreciation are disclosed in historical cost terms, although there is no obvious reason why current cost accounting (CCA) could not be used. However, the published accounting policies explain that the BBC's

Royal Charter requires the BBC to charge capital cost fully in the year of expenditure, and it is thus felt that CCA is not necessary, while exemption from CCA is also justified by the clause in SSAP 16 relating to 'entities whose long-term primary financial objective is other than to achieve an operating profit'. The BBC provides several similarities to the objectives and financial circumstances of health authorities, and its accounts illustrate how other non-profit public bodies could improve their public financial reporting on the use of capital.

The branch of the public sector which is most individualistic in its conduct of accounting for capital assets is local government. Most major capital expenditure is matched by loan finance, and typically major fixed assets are recorded and kept on the books at historical gross cost at least until the matching loan is repaid. However, local authorities can also establish capital funds from revenue contributions etc., to finance fixed assets, with subsequent repayment to the capital fund from period changes to the revenue budgets of services. In addition, they can purchase fixed assets directly from revenue funds (though in general it is illegal for borrowed capital funds to be converted in the opposite direction to revenue expenditure). Revenue finance also can be voted to Repairs and Renewals Funds, to be used for the replacement of short-life fixed assets such as vehicles and equipment, or of longer-life plant forming part of major facilities of still longer life (for example, lifts in multi-storey buildings). Of these four channels for fixed asset expenditure, the last three provide a form of self-financing largely independent of the views of the government or other lenders. This complexity may be contrasted directly with the NHS. The NHS is not allowed to borrow either capital or revenue funds, and health authorities are not allowed to invest in capital funds or repairs and renewals funds, though the offsetting of annual balances between Districts within a Regional Health Authority may achieve this to some extent by informal means.

We have not space here to explore the full complexities of fixed assets and capital accounting in local authorities. For the financial environment of this see Hepworth (1979); for additional accounting detail see CIPFA (1975, 1981a and 1981b); and for a combination of both these aspects see Holtham (1983).

In conclusion we may observe two main points. First, the definitions of what constitute capital expenditure and capital assets are very diverse within the non-trading public sector, and this makes cross-comparison and the assessment of relative performance difficult. Second, these definitions very often depend upon the official label and regulations attached to the source of funds, rather than upon the nature of the assets acquired. Both of these characteristics owe much to tradition, but the factor probably of greatest importance is the influence of legislation and governmental regulations promulgated at different points in time and with different political emphases regarding what should be controlled, and how.

(2) Is Capital Expenditure Wisely Decided and Controlled?

Political priorities and choices guide investment in the public sector, particularly in the non-trading public services where objective and definitive capital appraisal results are often impossible to provide due to the largely subjective and non-quantifiable nature of the social benefits which substitute for financial gain in conventional capital appraisals. There is concern, however, that, lacking a market discipline, capital (and consequently revenue) may be wasted. Often not only is there no market discipline, but also no charge is made for the use of capital in the accounts of non-trading organisations, or of their internal segments. For example, in central government and the NHS no depreciation, rent or interest is charged to authorities or their internal budget-holders for the use of capital. Chapman (1979) has speculated on the level of waste in hospital construction for the NHS. The study in Cheshire, commissioned by the CBI (1979), exemplifies concern for local authority expenditure, where loan charges are used in lieu of depreciation charges. Webb (1979) explores some of the areas of concern over the use of capital in the nationalised industries — where problems of optimising the use of capital persist in spite of their trading status (i.e. partly because of political interference, but also partly because of quasi-monopolistic roles in imperfect markets).

Capital Appraisal

Capital appraisal is known also as 'investment appraisal' or 'capital option appraisal'. The latter term is currently in especial favour because it highlights the general case that there are a variety of services, locations, scale choices, etc., to be considered in most major capital programmes, and it is emphasised that close attention should be given to identifying and then analytically comparing the alternatives or options, in order to find the best option. Each alternative should be appraised by some combination of discounted-cash-flow analysis (where feasible), cost-effectiveness analysis, cost–benefit analysis, and the evaluation of any largely non-quantifiable factors (such as the amenity factor for patients in building a hospital overlooking a park rather than a steel mill).

The Treasury (1982) provides a booklet of guidance on the conduct of option appraisals in the public sector, developing the above points in more detail. Most of the technical advice given in the Treasury (1982) booklet is broadly in line with that in good economics and financial textbooks. What is unique in the booklet is the advice on discount rates to be used in capital appraisals in the public sector: this follows a long history of government attempts to define the optimal discount rate, with the nationalised industries especially in mind (See Treasury (1961, 1967, 1978) and Jewers (1979)). Since Cmnd. 7131 (Treasury, 1978) the discount rate for individual projects has not been specified centrally: it is recognised that some investments are for safety reasons, that some are unavoidable and anyway not separately measurable because they are parts of a larger, integrated system, and that other investments (in the profit-seeking parts of the public sector) must achieve a higher rate of return to compensate for the uncertain returns of the first two kinds of investment. In place of a Test Discount Rate (TDR) for individual projects, the main focus now is on trading organisations earning a real-terms Required Rate of Return (RRR) of five per cent on their investment programme as a whole.

In non-trading activities there is, by definition, no overall return or profit to be measured in the above way. Most major non-trading public service investments have an improved-service objective and are likely (certainly this is so in the NHS) to turn out more and not less costly in revenue terms. Nevertheless, even in the non-trading services some investments are made mainly on grounds of efficiency or cost saving: new boiler systems or other energy-saving schemes are examples. It had been suggested originally that a discount rate of 5 per cent (i.e. the RRR), plus a 2 per cent 'premium' to offset appraisal optimism, totalling 7 per cent, should be used as the discount rate for a net-present-value test in non-trading activities.

Currently the Treasury (1982) advice is to use the five per cent discount rate even in non-trading organisations and to make full use of sensitivity analysis to explore alternative outcomes. The five per cent (in real terms) rate of discount or return is broadly intended to discipline the use of capital in the public sector to meet the opportunity cost of not using those capital funds in the private industrial and business sector. However, the logic of the method as a control system breaks down in, for example, the NHS where all revenue and capital is supplied 'free', with no interest costs or repayment of capital principal (Perrin (1978), Owen (1978), DHSS (1981)). Thus, within their own organisation, NHS District managers face the simple fact that any investment saving revenue costs and yielding a positive NPV at a discount rate of even 1 per cent or less, is advantageous given what is for them a 0 per cent cost of capital — especially if the capital funds can sometimes be obtained incrementally from Regional Health Authorities for such uses and are thus not (as far as local discretion is concerned) being diverted from capital service developments which authority members, managers and the local community might feel should have higher priority than marginal cost-saving returns to capital.

Financial Targets

Financial targets are levels of profits or rates of profitability (wherever practicable to be applied to current-cost valuations of assets) which shall be reviewed and agreed periodically for each nationalised industry, water authority and certain other public corporations and trading funds, including direct labour organisations (DLOs) in local authorities (Dick, 1981). The assumed normal financial target is the five per cent real-terms RRR discussed in preceding paragraphs. However, market forces or political pressures have prevented the prices/charges of many of the organisations concerned from rising to a level to yield this RRR, and so the financial targets in use have included a variety of alternative measures, generally involving a return well below a five per cent RRR. (See Foster (1971) and NEDO (1976) for some of the history and flavour of this.) Difficulties in balancing the financial and social accountability performances of nationalised industries have also exercised the interest of Parliamentary Committees (for example, see Select Committee on Nationalised Industries (1978), Webb (1979) and Lapsley (1981a)).

Triggered partly by the NEDO (1976) report, the 1978 White Paper (Treasury, 1978) laid down a framework within which the public trading sector should work (See Heath (1978), Heald (1980), Davies and McInnes (1982)). It prescribed that the practicable level of financial target should be decided industry by industry, and should take account of the expected return from good management of existing and new assets, market prospects, the scope for improved productivity and efficiency, the opportunity cost of capital, the implications of public sector borrowing and counter-inflation policies, and social or sectoral objectives. Most nationalised industries' legislation generally requires an industry to obtain ministerial approval for major programmes of capital expenditure. In these cases the above factors will all be taken into account, but the starting presumption is that all public sector trading organisations should earn at least the five per cent real-terms RRR. This includes DLOs, which are asked to tender for local authority business on prices allowing for recovery of the RRR (to be measured separately on each of four main categories of work). The DLO situation may be an extreme example, but it is certainly a worrying one for local authorities: their DLOs are competing in bidding with private contractors who, (a) would not necessarily expect to earn five per cent in real terms, certainly during a recession; and (b) can bid on private business to cover their fixed costs, and then bid on public sector business at marginal-cost-plus without either regulation or market forces requiring them to reach, or even approach, a five per cent real-terms return on their average capital employed.

Nationalised industries' financial management and accounting are considered in detail in Likierman (1979, 1980, 1981b, 1983). We return to aspects of the RRR and financial targets again towards the end of this chapter when considering the problems of self-financing by public bodies.

(3) Is Capital Stock Being Maintained?

As worded, the above question has two contexts. First, are the *physical assets* of the public sector receiving physical maintenance (and replacement as needful) so as to maintain a constant level of service performance and cost-efficiency? Accounting information alone cannot give a full answer to this, and anyway the accounting information available in most of at least the non-trading public sector falls short of what could be provided if complete asset registers and optimal/planned maintenance programmes and standard costs were in general use.

Second, is the *value* of the public sector's stock of capital assets being kept to a constant real value? In absolute terms this question is unanswerable because the opportunity costs (or, opportunity values) of most fixed assets are not objectively assessed, and relative cost–benefit trade-offs at the margin between different combinations of resource uses are not known. At the level of the practical, second-best solution, this question should be answerable in approximate terms by the use of CCA asset valuation and depreciation, supported by good asset registers and inventories of the state of capital stock.

Capital Maintenance and Depreciation Accounting

Capital maintenance began as the notion that the financial (i.e. money) capital of an entity should be maintained or preserved, year on year through time, before any profits are declared (or, by extension, before any deduction of relevant taxes, rates, charges or borrowings is allowed). The capital maintenance concept evolved over the last century in private sector accounting and finance, probably mainly because of concern for the spread of shareholdings in public companies to large numbers of small investors with limited knowledge of the business concerned, and the sad experience of some companies in which shareholders' interests were abused by directors not providing sufficient appropriation for depreciation but instead distributing cash in excess of true profits until the companies' resources were exhausted and they collapsed.

However, for central government and most other parts of the non-trading public sector, the concepts of capital maintenance and its application through depreciation accounting have largely been unknown, or rejected. In part, this may be because the notion of a continuing obligation to maintain capital stock has appeared to conflict with the notion of the supremacy of Parliament. It may also be partly because, at a more practical level, it is obvious that the government's financial resources are soundly based, through the power of taxation. Thus, even if, for a particular period, the government does not spend on capital assets at a rate to maintain the stock, this has no necessary implications for its taxation powers, credit rating or ability to make good any contractions in capital stock at some future time, should it choose to do so. Nevertheless, it might seem only fair that governments should be made to report on their capital maintenance via depreciation accounting, so that electors may better know, for example, how far public spending cuts involve running down the public sector's capital stock (Perrin, 1978, 1979, 1981, 1982).

Historically, in times of low inflation, it was generally sufficient for achieving capital maintenance in any organisation to charge the historical-cost depreciation of assets against revenue. Depreciation is defined in SSAP 12 (Accounting Standards Committee, 1977 and 1982) as 'the measure of the wearing out, consumption or other loss of value of a fixed asset whether arising from use, effluxion of time or obsolescence through technology and market changes'. Depreciation is determined annually, as a charge against revenue. This chapter cannot probe deeply the concept of, or alternative approaches and calculations in, depreciation accounting, but see Baxter (1971).

It has been noted previously that central government does not practise fixed asset accounting or depreciation accounting, except in certain trading funds which represent a tiny fraction of its total volume of expenditure. Similarly, the NHS does not use fixed asset accounting or depreciation accounting, though here there is at least concern about this among some NHS Treasurers as well as academics (Perrin (1978), Lapsley (1981b)). In addition, while nationalised industries and other public-sector trading activities generally conform to commercial practices in asset accounting and depreciation accounting, it is questionable whether or not all their published accounts have fully reflected their problems in maintaining capital stock: the latter may be more clearly shown by longitudinal cash flow analysis (Lee and Stark, 1984). Unlike several of the nationalised industries, the regional water authorities are cost-plus monopolists and have no great difficulty in covering their depreciation costs in charging policy, subject to ministerial approval. Instead, their depreciation problems are those of determining what is their real stock of fixed assets, and what is its physical state, its expected physical life, and its expected economic life given changes in technology of pipeline and sewer renovation, population movements, and changes in the scale and nature of industrial activity which affect demand for water and for effluent disposal.

Local authorities have never practised depreciation accounting in the strict sense, except on a limited basis for certain trading activities, and notably for DLOs at the present time. Local authority finance and accounting is very distinctive (see Hepworth (1979), Holtham (1983), CIPFA (1975, 1981a, 1981b)). It is based on a nineteenth century system of segregating capital and revenue finance into separate funds. As earlier noted, some capital assets can be purchased from capital funds, from repairs and renewals funds, or even direct from revenue funds, but nevertheless the major local authority fixed capital investments are financed by borrowed capital, accounted for on the loan-charge system. This involves the creation of historical asset accounts on the one hand, and of loan debt accounts on the other hand. While methods of handling loan charges may differ somewhat in detail between local authorities, the general principles are consistent. These involve the charging of the authority, and of the individual services within the authority, with annual loan-charge costs comprising the capital contribution necessary to fund repayment of the borrowed capital at redemption date, plus interest charges at the average rate borne by all the capital borrowing (for the time being) of the authority as a whole. Obviously this practice does not constitute depreciation accounting *per se*, but it is interesting that the practical effect on the revenue accounts of the authority and on its individual service accounts is that they are charged with approximately the same amounts as would be charged for capital consumption plus interest if (historical cost) annuity-base depreciation were in use.

Capital Accounting with Changing Prices

The professional debate and proposals for accounting reform to deal with changing prices and inflation first became strong in Britain in connection with Current Purchasing Power accounting (CPP), but via the entity approach of the Sandilands Report this gave way to Current Cost Accounting (CCA). The latter approach was finally given authority as an accounting standard in SSAP 16 (Accounting Standards Committee, 1980a), but with the addition of the 'gearing adjustment', which made a broadbrush compensating adjustment to operating profits, to meet partially the objections of the proprietary school of thought. However, nationalised industries and other public trading bodies (other than nationally-owned organisations already under the Companies Acts or about to be sold off, or privatised) were specifically excluded by the Standard from applying the gearing adjustment, though relevant details should be disclosed in a note to the accounts. We will return to this gearing adjustment and its implications for the nationalised industries and the water authorities, in the next section.

Government trading funds such as the Royal Ordnance Factories, and also the Post Office (even while still a government department prior to its redesignation as a nationalised industry and its later subdivision between posts and telecommunications) were pioneers in introducing replacement cost depreciation to cope with inflation. Other nationalised industries have been diverse in their interest and promptness in introducing accounting and public reporting on a basis adjusted for inflation or changing prices (Wright, 1979). In general, the industries with stronger profits (or stronger monopolistic positions) were quicker to introduce the new methods; but for 1981–82 all 17 nationalised industries published accounts on a CCA basis, though with differing degrees of prominence and detail (Morgan, 1983). Aside from the omission of the gearing adjustment (except in footnote disclosure) the main difference in the CCA accounts of the nationalised industries, and of the water authorities (Hill, 1981) and certain other public corporations, from commercial practice is the designation of the main profit measure as CCA profit after taxation and extraordinary items, but *before* interest on long-term capital. This arises because most nationalised industries have no equity capital (though a few have a small proportion of government-owned equity termed Public Dividend Capital), and the loan capital of the industries, which is mainly provided by the government (the owner), thus stands in lieu of equity capital.

DLOs and some other trading activities aside, local authorities' asset accounts are not adjusted to reflect the annual decline in net values of fixed assets between the dates of acquisition and of discharge (i.e. the writing out of the books of asset values upon repayment of the relevant loan). In addition, the loan periods may not match closely with the asset lives which would be chosen for depreciation accounting, though in broad terms this matching is understood to be generally sought. We have previously noted that in the absence of inflation the loan charges made to revenue accounts in local authorities approximate to annuity-base depreciation plus interest charges. With significant inflation, however, this matching becomes increasingly imperfect. Interest rates will rise and thus increase the new loan charges. However, interest rates in recent times have tended to lag behind the full impact of inflation and, in any case, at any point in time the average rate of interest of an authority's total borrowing is affected more by the volume of past borrowing than by the current interest rates. In addition, given that the principal of loans is fixed in money terms, that element in the loan charges does not alter with inflation. Thus, in general terms, the higher the rate of inflation and the less the degree to which current and recent interest rates on borrowing fully reflect inflation, then the greater the degree to which loan charges will fall short of charging the equivalent of current cost or other price-level-adjusted depreciation charges against the service accounts and the overall revenue accounts of local authorities.

The above situation has caused increasing concern to many accountants in local authorities. A research study and report by Jack Woodham (1982, 1983) has suggested a modified form of current cost accounting which might be compatible with local authority financial traditions, if supported by modest amendments to statutes. However, this is seen by some as a premature if not unnecessary innovation, and a counter-suggestion is that notional rents should be used by local authorities to charge their service accounts (CIPFA, 1983). The bulk of local authority non-trading assets (aside from highways) are in land, buildings and their fittings. Rent could be estimated by assessors on a current market basis so as to capture the main effects of inflation and/or the opportunity-cost valuation of the resources in use. By definition, market rents are an amalgam of depreciation or capital repatriation, current interest rates, and some premium or discount reflecting risk, market conditions and the opportunity-cost uses of particular resources. This suggestion is attractive with regard to a more sensitive financial discipline upon individual service committees and budgets, but at the level of the authority as a whole it achieves little in the improvement of financial information, since the aggregate rent figures will presumably not be capable of subdivision between the depreciation factor and other factors, and there will be no information on annual capital consumption (i.e. depreciation) costs, or on capital maintenance (i.e. current-cost net asset valuations of the capital stock). Nevertheless, even the use of notional rents should improve the quality of the information available on capital utilisation and opportunity cost, and interest in this approach has now spread to the NHS as a result of the Enquiry into Underused and Surplus Property in the NHS (1983).

(4) Is the Cost of Maintaining Capital Stock Equitably Shared?

Equity is, properly, an important principle in the financial management of the public sector in the UK, and geographical equity is widely recognised in practice. The financial resource allocation system for the NHS (Royal Commission, 1978) aims to equalise resources on a weighted population basis within all the Regions of England and Wales, and eventually to equalise resources also at the District level. The Rate Support Grant augments locally-raised rates income to assist local authorities to provide a standard level of service at a standard cost. Water authorities are asked to set their charges fairly having regard to the costs of performing services. The dimension of equity, which is less frequently discussed (except occasionally in academic and higher professional deliberations), is the question of the distribution of payment for the cost of capital assets between the tax/ratepayers or consumers in the current year as compared to those in future years. If rates, taxes or charges are set too low either because accurate information on the real costs of capital maintenance is not available, or because political expediency ignores this information, then future generations will have to pay more than their fair share in order to restore the capital infrastructure of service provision. Of course, it can also work the other way: if depreciation is excessive and fully reflected in charges or rates, or if, for any other reason, charges or rates are high enough to permit self-financed capital investment in excess of current need, then current consumers will be paying more than their fair share, to the benefit (presumably) of future generations.

Accounting, Self-Financing and Equity

In the competitive commercial sector, prices (as alternatives to charges, rates and other taxes) are not directly determined by accounting practices or numbers. Instead, they are typically determined by market forces combining various sources of information, only one of which is on accounting costs. In commercial monopolies, and in those parts of the public sector which are monopolies, the situation can be quite different. Policy decisions can be taken to set charges, rates or taxes (or at least the allocation of some portion thereof, as for the NHS) high enough for current operational income to cover all approved capital requirements. Thus, although government borrows part of its central funds, at the level of subsequent allocation within the NHS it is as if all funds were costless. The decision on the proportion of available NHS funding to be spent on capital, as distinct from revenue, is made by government (though there is local discretion within the NHS to vire up to 1 per cent of revenue to capital, or up to 10 per cent of capital to revenue, to meet local needs in the phasing and completion of developments). The NHS is 100 per cent self-financing of its capital needs, in the sense that these are all a free gift from government and no capital repayments, or interest on capital, need be paid: it is as if there were 100 per cent first-year depreciation, with immediate and total write-off asset values from the books of account.

Nationalised industries and water authorities will, in general, finance the replacement of a given level of capital stock mainly out of operational cash flow, but any net capital growth, or shortfall in available cash owing to market factors or inflation effects, will normally have to be met by borrowing — usually from government sources (e.g. the National Loans Fund). All major capital spending by local authorities will normally be financed in this way. Naturally the government, like any influential lender/investor, aims to protect its investment with conditions and guidelines, and its willingness to approve capital expenditure and borrowing by public bodies is heavily influenced by the PSBR and the political and economic pressures and priorities of the day. It is equally natural that the governing boards and professional managers of the industries or authorities concerned often regret these constraints on their professional discretion over operational and financial needs, and would gladly escape from them. An attractive way to escape from such constraints, at least at times when central controls are only on capital borrowing as distinct from capital expenditure, is to increase the self-financing ratio — the proportion of capital requirements met from funds generated internally through charges, rates and service prices, etc. — thus reducing dependence upon government departments for approval of new borrowing. One concern here is that new borrowing by public bodies enters directly into the political and macroeconomic policy arena of the Public Sector Borrowing Requirement (PSBR), with the attendant risks that the apparently justified capital needs of individual public bodies (which may indeed be endorsed by their sponsoring government departments) will be overridden by the Treasury on national economic grounds, or by the Cabinet on party-political grounds. Thus, any reduction in dependence upon borrowing clearly increases the freedom, stability and continuity of capital programme policy in individual public bodies.

In local authorities also, there is a desire for greater independence from central government, and therefore an interest in means of increasing their self-financing. The use of capital funds and repairs and renewals funds, and of direct capital expenditures from revenue funds, are all methods of raising the level of self-financing. But these are on a relatively small scale. The only means by which local authorities can achieve a major increase in their self-financing ratio would be to increase rates substantially and earmark the increment for capital rather than revenue expenditure. There are obvious local political constraints on the feasibility of this, aside from constraints sometimes imposed by central government — as currently under the 1980 Local Government Planning and Land Act.

The Capital Gearing Adjustment

SSAP 16 (para. 51) states, 'No gearing adjustment should be made in the profit and loss accounts of Nationalised Industries in view of the special nature of their capital structure. Accordingly, in such cases interest on their net borrowing should be shown after taxation and extraordinary items.' The latter advice seems reasonable, especially if one supports the entity approach to financial reporting. But the former advice, to make no CCA gearing adjustment in the accounts of nationalised industries (and, by extension, in the accounts of RWAs), is perhaps less easily defensible. SSAP 16 and its supplementary Guidance Notes (Accounting Standards Committee, 1980a and 1980b) do not provide any conceptual justification for the SSAP 16 advice on the gearing adjustment, beyond a laconic comment on 'the special nature of their capital structure'.

This is not a text on the theory of accounting for changing price levels (but see Whittington (1983); and for some problems regarding interest costs and holding gains see 'Inflation Accounting Special Issue' (1976), and Perrin (1977)). However, let us note at least some of the practical complications arising from the different arrangements for the gearing adjustment prescribed for the public and private sectors. RWAs are expected to manage their pricing policies to recover net operating cost, plus CCA depreciation, plus the government's financial target determined upon CCA asset values (and no gearing gain offset is allowed to reduce the total income requirement). But in the small number of private water authorities operating under the Companies Acts and alongside the RWAs, it appears that gearing adjustments are allowed and may be taken into account to set lower water charges than RWAs are allowed to set (if they are to meet their financial targets). Similarly, in the nationalised industries, those industries in competition with the private sector will, *ceteris paribus*, either have to set higher prices than their private competitors may choose to use, or else set competitive prices but fail to meet their financial targets, with all the risk of opprobrium this may involve. Only those industries in monopoly positions, like RWAs, can be reasonably assured of meeting their targets. The effect of all this, if inflation continues at even a modest rate, would appear to be a continuous increase in the self-financing ratios of the water authorities, of at least some of the nationalised industries and some other public corporations, until the point is reached when (at least in the absence of major systems expansion or any sudden change to a much more capital-intensive mode of operation) these public bodies become 100 per cent self-financing — with no need to go to the government or any financial marketplace to expose themselves to the discipline of scrutiny regarding the credibility and general efficiency of their operations and, in particular, their level and specific uses of capital funds. If this scenario is correctly interpreted, then it is a matter for both public and professional concern whether or not, first, the anticipated outcome is desirable, and second, the present government policies for nationalised industries and water authorities on financial targets, self-financing, and the CCA gearing adjustment should be reviewed with concern for an equitable division of capital costs between present and future consumers and taxpayers (see Monopolies and Mergers Commission, 1981a, 1981b).

Conclusion

The basic function of this chapter has been to convey information regarding the wide variety of capital accounting and related financial practices in the public sector, and to give guidance on specialised sources for additional reading. A second function has been to draw attention to some key issues; these are set out in question form as the four main section headings of the chapter. Readers will have noted that, in general, explicit answers to the questions posed in the text have not been given. In fact, no absolute answers can be given to the questions. This is partly because the accounting and other relevant information is not sufficiently comprehensive and consistently comparable across the wide diversity of the public sector for sweeping judgements to be meaningful. Academics and practitioners (and politicians) more accustomed to the private sector often tend to be highly critical of the quality of public sector accounting systems as regards their usefulness for efficient and effective decision making and control, and, as we have noted, they doubt the need for such diversity of accounting methods. But those who work as professional accountants in, for example, local authorities, will typically strongly defend the distinctive features of their own systems.

Nobody has as yet written a definitive treatise to 'prove' one way or the other whether, on balance, it would be better for local authorities to continue with their present accounting methods (including loan-charge accounting in lieu of depreciation accounting), or to convert to 'mainstream' accounting methods (assuming that Parliament would agree to amend the relevant Acts which govern parts of local government accounting practice). This author's personal views on the answers to the four questions are that they vary widely between different parts of the public sector, but that in most cases there remains much scope for improvement in accounting systems and information so that the questions *can* be better answered. As for the diversity of accounting methods, this writer and researcher personally feels that there is probably no good case for perpetuating the diversity, so that effort should continue to be made to bring public sector accounting (for example, in the treatment of capital, fixed assets, depreciation and adjustments for changing prices) into full conformity with 'generally-accepted' accounting practice and with all relevant Accounting Standards.

References

Baxter, W. T. (1971) *Depreciation*, Sweet and Maxwell.

British Broadcasting Corporation (1983) *Annual Report and Handbook 1983*.

Chapman, L. (1979) *Your Disobedient Servant*, Penguin Books.

Davies, J. R. and McInnes, W. M. (1982) 'The efficiency and the accountability of UK nationalised industries, *Accounting and Business Research*, Winter, pp. 29–41.

Dick, M. (1981) Problems for financing local authority DLOs, *Public Finance and Accountancy*, November, pp. 18–19.

Foster, C. D. (1971) *Politics, Finance and the Role of Economics*, George Allen and Unwin.

Gibbs, M. and Tailor, B. (1979) *Nationalised Industries' Accounting Policies*, Consumers' Association.

Griffin, T. (1975) 'Revised estimates of the consumption and stock of fixed capital, *Economic Trends*, October, HMSO.

Griffin, T. (1976) 'The stock of fixed assets in the United Kingdom: how to make best use of the statistics', *Economic Trends*, October, HMSO.

Heald, D. (1980) 'The economic and financial control of UK nationalised industries', *Economic Journal*, June, pp. 243–265.

Heath, J. (1978) 'Accountability and control in nationalised industries', in Sixth Special Report from the Select Committee on Nationalised Industries, Session 1977–78, *Comment by Nationalised Industries and Others on the Government White Paper on the Nationalised Industries*, HCP 638, pp. 94–127.

Hepworth, N. P. (1979) *The Finance of Local Government*, George Allen and Unwin.

Hill, K. (1981) 'Water authorities and the impact of CCA', *Public Finance and Accountancy*, November, pp. 14–18.

Holtham, C. (1983) 'Local government: its financing, internal control and external reporting', in Sir D. Henley *et al., Public Sector Accounting and Financial Control*, Van Nostrand Reinhold.

Jewers, W. G. (1979) 'Required rate of return/test discount rate, pricing policies and financial targets', in *Financial Targets of Public Corporations*, CIPFA.

Lapsley, I. (1980) 'Towards public sector capital maintenance, *Public Finance and Accountancy*, October, pp. 27–28.

Lapsley, I. (1981a) *The Role of Accounting Measures in the Financial Regulation of UK Nationalised Industries*, University of Glasgow Accounting Research Workshop Paper.

Lapsley, I. (1981b) 'A case for depreciation accounting in UK health authorities', *Accounting and Business Research*, Winter, pp. 21–29.

Lee, T. A. and Stark, A. W. (1984) 'A cash flow disclosure of government-supported enterprises' results', *Journal of Business Finance and Accounting*, Spring, Vol. 11, No. 1.

Likierman, A. (1979) *The Reports and Accounts of Nationalised Industries*, Civil Service College Handbook, 20.

Likierman, A. (1980) 'Where politics dominate accounting theory', *Public Finance and Accountancy*, October, pp. 23–27.

Likierman, A. (1981a) *Cash Limits and External Financing Limits*, Civil Service College Handbook, No. 22, HMSO.

Likierman, A. (1981b) 'The history and problems of targetry', *Public Finance and Accountancy*, November, pp. 11–13.

Likierman, A. (1982) *Appendix 1: Report on The Form of the Nationalised Industries' Reports and Accounts*, Third Report from the Transport Committee, HMSO.

Likierman, A. (1983) 'Nationalised industries', in Sir D. Henley *et al., Public Sector Accounting and Financial Control*, Van Nostrand Reinhold.

Morgan, C. (1983) 'Accounting standards and the public sector, *Public Finance and Accountancy*, January, pp. 16–18.

Owen, A. J. (1978) *Health Authority Capital Budgeting: the State of the Art in Theory and Practice*, Technical Paper for the Royal Commission on the NHS, University of Warwick, Centre for Industrial, Economic and Business Research.

Perrin, J. R. (1977) 'CCA and the appropriation account', *Accounting and Business Research*, Summer, pp. 193–202.

Perrin, J. R. (1978) *Capital Maintenance and Allocation in the Health Service*, Technical Paper for the Royal Commission on the NHS, University of Warwick, Centre for Industrial, Economic and Business Research.

Perrin, J. R. (1979) *Accounting for Depreciation in the Public Sector*, in Papers presented at the 94th Annual Conference, CIPFA, pp. 37–44.

Perrin, J. R. (1981) 'Accounting research in the public sector', in M. Bromwich and A. G. Hopwood (eds), *Essays in British Accounting Research*, Pitman, pp. 297–322.

Perrin, J. R. (1982) 'Introduction—to why depreciation is an issue in the public sector', *Public Finance and Accountancy*, pp. 32–34.

Perrin, J. R. (1983) 'The National Health Service', in Sir D. Henley *et al.*, *Public Sector Accounting and Financial Control*, Van Nostrand Reinhold.

Webb, M. G. (1979) *A Critical Appraisal of UK Government Control of Nationalised Industries*, Discussion Paper 37, University of York, Institute of Social and Economic Research.

Whittington, G. (1983) *Inflation Accounting: an Introduction to the Debate*, Cambridge University Press (with the Social Science Research Council).

Wilson, A. (1980) 'Capital problems stem from split responsibility', *Public Finance and Accountancy*, October, pp. 20–21.

Woodham, J. B. (1982) 'Local government: the impact of depreciation', *Public Finance and Accountancy*, May, pp. 34–36.

Woodham, J. B. (1983) *Current Cost Accounting in the Non-trading Services of Local Authorities*, CIPFA.

Wright, D. M. (1979) 'Inflation accounting in the nationalised industries: a survey and appraisal', *Accounting and Business Research*, Winter, pp. 65–73.

ASC (1977) *Accounting for Depreciation*, SSAP 12.

ASC (1980a) *Current Cost Accounting*, SSAP 16

ASC (1980b) *Guidance Notes on SSAP 16: Current Cost Accounting*.

ASC (1982) *A Review of SSAP 12—Accounting for Depreciation*.

CIPFA (1975) *Local Authority Accounting I: Accounting Principles*.

CIPFA (1981a) *Accounting Methods in Local and Public Authorities*.

CIPFA (1981b) *Implications of Capital Expenditure Controls for Local Authority Capital Programming*.

CIPFA (1982) with the Assn. of Health Service Treasurers, *Local Accountability: the Need and Scope for Health Authority Published Annual Financial Reports*.

CIPFA (1983) *Capital Accounting in the Non-trading Sector*.

Confederation of British Industry (1979) *Value for Money*, Report on Cheshire County Council, Manchester, CBI North-West Region.

Department of Health and Social Security (1981), HN (81) 30.

Department of Health and Social Security (1983) *Under-used and Surplus Property in the National Health Service*, Report of the Enquiry, HMSO.

Inflation Accounting Special Issue (1976), including editorial and papers by G. H. Lawson, G. Briscoe and G. Hawke, and M. Bourn relevant to defects of the gearing adjustment, *Journal of Business Finance and Accounting*, Spring, Vol. 3, No. 1.

Monopolies and Mergers Commission (1981a) *Central Electricity Generating Board*, HC 315, HMSO.

Monopolies and Mergers Commission (1981b) *Severn–Trent Water Authority . . .*, HC 339, HMSO.

National Economic Development Office (1976) *A Study of UK Nationalised Industries*, HMSO.

Royal Commission on the National Health Service (1978) *Management of*

Financial Resources in the National Health Service, Research Paper No. 2, HMSO.

Select Committee on Nationalised Industries (1978) *Reports and Accounts of the Energy Industries, Session 1977-78*, Seventh Report, HC 583, HMSO.

Treasury, HM (1961) *The Financial and Economic Obligations of the Nationalised Industries*, Cmnd 1337, HMSO.

Treasury, HM (1967) *Nationalised Industries: a Review of Economic and Financial Objectives*, Cmnd 3437, HMSO.

Treasury, HM (1978) *The Nationalised Industries*, Cmnd 7131, HMSO.

Treasury, HM (1982) *Investment Appraisal in the Public Sector*, 3rd Edition.

Part 2
Financial Planning and Control

5
The Role of Accounting in Local Government: Some Illustrations from Practice

CYRIL TOMKINS and IAN COLVILLE[1]

Most of the literature on management accounting was written from a normative perspective. That is, it was written as though there was one correct way, even if not yet discovered, to analyse certain financial decisions. The literature on local government accounting, although less extensive, is no exception to this phenomenon. The purpose of this chapter is to emphasise that the value placed upon accounting information, the impact it has upon decisions and the design of the accounting information system itself, must depend to a large extent upon the context within which that accounting information is produced and offered for use. By context, one does not just mean the type of industry or whether the concern is with the public or private sector, though clearly those factors have some impact on the nature of accounting; one means, in addition to these broader contextual factors, the full local circumstances of the organisation in question. This includes the nature of tasks performed, perceptions of those tasks and the status of people involved in the organisation, and the scope relevant individuals have for choice and action. This is not intended to suggest that

[1]This chapter is one of a series of contributions on local authority financial control arising out of a project financed by the Social Sciences Research Council.

normative analysis is of no value: rather, that one needs to have a good description of the context within which accounting is to work before one attempts normative prescription of what the accounting system for a particular organisation should be.

This chapter, therefore, sets out to describe how accounting information is used (or not used) in two particular local authority departments: a social services department and a police force. While, following the comments above, it would be dangerous to generalise too far from descriptions of accounting in action to all similar local authority services, it is felt that the descriptions which follow do advance our understanding of both the general nature of accounting in the local authority domain and the way that specific local circumstances affect the way accounting is used.

To even a general observer it seems clear that there is likely to be a marked difference in organisational characteristics and operational philosophy between a police force and a social services department. The police force seems to consist mainly of uniformed officers who are subject to very tight discipline and often expected to follow orders in a similar way to armed service personnel. An outsider gets the impression of strong central direction and co-ordination (Colville, 1982a). Of course, the Police have a consideration for social welfare and the policeman on the beat is especially aware of the need to have this in mind in order to provide a comprehensive policing service. Nevertheless, it does seem likely that there will be a lesser degree of delegation of authority and a greater exercise of control by discipline in the Police than within a social services department, where concern to provide service tends to focus more on the individual than the broader needs of order in society. As a consequence, the question arises as to whether or not the different traditions of discipline and authority within these two departments give rise to a different use of financial control information and procedures.

It is also interesting to compare the public image of an accountant with that of a policeman. Is not the accountant often referred to as a 'policeman' in both an audit or financial control role? Is not the logic of the accounting profession the establishment of control systems, the structuring of a series of accounts with clear responsibilities designated as to who is responsible for each one and the establishment of an organisational network of accountability? Such a rule-orientated control philosophy seems more akin to a police perspective on the world than the individualistic, less regimented, procedures of a social services department. Consequently, it will be interesting to examine whether a police force might adapt more easily than social services officers to notions of accountability in a financial sense and, therefore, have a more developed and systematic accounting system.

Despite the apparent logic of such an argument, the following descriptions of 'accounting in action' do not lend themselves to such easy prescriptions.

The Relationships of Departmental Structures and Management Processes to Financial Control

Before describing and comparing the accounting systems of the two local authority services it is important to give some background information about the external influences upon them, to whom the senior members of these services see themselves as accountable and the type of organisational and management process each uses. Just brief elements of these factors should be sufficient for the purposes of this paper.

The Police Force is accountable both to the Police Authority and the Home Office. The Home Office is a significant influence in overseeing the execution of policing activities through its inspectorate, but also has considerable power through its provision of a grant that amounts to 50 per cent of police expenditure. In addition, the Police Authority precepts upon two separate County Councils for the other 50 per cent. The Police Force, therefore, has three prime 'masters' to serve, though the Chief Constable considers himself first and foremost a policeman with main responsibility to the Home Office for policing, and only weaker responsibility for professional police activities to the Police Authority.

In contrast, the Social Services Department sees itself as almost entirely accountable to just one of the County Councils which form the Police Authority.[2] The Department does, of course, have many statutory duties and does have finance provided from bodies outside the Council. The Area Health Authority, for example,

---

[2]The Police Authority consists, in this instance, of two County Councils which both contribute to the Authority's expenditure.

provides 'joint finance', the Manpower Services Commission gives a per capita grant for sheltered employment, and the Department of Health and Social Security plays a part in control over capital expenditure. The total funds provided directly by these outside bodies are, however, quite small when compared to the size of the revenue budget. These outside sources supply funding for about only 3 per cent of the total revenue expenditure, and a large part of that from the Area Health Authority is continuing revenue agreed and committed in earlier years. These facts mean the Social Services Department definitely sees itself as a *County Council* service. In particular these outside bodies have practically no influence on internal control processes. As a senior member of the Department said:

> We do have to produce accounts for the sheltered workshop in the form required by the Manpower Services Commission, but they are 'knocked off' in a couple of hours each year to satisfy them . . . [and] not used for control, monitoring or management purposes. They are something you've got to do to get the grant. And its the same with the Area Health Authority.

The Police Force looks primarily to the Home Office and secondly to the Police Authority, consisting of two County Councils, as the main control devices upon it. The Force sees itself as a quasi-autonomous regional service not too tightly coupled with either County Council, whereas the Social Services Department is a part of the County Council. The Headquarters of the Social Services Department are in the County Council main offices, but the Police Headquarters are miles away.

As a result of the structure of accountability just described, the Treasurer of the County Council has a dual responsibility. He is treasurer to both the County Council and the Police Authority and, as the County Council pays a proportion of the police expenditure, the interests of the County and the Police Authority may well conflict. On the other hand, the County Council only bears 20 per cent of the Police expenditure and the Police Force do not seem to be directly competing for resources with other County Council departments. The Treasurer's relationship to the Social Services is different. In agreeing to expenditure by Social Services he is aware that the County Council must usually provide 100 per cent of the sum and that this will be more clearly visible to other departments.[3] Moreover, the Treasurer is much more intimately involved with

County Council matters, not only through having his office located there, but also because of his close relationship with the Chief Officers of the County Council Services and their problems. The Treasurer meets the Chief Officer of the largest services regularly each week with the Chief Executive and the Chief Officers Group, and will often see them informally. Both the Treasurer and the other Chief Officers see themselves as within the same organisation even if they have departmental differences. Contact between the Treasurer and the Police Force is more formal. The Police Force will keep him at a distance from professional policing matters whereas the Social Services Department states that it makes a point of trying to involve the Treasurer, and more particularly his staff, in their professional activities. A senior officer in Social Services stated:

> We deliberately try to involve anybody and everybody in the Treasurer's Department in the care philosophy of this Department.

It is clear that the Social Services Department feels that Treasury personnel have to understand social care and work before they can expect co-operation and understanding. This difference in emphasis is also apparent in levels of contact between departments. The Treasurer (and the Social Services Director) will often have contact with the *Deputy* Chief Constable. 'It is as though,' it has been said, 'the police pyramid has a slightly higher peak than ours' (i.e. the County Council).

There is also a difference in terms of the financial regulations governing the Treasurer's position with regard to each of the departments. The Treasurer has to consult with the Chief Constable over records maintained by the Police Force, but the Chief Constable has the right to define his own needs. In Social Services, however, the Treasurer could exert stronger pressure to satisfy himself that the accounting records of the department are adequate for the needs of the County.

For both the Police Force and the Social Services there are considerable degrees of autonomy in managing operational procedures. While the Police Force has very strong central direction

---

[3]The Council will, of course, receive rate support grant equal to approximately half revenue expenditure, but it is not earmarked for social services and so 100 per cent of the demands for that department are in competition with demands of other departments.

from the Chief Constable in setting the tone and manner of policing, the area covered is so large that it must be divisionalised geographically and the Divisional commanders have a considerable degree of discretion in operating a full variety of police activities in their divisions — being able to call upon specialist headquarters services if required. Operating responsibility in the Social Services is also decentralised but follows a more functional structure dividing into Services for the Elderly, Children and their Families, the Disabled and Fieldwork Related Services. Much of this care is provided in residential accommodation and it is clearly in the clients' interests to have each home managed and run as autonomously as possible in order to create 'the right atmosphere' and avoid notions of institutionalisation and bureaucracy.

It is interesting to see where responsibility for financial control fits into this framework. In the Police Force there is an Assistant Chief Constable (Administration), but the person taking operating control of accounting and financial management is a civilian at about the fourth tier level in the Force. He is not a qualified accountant. In the Social Services the person directly responsible, and actually operating financial control, is a qualified accountant and holds the rank of Deputy Director of Social Services. There are two such Deputy Directors: the Director responsible for Administration (the accountant) and a Director of Operations who then has beneath him the Directors of different elements of the Service. The person with most direct influence over accounting matters is, therefore, placed at a far more powerful level in the organisational hierarchy in the Social Services, indicating that the Director himself sees finance as being very central to the management of his Department.

The location of the accounting/finance officer and his professional background can vary between police forces and social service departments. Any differences in the use of accounting information related to these factors must not, therefore, be automatically applied to such departments in general. Indeed, six or seven years ago they would not have been relevant to this particular Social Services Department. Prior to the appointment of the current Deputy Director (Administration) there was a non-accountant responsible for financial administration at about the fourth tier down in the hierarchy, but it was clear that he had not provided the type of financial control the Director wanted. The Director, therefore, recruited an accountant and, while the status of Deputy or Assistant Director was probably needed to induce a qualified accountant to move out of the Treasurer's Department permanently, the fact that the Director appointed at such a level indicates his awareness of the centrality of financial management for Social Services. This can be contrasted with the Chief Constable's perspective on finance. As described by Colville (1982a) the Chief Constable sees finance more as a broad operating constraint setting the boundaries on total activity.

This difference in perspective shows through in the way the Chief Constable and Director of Social Services operate in financial meetings. It would be extremely rare for the Chief Constable to meet the Treasurer to discuss budget matters without having his financial administrator present. The Director of Social Services, on the other hand, would often see the Treasurer to discuss financial matters without the presence of the Deputy Director (Administration). As his Deputy Director (Administration) says, the Director of Social Services is extremely capable at grasping the financial management needs of the Department and handles the financial questions at committees extremely well.

The descriptions given so far suggest that, with regard to the gaze of the Treasurer, the Police Force has a position of greater operating independence than Social Services, and that Social Services see financial management as more central to the management of their activities than do the Police. Already, therefore, the insights emerging from trying to understand practice do not support the apparently sensible initial expectation that, because the 'control philosophy' of the Police was closer to that of accountants than was the attitude of social service officers, the Police were likely to place greater reliance on good financial management. If one wants to understand attitudes towards financial management, then one also needs to understand the ways in which financial control is embedded in the organisational structure and the beliefs of the people within it.

These different service attitudes are also reflected in the way in which the financial management of those services is integrated with the staff of the Treasurer's Department. Because of the 'neater' professional distinction between policing and finance, the Police Force relies to a much greater extent on the Treasurer's Department for advice and guidance on financial matters. Until a recent change in emphasis, as a result of a re-organisation of the Treasurer's office, the Treasury Group accountant responsible for police matters spent about 70 per cent of his time on police finance and financial control. (With the re-organisation of the Treasurer's Department, the same amount of work for police is still done within the Treasury.) That Group accountant and the relevant civilian administrator in the Police Force have a very close and continual working relationship. In contrast, the Social Services Department feels that 95 per cent of financial control related to their services is exercised by that Department itself. The Deputy Director (Administration) has friendly personal relationships with Treasury staff at several levels – they work in the same buildings and some are ex-colleagues of his in the Treasury – but, while co-operation is good, he explains the relationship as one of 'co-existence rather than dependence.' In addition, by undertaking 95 per cent of financial control activities itself, the Social Services Department manages to establish a large degree of independence from the Treasury.

It would seem that the possession of an independent financial control system in Social Services can provide that department with the degree of independence and self-determination from others within the same organisation (the County Council) that can be achieved by a police force by virtue of its separable organisational status and more distinctive professional boundary. An apparent paradox arises in the case of the Social Services Department in that it seeks independence by exercising financial control itself while simultaneously seeking to 'involve' the Treasury in care considerations. The resolution of this paradox comes from recognising that it may be to the advantage of Social Services to select the areas in which the Treasury needs to be 'involved' and educated. No Machiavellian intent is suggested. It may well be in the best interests of the County Council and its Social Services to allow this form of interaction, especially if the Treasurer ensures that a fairly tight *aggregate* expenditure limit is observed by Social Services. Tomkins (1982) describes how virement has been relaxed with the Treasurer *consciously* following just this sort of policy.

The Centrality of the Budget, Budget Construction and General Form of the Accounting System

In both the Police and Social Services Departments all decisions having financial effect are considered through their impact on the budget. Indeed, Colville (1982a) stresses that accounting processes in the Police Force can only be understood by seeing that essentially they serve budget compliance purposes. Exactly the same is true of Social Services.[4] However, following remarks above regarding independence in operating financial control, there is a marked difference between the two departments in terms of the degree of collaboration with the Treasury over budget construction. The Treasury Group Accountant with police responsibilities will liaise closely with the police administrator in constructing the detail of the budget. While budget requests are collated within the Police Force, the Group accountant will sit in on the Police management team discussions relating to budget construction and he will, for example, check carefully that requests being made for increased or even sustained expenditure at a fairly detailed level were not under-spent in the previous year indicating, perhaps, that the budget request is not needed. This can lead to intensive negotiation over some budget items.[5]

The practice of Social Service budget construction is quite different. Budget requests are collated within the Social Services Department and discussed and adjusted by the Departmental Management team without any reference to the Treasury. The complete budget, including continuation and development activities, is then given to the Treasury. The budget document submitted is also in highly aggregated form and has become more so in recent years having been reduced in length (and hence detail) to about one-third of what it was before. Subsequently, discussion and negotiation occurs with the Treasury on what information on developments the Social Services chooses to give and what questions the Treasury Budget Liaison Officer can raise from the broad

---

[4]This is not necessarily true for other local authority services which have a trading or competitive aspect to their operations. See Tomkins (1982) for a discussion of recent accounting developments in direct labour organisations which are not so closely budget related.

[5]See Colville (1982b) for a more detailed discussion.

total provided. Otherwise, unless the Budget Liaison Officer chooses to force the issue, he or she can do little except check that the total budgeted expenditure is within the target expenditure set for Social Services by the County Council and its Policy and Resources Committee on the bases of central government White Paper guidelines, the expected government grant position and local political arguments. The degree of involvement of the Budget Liaison Officer on details of the Social Services budget has, in fact, declined over recent years—especially as there has been less scope for development with the financial cuts imposed by central government.

It has already been argued at a broad level that financial control can be embedded in organisations in different ways. This view is reinforced as one moves to a more detailed investigation of budgetary control, even though the main technical accounting records supporting the budget system appear, in general terms, quite similar. Both the Police and Social Service Departments rely on two major components of the accounting system: the 'official' computer tabulations of income and expenditure issued by the Treasury, and the commitment accounting records kept wholly within the service departments. The tabulations received from the Treasury in both departments provide comprehensive coverage of all expenditure for the relevant department. They are routinely updated each month and are very simple in terms of accounting technology being merely aggregations of expenditure incurred. They provide a minimum breakdown of information for departmental management purposes and are, therefore, budget custodial in orientation rather than management orientated. In addition, both departments have a large proportion of expenditure incurred on employee costs: being 50 per cent of revenue expenditure in the Police and 74 per cent in Social Services. Also in neither department was there any evidence of extensive use of further informal records kept by particular individuals (often called 'black books') in addition to the 'official' tabulations and commitment records. Moreover, both commitment accounting systems were installed to compensate for shortcomings in the Treasurer's tabulations for management control purposes and both are *wholly* directed towards keeping expenditure within prescribed budget allowances, searching for savings under one budget head which could be transferred (with appropriate approval where necessary) to another heading, and searching for likely overspendings. The general structure and purpose of technical accounting systems appears, therefore, to be very similar for each department. Consequently one might expect to find that the budget compliance controls within departments are similar; it will be seen that this is not the case.

Ensuring Budget Compliance

The major difference between financial control in the Police and Social Services Departments can be seen in the different degrees of sophistication and comprehensiveness of their commitment accounting systems. In the Police Force the commitment records are not consolidated to show a comprehensive practice, nor are regular reports produced from them, though individual spending officers may be called upon to give details of commitments under any head of expenditure in response to an *ad hoc* enquiry. In addition, these spending officers are not usually budget holders, hence there is no automatic incentive for them to seek savings and they are most likely to undertake such action when directed to do so from the centre. In contrast, in Social Services the commitment accounting records constitute a co-ordinated accounting system covering the whole Department's activities and the managers of most 'outlying stations' providing data input to the system are budget holders. Regular consolidated reports from this system are discussed by the Departmental Management Team and a monthly report (including expenditure to date and commitments and departmental projections to the end of the year, based on seasonal expenditure profiles) is discussed by the Departmental Management Team after each month ends. There are, therefore, clearly different degrees of 'importance' or 'emphasis' on accounting matters exhibited by the two Departments and it is becoming increasingly apparent that accounting controls are grafted into the control processes in these two organisations in ways which are consistent with more general management attitudes. Recall, for example, the difference in ranking of the principal financial officers within these two departments.

The major budget item to be controlled in both departments is, as already stated, employee costs. For this purpose the Police Department finds the Treasury computer tabulations an adequate monitoring device. The information is sufficiently up-to-date for exercising control. This is not the case with Social Services.

In the Police Department the employee costs budget was costed at full establishment level. Given the difficulties of recruiting police officers at that time, the senior police officers knew that the full establishment would not be reached and that, consequently, there would be savings under that heading for use as a contingency cover for unexpected costs and overspendings in other areas. The budget control process was, therefore, geared primarily to watching for overspendings and trying to ensure that they were within likely savings on employee costs.

The situation is different in Social Services. First, for reasons given below, that Department considers the computer tabulations to be an adequate control device only for salaries (as distinct from wages). Second, budgeted employee costs are based on establishment figures less expected vacant positions; hence, one cannot assume that there will be slack under this budget heading.

This is an example of how external pressures can influence attitudes towards financial control. Basing the budget on the establishment, rather than the expected, employee level gives the Police Force a regular source of savings and lessens their need to search rigorously for savings over all other heads. There is, therefore, no necessity, from a police viewpoint, for an extensive and sophisticated commitment accounting system. This might well be different if the basis for budgeting police employees was changed; but with the current political pressure for improving the police, and with Home Office influence, it seems difficult to plan for a below-strength Police Force. In contrast, there is no prime source of budget slack in Social Services. Thus a more comprehensive system is needed to ensure savings are identified, in whatever pocket they might occur, well before the end of the year and before the budget holders spend them on what are, perhaps, less vital purposes.

This conclusion, and the general motivation for the commitment accounting system as a vehicle to facilitate virement, was corroborated in a discussion with the Deputy Director (Administration) of the Social Services. He said:

> If I could build in 3 to 4 per cent of additional money into the budget, I would not need a commitment accounting system at all . . . I wouldn't need this financial control system. All I would need to do is to have a monitoring control on overtime . . . a monitoring control on develop-

ments and a monitoring control over the largest item of income which is personal charges. These three would do if 3 to 4 per cent was in the budget as fat . . . By controlling those aspects, I could ensure that we came within the target.

This seems very similar to what happens in the Police Force. It also suggests that financial managers have a choice between designing elaborate and more expensive accounting systems which enable 'tight control,' or allowing more slack in budgets and operating with fewer, broader and less expensive accounting indices. It may not be clear, unless one looks at specific situations, which results in the most effective management of the department; in other words, is the 'tighter control' worth the extra cost? For wages costs the Social Services see the computer tabulations as inadequate for management purposes because, while employee costs are broken down into service groups and establishments, the data do not tell the Deputy Director why that amount of money was spent as it was. For example, the Deputy Director explained that he needed to know why Sunday overtime (paid at a higher rate) had increased rather than weekday overtime. This reflects the differences between Social Services and the Police in terms of where the decision point is located for incurring overtime.

It has been described how there is a perceived need for tighter budget control over individual headings in the Social Services in comparison with the Police, but this in itself does not explain another key difference. It has already been stated that there are many more separate budget holders in Social Services than in the Police. Colville (1982a) stresses that while the operations of the Police are semi-decentralised, there is no attempt to do the same for the financial control structure. In contrast the financial control structure in Social Services is very tightly coupled with the operational structure; a system of responsibility accounting has been installed with budget independence and responsibility closely following operational responsibility.

The value of responsibility accounting in the Social Services seems to lie partly in the managerial philosophy of the Director and his deputies and partly in the nature of the service tasks to be carried out. As already stated, the Director believes that financial management should run a close second to service need in running his service. Certainly the need for care is placed a clear first, but he recognises how good husbanding of resources can lead, in turn, to better service provision. In association with this there is a management philosophy in that department that people will act more responsibly if given more independence within broader constraints, like an aggregate budget, rather than being instructed what to do and controlled over each detailed budget head.

Since going over to this decentralised responsibility budgeting, the Deputy Director (Administration) stated that large savings have been forthcoming. He felt that this was a direct corroboration of this philosophy of making people responsible; without that responsibility for managing resources people are placed in the position of asking for things and the custom of asking for as much as possible in order to get as much as you can becomes established.

Such decentralisation of budgets is not, apparently, adopted in all, or even the majority, of social services departments in other local authorities. However, there do seem to be task and local cultural organisational factors encouraging such a design in *this* authority compared with that which exists in the Police Department. First, in the Police, the profession is accustomed to being far more disciplined, in a 'rule-governed' sense, than are Social Service employees. Moreover, the nature of the employees suggests differences in the practice of management. For example, it is inevitable, with many domestics and cooks in social service homes being women with family responsibilities and employed part time, that social service managers have to be flexible in allowing altered shifts, occasional (approved) absenteeism and so on. This is not likely to be tolerated on the same scale among police officers, nor, indeed, among the professional ranks of the Social Service Departments. Such flexibility cannot be managed (i.e. detailed changes and absentees authorised) from the County Council Head Office, even though there may be effects in terms of incurring increased overtime rates, paying replacements, etc. The easiest way to control expenditure, while allowing flexibility in operations, seems to be to pass such operational responsibility to the head of the residential home, provided that a total budget and general controlling determined policies are observed. Similarly, a person responsible for aids to handicapped persons in a particular part of the County may be faced with two clients each needing walking aids. It would be impossible for the decision to be taken centrally about the allocation of the available budget in specific cases. Consequently, budgets are allocated to different areas according to their characteristics and then the person in the field has to make choices within that budget.

The Social Services Deputy Director (Administration) also feels that to try to control such matters centrally by providing rigid rules of operation will induce people in the field to 'set you up' and find ways around the rules which they will find irksome and, from the point of view of providing good care to old people, the disabled and children, bureaucratic and meaningless. In the police, by contrast, a willingness to take central discipline and a desire not to be seen manipulating the system (with the implications regarding honesty that that entails) may make responsibility budgets unnecessary. Of course, the central police headquarters will not direct detailed placing of police officers. This must be done at divisional level, but the Police Force seems more able, within divisions, to operate much more upon a pool of resources (mainly policemen and vehicles) basis, rather than having specific detailed activities always directly associated with specific local resources. In this way the allocation of a policeman to a car and a particular route draws upon different budgets which are controlled in aggregate at Head Office. Moreover, there is not even a budget for each Police Division.

The nature of financial control and the detailed aspects of the commitment accounting system and the way it is used reflect, therefore, an amalgam of pressures including: external pressures on maintaining employee establishments; professional attitudes; internal managerial philosophies; and the nature of tasks performed. The effectiveness of an accounting division cannot be justified on purely technical accounting criteria.

Cost Behaviour Analysis and Standards

The main emphasis of this chapter has been to examine the extent to which accounting control was exercised differently within the Police and Social Services Departments given their apparently very different tasks and cultures. In undertaking this analysis, however, some commonality of practice was noted which also seems to reflect their similarity in being part of the public *service* and distinct from public or private sector manufacturing organisations.

While both the Police and Social Services Departments

undertake accounting analyses of their own to facilitate their own control, it is immediately apparent to anyone familiar with cost accounting for manufacturing and marketing operations that there is no cost behaviour analysis, flexible budgeting or standard costing built into the acounting system. This stems from the dominance of ensuring budget compliance, but also implies that even simple cost analysis into fixed and variable variations has little meaning for those responsible for constructing budgets or evaluating performance. Colville (1982a) could find no evidence of such analyses or use of technique in the Police Force. Similarly there is no evidence of formal recognition of such concepts in designing systems in the Social Services. Moreover, it was categorically stated that such analysis was not done in constructing budgets.

It did appear, however, that the concepts of fixed and variable costs, capacity utilisation and cost behaviour generally, were used on an *ad hoc* basis in making specific investigations. There is a practice, outside of the budget construction activity, of selecting certain budget heads each year and 'taking them down to zero base.' This is not a formal zero-base budget system, but merely a detailed questioning of the activities under the relevant heading and of how the money is being spent. In carrying out such analyses any techniques deemed desirable are used. For example, a recent analysis disclosed that coaches used regularly to transport children along given routes are usually two-thirds empty. This was disclosed by calling for capacity utilisation data which, indirectly, recognises the separation of fixed and variable costs. Such a discovery will lead to a re-planning of that activity and an adjustment of budgets in future, but there appears to be no attempt to collect such information systematically.

It is difficult to know the extent to which such systematic analyses would be useful in either Social Services or the Police. All one can say is that, to date, they are not used systematically in these particular departments nor is there a perceived need for their use on a systematic basis. This may well be quite justified if there is little variation in units of service delivered (if they can, in fact, be measured) and static budgets updated incrementally according to new developments may be cost-effective.

Summary and Conclusions

The clear message coming through from investigating the way in which accounting controls operate in the two Departments examined is that if one wishes to understand accounting practices and attempt to evaluate what impact they have, one must see that those practices are established within a broader process of management practice. The significance of specific aspects of the system cannot reliably be deduced without seeing the relationship between the accounting operation and that broader management practice. At a very general level this has been recognised by consultants for years and by contingency theorists amongst academics. But it seems, from this enquiry, that it may often be necessary to explore very closely the *specific* pressures, interests and areas of discretion which managers feel they have, rather than rely on very broad descriptions of tasks and the nature of organisations – though we would be quite ready to agree that broad categorisations can yield useful information about *some* features, as was shown in the penultimate section of this chapter. Systems designers should be aware of influences of local specificities as well as broad contingent factors.

For example, one may summarise the Police Force's use of accounting as follows. The Police want increased flexibility in budgeting without having to rely on the employee's pay heading to meet their virement needs. In addition, it was vital to understand the political and organisational context (even down to specific local issues and ways of budgeting) in order to see why accounting was treated as it was. In the Police Force, the Chief Constable has a dominating service quality orientation whereas the Treasurer acts as a budget custodian – the two functions are largely divorced from each other with the Chief Constable only being concerned with finance to the extent that he must see that his department complies with the aggregate budget figure and does not violate virement rules which are, in fact, quite liberal in this authority. The budget, therefore, defines the boundaries around policing activities and is not the prime focus of anyone in the Police except the fourth tier administrator. The budget is both enabling and constraining at broad levels, but no more than that. This 'professional' separation of policing and financial control is reflected down through the organisation so that there is hardly any coupling of operational and budget responsibility, though it has also been suggested in this paper that this may additionally reflect the nature of the management tasks as well as professionalism. It is stressed that the authors are not arguing that these responsibilities should be tightly coupled; it is merely a fact that they are not and no one seems to want the situation changed.

It is clear that financial control is also boundary defining for the Social Services, but it is also far more than that. The Social Services strategy is to maintain as much independence from the Treasurer (in operating its own financial control) as possible, while at the same time 'involving' him and his staff in care considerations. As the Treasury recognises that the Social Services can exercise good financial control through its five-year-old commitment accounting system, it appears to be more happy to go along with the Social Services Department's approach than it was a few years ago. The Social Services Department, therefore, seems to want to establish that the Treasurer can only use the budget to be broadly 'boundary defining' upon them, but, unlike the Police, it then also sees that it can use accounting procedures to exercise control within this boundary over the subordinate part of its service. As a result, the internal accounting system *within* the Social Services Department is very tightly coupled with operational responsibility. The Social Service Department would also be delighted to have the flexibility it perceives the Police having through the employee cost heading.

The reasons for this contrast between Social Services and Police are difficult to unravel with just one case study of each service and it is not known how different these practices are in other local authorities. Nevertheless, the use of accounting in this way seems to reflect a mixture of external pressure, professional differences and the contrasting nature of their activities, though it may well also be influenced by local management philosophies and characteristics. In the case of the Social Services Department examined, the Director's personality, his awareness of what can be achieved in his department by good financial management and his decision to hire a qualified accountant at Deputy Director level, seemed most important. Many Social Service Departments have not done this, in which case it is possible that the contrast between the Police and Social Services is not so marked.

Finally, it should be stressed that the findings of this research contradict the general hypothesis with which it started. The more rule-orientated control philosophy of the Police Force does *not* lead to a more ready acceptance of accounting means of financial control. Paradoxically, the less tightly controlled, more 'democratic', Social Services see greater benefits in the use of responsibility accounting. It also seems that tight *central* control of service delivery can be maintained (e.g. in the Police) without elaborate financial control systems. This chapter suggests that relationships between 'tight' and 'loose' delegation and the extensiveness of accounting systems may not be as straightforward as one might imagine.

References

Colville, Ian (1982a) *Accounting Information Systems in a Police Force*, Working Paper No. 38, School of Management, University of Bath.
Colville, Ian (1982b) *Budgets and Their Men; Men and Their Budgets*, Working Paper No. 41, School of Management, University of Bath.
Tomkins, Cyril (1982) *The Effect of Political and Economic Changes (1974–82) on Financial Control Processes in Some UK Local Authorities*, Working Paper No. 40, School of Management, University of Bath.

6
Financial Planning and Control

CLIVE HOLTHAM

Context

In the climate of economic constraint which faces the public sector not only in the UK, but also in many other countries, it is perhaps hardly surprising that the tools and techniques for financial planning and control have come under increasing scrutiny. Specific areas such as budgeting, cash limits and efficiency studies are covered elsewhere in this book. The aim here is to give an overview of the broad area of financial planning and control; not to provide a fully comprehensive review, but rather to examine and assess selected key issues. The specific topics examined are: financial planning; project appraisal; budgetary control; and the use of information technology.

In public sector organisations, which typically have goals that are social, environmental, educational or economic in nature, the role of financial planning and control may be quite different from that in a commercial organisation. Of course, the public sector can encompass businesses, such as nationalised industries, but even in these, with a very dominant profit or financial target, account is taken of wider implications. Also, in the governmental sector, it is more appropriate to consider finance as in many ways a constraint rather than a target.

During the 1960s and 1970s there was a massive increase in the literature on public sector planning and control. There was an increasing interest in new systems and techniques to promote more rational approaches to public sector management; such as Planning

Programming Budgeting Systems (PPBS), Cost-Benefit Analysis (CBA) and Zero Base Budgeting (ZBB). There has been considerable experimentation with such approaches, particularly in the USA and UK. Much has been learnt from both the successes and the failures. What is now particularly noteworthy is the way in which many of the ideas, systems and techniques promulgated in the 1960s—an era of considerable growth in public expenditure—are now being 'recycled', in what is only a marginally altered form, as the solutions for the 1980s—an era of highly constrained public expenditure. Perhaps the clearest examples are the MINIS system (Minister's Information System), introduced by Mr. Michael Heseltine when Secretary of State for the Environment, and the related central government Financial Management Initiative. Both closely parallel processes implemented 10–15 years earlier, particularly in local government.

Before outlining approaches for improving planning and control which may be worth consideration, it is necessary to stress that one of the major lessons of the experimentation of the 1960s and 1970s was that there were few, if any, panaceas. Changes in structure or management systems or techniques were, *in themselves*, unlikely to promote the greater efficiency and effectiveness sought. Indeed, where introduced inappropriately, or inadequately, they could actually reduce efficiency and effectiveness. More attention needs to be placed first, on reviewing existing shortcomings (if any), and then on deciding the resources to be devoted to, and priorities for, change. There can be very heavy costs associated simply with the act of change, and these must be balanced against the hoped-for benefits.

In relation to governmental planning and control it is sometimes argued that because politicians have at most a 4–5 year period in office (and often in local government considerably less because of annual elections), they only have short-term horizons. It is argued that this limits the scope for improvements in planning and control. This can be and often is true, but it is not a universal truth. Many politicians actually have long-term goals, though these may be matched by short-term preoccupations. It must also be pointed out that if officials either accidentally or deliberately concentrate politicians on matters of short-term significance, then it will be more difficult for them to take a longer-term view.

Financial Planning

In a climate of economic constraint, the case for financial planning is not always clear. It is therefore felt to be important to state why there is a continuing need for financial planning.

It is important to make, at an early stage, a clear distinction between financial planning and budgeting. These are two separate processes, with differing objectives and requirements. Although neither is limited to a particular timescale, financial planning tends to have a perspective of more than one year ahead, while much of budgeting is concerned with the current and subsequent year.

Although financial planning and budgeting are different they are, of course, intimately related, and in practical terms link into each other in a variety of ways. Financial planning logically precedes, and provides the general framework and policies for, detailed budgeting. Budgeting can and does exist without effective financial planning, but financial planning needs to be able to make an impact on budgeting if it is itself to be effective.

Due to the fact that financial planning looks to the future, which is inevitably uncertain, some commentators argue that financial planning is worthless. They say, quite rightly, that inflation cannot be precisely forecast 12 months ahead, that we do not know the resources that will be available next year (from Government Grant, rates, charges, etc.), and that political power, nationally or locally, can be subject to change or redirection. How, then, can anyone look ahead 3, 5 or 10 years with any accuracy? The budget should remain as the main planning vehicle.

This is a persuasive argument, but it overlooks several things. First, even the annual budget is subject to uncertainty in a variety of ways (demands, inflation, interest rates, the weather, etc.). Second, although uncertainty tends to increase the further one looks into the future, there are, in fact, differing degrees of uncertainty attached to different factors. It is usually possible to contain uncertainty within a range of, say, 'high', 'medium' and 'low' options. The implications of different assumptions can then be examined within the planning process. Strategies can then be devised to take account of a range of assumptions, rather than simply extrapolating the present position ahead under a single assumption.

There is no better demonstration of the need for effective

planning than the Department of Education and Science's failure in the area of teacher-training policies. Published 'planning' documents in the early 1970s used just one assumption about the birth rate and pupil-teacher ratios. Internal DES documents had contemplated quite wide variations in both assumptions, but these never surfaced to inform the policy debate in the early 1970s. It is hardly surprising that policies and capital programmes failed to take account of the range of uncertainty.

Effective planning must recognise the inevitability of uncertainty, rather than ignore it. This still does not, of course, guarantee the 'right' decisions because judgement still has to be applied and, indeed, risks taken. But it can be seen that, in many ways, uncertainty increases the need for planning, rather than stands as an objection to it. Planning allows organisations to respond to changing circumstances by anticipating potential changes.

Objectives of Financial Planning

There are six main objectives of financial planning:

(1) To Enable Priorities to be Determined and Exercised in Key Policy Areas   One of the great limitations of budgeting as a policy planning tool is that usually it only looks one year ahead. Yet significant policy changes in the public sector are rarely capable of implementation wholly within the next budget period. This is most visible in the case of capital schemes. In many cases in the public sector it is only over a 3–6 year period that major changes of direction can be planned and implemented.

(2) To Examine the Impact of Possible Changes in Demand, Particularly Demographic Changes   The public sector responds to demands, whether for refuse collection or hospital places. It does not necessarily fulfil all demands; there can often be disagreement over the measurement of demand, and public sector bodies can influence demand through pricing and administrative policies. Nevertheless, in order to meet future demands, decisions need to be made now. A very clear example of this is expanding towns where, to meet targets for houses and jobs several years ahead, infrastructure needs to be constructed well in advance.

Many public services are influenced by demographic change. Some aspects of demography, particularly the birth rate and migration rates, are highly uncertain even in the short-term. Yet in, say, 1984, the total number of 12–16 year olds in an education authority could have been forecast up to 1996 fairly accurately, assuming no significant in-or-out migration. The secondary school children of the mid-1990s were already born in 1984. The financial implications of such demographic trends can then be forecast using assumptions about service levels and use of the capital stock.

(3) To Identify the Medium-Term Effects of Both Capital and Revenue Proposals Within an annual budgeting system it is usually only possible to demonstrate the first-year impact of new growth proposals. At constant prices it is relatively straightforward to identify the medium-term costs of new schemes; in many cases the costing will derive from a project appraisal exercise. With innovative, or indeed highly complex schemes, the degree of uncertainty increases. A budgetary system which only looks one year ahead in, say, Year 0 (when the 'go ahead' to build a major scheme in Year 1 is given) will not bring out the full commitments being entered into five years ahead.

(4) To Relate Policy Making to National or Other Guidelines In the public sector, the Public Expenditure White Paper contains the central government's plans for public spending, including that for local government and the public corporations which is not necessarily under the government's direct control. Despite the shortcomings of the White Paper, it remains an important source of guidance on current thinking at national level for two years beyond the next budget year.

(5) To Display the Cumulative Effect of Existing Committed Growth and Savings The cost of existing policies and commitments forms an important baseline to the financial planning exercise. At a time of no growth or restraint they can, by themselves, considerably constrain the budgeting exercise.

(6) To Provide a Framework for the Programming of Activities by Individual Services A major orientation of financial planning is towards present decisions. It enables resources to be programmed

this year to achieve a goal in some future year. This refers not only to the allocation of financial resources, but also to the programming of staff time, training needs, land acquisition and maintenance policies.

Medium-term financial planning should not be about building castles in the air. At the end of the day it must have a direct influence on detailed resource allocation, that is, the annual budget. The annual budget should be the short-term, primarily financial, representation of the financial or policy plan. In the past, the annual budget was the only approximation to a policy plan. But a budget has a short-term orientation, an emphasis on control needs and on detailed accountability. In a few organisations it may serve well enough as a policy plan, but this will not typically be so in most of the public sector.

In a climate of economic constraint the need is to develop a selective rather than comprehensive approach to financial planning. It may be neither possible, nor necessary, to meet all the above objectives in full, but public sector organisations should aim to cover at least the key aspects for their own areas of concern.

Project Appraisal and Review

During the 1960s and 1970s, when more rational planning, budgeting and control systems were being introduced or experimented with by national and local governments in the UK, USA and elsewhere, there was also interest in improved project appraisal techniques. Part of the impetus for this had come from welfare economics and in particular the development of the theory of cost–benefit analysis. A considerable amount was learnt from the experimentation and development which took place, and cost–benefit studies found a role in projects where the quantification of both costs and benefits was possible even if uncertain or not reducible to financial terms. They have also been used by agencies such as the World Bank to provide a framework for decisions of some consistency across widely differing circumstances (though mostly in 'economic' projects expected to have some significant financial returns). In the UK the Roskill Commision's study into a third London airport also attempted a quantification of social and environmental costs, but this did not inform the public debate in the way intended.

Subsequent attempts to improve project appraisal have tended to examine a more broad based approach. At one level project appraisal should be one part only of a rational management system, where objectives are clear, alternative strategies are carefully examined and individual schemes for approval flow from this. The real world is rarely so straightforward. Where objectives and strategies are not altogether clear, this should highlight even more strongly the need for good project appraisal methods. But in practice the record for the governmental parts of the public sector is distinctly patchy. There are areas of central government where project appraisal has been developed, but in local government and the health service it is relatively underdeveloped.

This is not to say that the reports produced on new schemes and projects are hopelessly inadequate; by and large this is not the case. What is lacking is a systematic approach to appraising projects. This is not necessarily easy in the governmental sector where social and environmental considerations are so important. It is not promoted by centrally imposed planning systems (as in the Health Service or Housing Investment Programme) which aim to increase strategic thinking and rigorous appraisal, but can at times prevent it through an over-mechanistic approach and unrealistic timescales or resource assumptions.

Within an individual organisation, improved project appraisal can be promoted in a variety of ways.

(1) Strategic Analysis   It is very difficult to make judgements on individual schemes (capital or revenue) without some kind of broad policy framework. The worst situation is, perhaps, where capital and revenue are treated as separate, and resource allocations are made in each area on differing bases. This can occur both in central and local government and in the Health Service. Decisions on major capital or revenue schemes should, ideally, have been preceded by at least some analysis of the broad policy alternatives and their implications, as between capital- and revenue-based strategies (and probably more than one of each).

(2) Appropriate Timescales   Project appraisals should show the full costs and benefits quantified, as far as possible, for as many future years as are necessary to show the full impact of the scheme.

For major capital schemes, the full revenue costs may not be incurred for 3, 5 or even 10 years ahead.

(3) Statement of Risk The future is uncertain, yet reading through project appraisals one is not always made aware of this. It is common for both costs and benefits to be expressed as single estimates. In reality there is always a degree of risk either way in relation to both costs and benefits. It is, however, not completely unknown for both costs and benefits to be assessed in an optimistic light. Obviously it is a key task of the finance officer to try to prevent this. Ideally there should be a formal record of the people responsible for all technical, financial and non-financial assumptions and forecasts, from the initial emergence of a project to its actual operation. In addition, schemes should contain some indication of the risks involved, perhaps by showing high, medium and low risk outcomes for key factors and their implications.

(4) Formal System and Data Presentation Project appraisal is promoted by a formal system which all projects and schemes must pass through, and also by a uniform method of documentation, evaluation methods and criteria. These should not operate as a strait-jacket and different approaches may be needed for different types of scheme. Industrial development schemes are different from social services ones; large schemes from small ones; building projects from new technology. But a good project appraisal system will allow for diversity while also drawing together common elements.

For a large scale capital programme (or major revenue projects) a six-year system could be outlined, which might be truncated for smaller schemes.

(1) Five Years Before Scheme Starts—Project Identification by Services This step involves the identification of a problem or idea, which needs resources to be solved or exploited. It is the time for a broad examination of options. It is the type of work on which, for example, broad policy reviews may concentrate.

(2) Four Years Before Scheme Starts—Project Justification This is the step where detailed work is required, and by which time a commitment of staff resources is needed. The scheme will appear in

the organisation's medium term plan if it is a sufficiently high priority, in the work programmes of the departments if it is not.

(3) Three Years Before Scheme Starts — Probable Programme
Detailed work on programming is continuing and the need to review, and if necessary revise, previous assumptions is essential. The scheme should be appearing in the medium term plan with, for example, a firmer specification and perhaps advance land purchases or de-commissioning plans being drawn up.

(4) Two Years Before Scheme Starts — Provisional Programme
Where there is a capital scheme, the architects will require a firm brief by this stage. There should be a clear idea of the key steps needed for implementation, their timing, sequencing and resource impacts.

(5) One Year Before Scheme Starts — Committed Programme
The scheme will now be in the first year of the medium-term plan and is therefore to be formally approved, deferred or rejected. For schemes designated as 'Firm' early approval may be given, other schemes may be designated 'Subject to Finance' and finally approved or otherwise as part of the conclusion of the detailed budgeting exercise.

(6) Programme Starts   The Scheme has finally been approved and departments implement it.

Post-Project Review

One area that has been very seriously neglected in the public sector (and also where the private sector is not free from criticism) is post-project review, also known as post-project audit. This involves examining, after the project is complete and in operation, whether the actual results vary from those planned. The review should not be solely of a financial nature; indeed, it may be in the non-financial area that most is gained from the review.

A post-project review undoubtedly assists an organisation to learn from experience, to minimise future errors, and to stimulate improvements in forecasting and decision-making processes.

However, the behavioural barriers to post-project review are considerable, particularly in some public sector bodies, and account for the limited introduction of the approach. No one likes admitting mistakes, particularly where professional and/or political judgement was involved, and most particularly where organisations are in the public eye. In addition, where projects are successful in one dimension (such as architectural acclaim) it can become more difficult to review them on other, possibly conflicting, dimensions (e.g. poor workmanship, failure to achieve throughput anticipated).

It is better to create a constructive atmosphere based on an objective approach than to apportion blame or praise. The projects selected should tend to be those of key importance to the organisation, both repetitive and one-off. Post-project review can be resource intensive and it is probably more important to look at a small number of carefully chosen projects in depth, than to adopt a mechanistic approach to all schemes. Post-project review requires a clear statement of accountability for assumptions and project management.

The method of undertaking post-project reviews will vary between organisations but one approach, based in part upon the approach of the British Gas Corporation, is:

(i) Identify 'critical factors' upon which the decision to proceed turns; for example, staff reduction, sale of land, reduction in delays.

(ii) Clarify basis for review at the time the project is approved, together with reporting timetable and reporting responsibilities.

(iii) Produce review report, including variances (if any) between project approval and actual for financial and manpower assumptions, and key dates, together with reason for variance.

(iv) Compare each critical factor between that assumed for project approval and achievement, together with reason for variance.

If substantial progress could be made in undertaking post-project reviews, there could be subsequent benefit from comparison of such reviews, particularly between individual local or health authorities. Unfortunately, given the behavioural problems associated with reviews, even within an organisation, frankness of a broader type might be even more difficult to achieve. However, there are, even now, informal methods of passing information between authorities on what has not gone wholly right (particularly on large and/or innovative schemes).

Budgetary Control

Budgetary Control does not exist in a vacuum. It is part of, and reflects, the whole management philosophy and system of an organisation. Looking across the public sector it is noticeable how there have been many changes in management philosophy and systems over the last 20 years. They are probably more diverse than ever before. At one end of the spectrum are the nationalised industries. Several of these have developed some of the most sophisticated control systems in any part of the public or private sector. This has been necessitated by their size, functional specialisation, and the quantifiability of their targets, and their regular exposure to financially orientated scrutiny by consultants, the Monopolies and Mergers Commission and the government.

At the other extreme is the central government where, despite considerable recent efforts, much of the management philosophy and systems is still rooted in the last quarter of the nineteenth century. (Notable exceptions are the trading funds.) This has been compounded by the split between administrators and professionals such as accountants, the absolute lack of financial expertise at all levels, the diversity of functions, the lack of measurable targets and the relative lack of scrutiny by Parliament, consultants or consumers.

Local authorities and the health service come in between these two ends of the spectrum. Some operate very sophisticated systems, others tend towards the central government philosophy and the health service is actually constrained to some extent by central government's own systems. Also, there is a very wide range of practice within each of the local government and health sectors.

Before examining good practice in public sector organisations, it is important to set a framework for the analysis of such practice. This framework will establish the objectives of budgetary control, and the factors regarded to be of significance in implementing budgetary control systems, and hence for evaluating them. An illustration of the relevant parts of a generalised management cycle is set out in Figure 6.1.

Most public bodies have formal or informal plans which reflect their strategies. The annual budget is the short-term, financially-orientated representation of these plans. In the implementation of the plans, control information will be produced which in turn allows control to be effected.

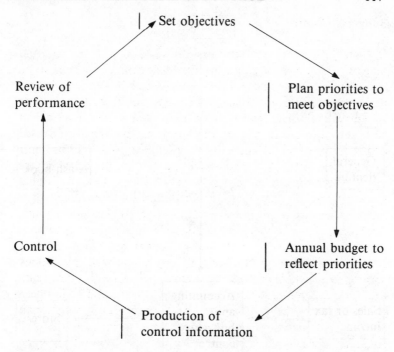

Figure 6.1 Management Cycle – The Context of Budgetary Control

Two main points can be drawn from this. The first is that where the objectives of an organisation are not purely financial – and this applies to most organisations, though more so in the public sector – budgetary control which is solely financial is only one component of the wider subject of *Management Control*. The aim of management control could be summarised as: *the effective use of resources in the achievement of objectives.*

Budgetary control is an important element of management control, but is not the only element. A good budgetary control system can in fact help managers in exercising management control in the widest sense.

The second point is that budgetary control systems do not exist in their own right. Unlike payroll, the payment of creditors systems, etc., budgetary control data is derived from feeder systems; it is essentially the by-product of the continuing management and financial administration of an organisation. Many systems feed

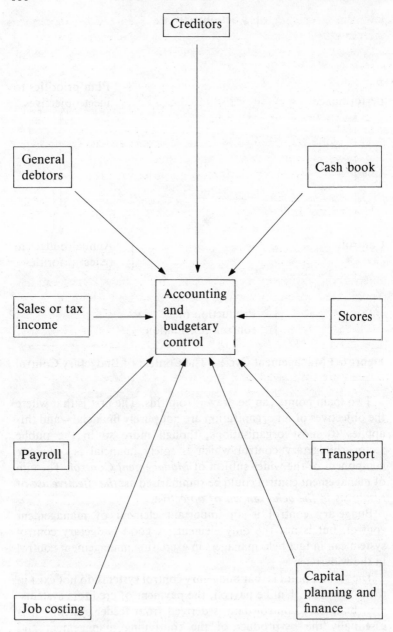

Figure 6.2 Budgetary Control and Feeder Systems

into the budgetary control system (see Figure 6.2). It cannot therefore be 'optimised' in isolation from these feeder systems.

A succinct definition of the objective of budgetary control systems could be:

> To provide relevant, intelligible, up-to-date and accurate information to all levels of management in order to help them make decisions in the areas for which they are accountable.

This is the objective which is related to management's use of budgetary control. However, accountants also need the same or similar information for accounting purposes such as:

(1) Ensuring authorisation, accountability and integrity (stewardship).
(2) The production of statistics for submission to government, CIPFA, regions, etc.

Budgetary control systems have often grown out of systems set up initially for book-keeping and accounting purposes. But the objectives of budgetary control are wider than those of accounting, though they are dependent on good accounting. In some organisations, the accounting and the budgetary control system are one and the same thing. For all but the smallest organisations, however, their differing requirements should be met in different but related ways. In the analysis below, 'accounting' and 'budgetary control' systems are contrasted as if they were quite discrete, though they rarely are. Nevertheless it is useful to adopt this stance to distinguish between features primarily geared to stewardship, and those aimed at management control.

Following on from the objective of budgetary control above, each feature within the objective will be examined in approximate order of importance.

(1) In Order to Help Make Decisions An accounting system is concerned with the correct recording of information. But the prime aim of budgetary control is the making of decisions, even if the decision is to do nothing. Most of the other features below flow from this overriding requirement.

(2) All Levels of Management The board or policy committee, directors or chief officers, and all line managers, accountants and administrative officers need budgetary control information. But the board does not (or should not) want the same information as the

first-line supervisor, though the information to all managers should derive from the same source and be reconcilable.

The differing needs of different managers inevitably means that, ideally, output should be personalised. Accounting-based systems have not always facilitated this, but the modern computer does allow it. It is assumed below that senior staff in the finance department are managers with needs for strategic financial information which do not directly relate to the detailed stewardship requirements with which most accountancy staff are concerned.

(3) In the Areas for which they are Accountable An essential feature in achieving control is that all individual components of a budget should have an identifiable person accountable for its control. When a budgetary control system has gradually derived from an accounting system, clear identification of individuals accountable for control may never have taken place. It should not be assumed that identification is necessarily a straightforward task. For an individual functional area, several managers even from different departments may be responsible for maintenance, central accommodation, transport services, depreciation and financing.

It is, however, possible to use the opportunity of systems review to ensure a correct structure of accountability. Indeed, even without any revision to computer systems, accountabilities can be made clear so that all expenditure has someone accountable for it. Where several people have a role in individual items of expenditure, the accountability for financial control should be made explicit.

(4) Relevant Different levels of management reflect the hierarchy or pyramid which is a recognisable feature of almost all public organisations. Budgetary control systems should take account of this and give management at each succeeding level the *minimum* of information required to exercise their accountability. Aggregation from one level of accountability to the next is essential.

People should get what they want to make decisions. This rarely implies bulky tabulations, but it means paying considerable attention to layout. Where the organisation is structured into accountable units or cost centres it is easier to determine relevance than where it is not.

(5) Intelligible Outputs designed for managers should be intelli-

gible to them. Few managers are acquainted with, or even interested in, financial codes. Output should therefore use narratives in English rather than codes. In an accounting system the opposite can be the case. Intelligibility means that outputs should be comprehensive in themselves, and many budgetary control systems include, for example, a facility for narratives to be included to describe individual creditor payments. Creditors' names are more intelligible than creditor numbers.

The form of presentation may affect intelligibility. Typed reports, tabulations, computer output, microfilm and visual display units each have different degrees of intelligibility for different purposes. Another feature of intelligibility is the comparison of like with like. Some budgetary control systems compare expenditure to date with the budget for the year. This is not comparing like with like. A comparison should be between actual and estimate up to a given period. This means re-analysing the annual budget into weeks, months or quarters by establishing a *PROFILE* of expected spending. Budgets should also be capable of coping with inflation during the year.

(6) Up to date　A manager is concerned not just with having an historical record, but with knowing whether corrective action is needed. Therefore, a basic requirement is that historical information is as up to date as possible. The development of on-line input and output of data has facilitated this.

However, the manager is also concerned not just with what has actually been spent, but with what will have been spent by the end of the budget period. If the system only contains and compares historical data, then this *forecasting*, which is an essential part of budgetary control, cannot be achieved.

The first step towards forecasting is to know not just what has been spent, but also the expenditure which is committed. Where a workable commitment accounting system does not exist, line managers often resort to 'black books' to record commitments as a basis for forecasting.

The next part of forecasting is to take payments and commitments and then, by applying the profiles referred to earlier, see if the year-end spending is likely to be above or below budget. Forecasting deviations from original budgets not only forms the basis for corrective action, but can be used as feedback for the revision of the budget itself.

(7) Accurate The greater the degree of integration between systems, and the more automated the transfer of data into the budgetary control system, the higher the chances of accuracy. The accounting system will usually contain the validity checks and error reporting (for example of mis-coding) which can be a great irritant if they reach the budgetary control system. Indeed, should data not be seen to be accurate and reliable, it can undermine confidence in the systems. It is also an issue of how people act. Figure 6.3 illustrates some of the most significant relationships in the production of budgetary control information.

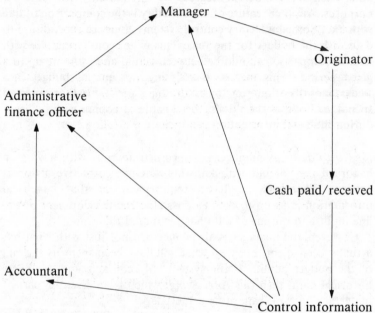

Note: → denotes information flow

Figure 6.3 Relationships in Budgetary Control

It is rarely the case that a manager actually *originates* spending or the receipt of income, even though he or she may have authorised it. A frequent source of error is at the 'origination' level – a task often carried out by clerical staff who may not be fully aware of the wider implications of their work. The reduction of errors can be helped by training both managers and originators in the needs for budgetary control. The more that managers actually use budgetary control information the more likely it is that they will make 'originators' responsible to them aware of the need for correct coding. The development of good relationships between all the people shown in Figure 6.3 aids the reduction of errors as well as ensuring that the information flows shown do exist.

(8) Information In an earlier reference to budgetary control it was suggested that it was one element in the wider question of management control. Management control invariably refers to non-financial factors and resources, as well as financial. The more that the budgetary control system can include reference to these factors, the more it will contribute to management control.

To measure efficiency and effectiveness there must be reference to outputs as well as inputs. It is important to know what unit costs are, and better to include such management information within the budgetary control system than to require the manager or his staff to relate financial and non-financial information manually.

Non-financial information can include the following:

(1) *Personnel* Numbers in post (estimate/actual), man-hours worked, data from bonus schemes.
(2) *Physical Units* Electricity consumed, numbers resident in establishments.
(3) *Outputs* Units of production, inspection visits undertaken, books issued.

The framework for budgetary control described above tends to discuss 'ideal requirements'. Few public authorities' systems would meet, or try to meet, all these requirements. They tend to be adequate rather than ideal, not least because there is a cost associated with meeting all objectives. In the real world the benefits of the ideal system have to be set against the costs of implementation.

It is not the purpose here to suggest that any organisation not meeting all objectives of budgetary control is failing in its duty. But it does provide a basis for examining current practice and deciding on features whose benefits are worth considering when systems are under review, as many presently are.

Some of the features highlighted in the framework are more easily implemented on advanced modern computers. It is quicker to input data through, and retrieve information from, visual display units than the 'traditional tabulation'. It is easier to obtain a variety of outputs, and achieve the inter-relation of data, from data-base systems. But it is not the purpose here to recommend the purchase of advanced computer hardware or software. Many features can be implemented by revising existing systems on existing hardware. Others, such as personalised reports, can be achieved, at least to a limited extent, by supplementing existing systems by file interrogation packages.

It should also be noted that the method of implementation may be just as important to the ultimate success of the system as the technical design of the system. Different users, both service managers and accountants, may have different needs and these are best established before, rather than after, implementation.

However, it is unrealistic to expect that all requirements are capable of precise specification in advance; indeed, personnel change while systems remain unchanged. An important criterion of design for budgetary control systems is flexibility. This too has a cost, but the ability to vary inputs and outputs either in total, or on an *ad hoc* basis, is important. Budgetary control is dependent on feeder systems such as payroll, creditors, etc. Since these can change independently of the budgetary control system, the latter needs to be sufficiently flexible to cope.

Information Technology

The public sector, particularly the nationalised industries and local government, have always been leaders in the development of new technology; first accounting machines, then computers and now the whole spectrum of electronic aids that receive the collective title of 'Information Technology' (IT). IT is only a means, not an end. But the whole process of financial planning and control can be analysed, albeit incompletely, as if they were systems which generate, process and present information on a vast scale. Indeed, such is the present complexity of the demands on planning and control systems in large organisations that information technology is indispensible to the creation of effective management systems.

Acquiring information technology is not, however, the only condition for its effective use (despite the impression to the contrary given by suppliers in advertisements). Considerable effort has to be put into:

(1) The Functional specification (What do we ideally want?)
(2) The Systems specification (What can we practically do?)
(3) Systems Development
(4) Implementation
(5) Maintenance

Before embarking on any systems development, the costs and benefits in all the above areas need to be properly appraised through a feasibility study.

The contribution of information technology to financial planning and control can be divided into three broad areas:

(1) Large-Scale Clerically-Based Systems   This covers 90 per cent of all financial systems. Computerisation here is labour-saving and provides a greater capability for the analysis of routinely produced information. This covers all the basic systems shown in Figure 6.2. To get the most out of these systems, the accountant and auditor *must* be involved from the beginning and build in their requirements for management information and management control respectively. There is much debate about the 'best' system for these areas, be it a package or in-house solution. The main general requirement is for a good feasibility study (as indicated above).

(2) Extraction of Data from Existing Systems (File Interrogation)
Under systems implemented in the 1980s, the system philosophy usually has the idea of *ad hoc* file interrogation built in from the start. Many existing systems do not. Hence there still remains a need for the use of file interrogation packages—most of which can be learnt by non-computer experts. In fact, to get the most out of file interrogation it is necessary to be proficient at interrogation and to learn a great deal about the basic financial systems. This has the spin-off that it increases awareness of what can be achieved.

There is really no limit to what can be achieved using the data available, but it does require training in the interrogation language, and an awareness of what the financial systems contain.

(3) Using the Computer for Working Papers Presently Manually-Based   This is nothing new; the reason for doing it is essentially to save time and effort. Most finance departments still do not make the maximum use of personal computing, particularly of the so-called 'spreadsheet' packages which run on microcomputers (and also now mainframes). These can be learnt in hours, not days, and allow staff at all levels in finance departments to directly use a computer, because the packages are so user-friendly. The names of

Table 6.1   VISICALC Applications in a District Coucil

Area health authority joint finance
Interpretation of company accounts by use of ratios
Housing association (estimated cost calculation)
Controlled car parking statement
Housing subsidy calculation
Service charge calculation
Select company list
Fleet list
Wages control statement
Catering statement
VAT calculation
Codebook
Form design
Draft revenue estimate working sheets
Cash flow forecast
Debt charge calculation
Inflation contingency model
Block grant model
Rate projection
Control budget
Personal accounts
DLO bonus calculation
Budget statements for voluntary organisations
Covenants register
Capital investment programme summary
Average rents calculation
Financial appraisals for economic development –
Schemes (workshops)
Company appraisals
Debt charges – capital fund
Debt management
Capital monitoring
Consolidated loans fund model
Investments register

such packages are, for example, VISICALC, SUPERCALC and MULTIPLAN.

The use of these very easy-to-learn packages is only limited by the imagination of the user, and the time available. Table 6.1 includes some of the areas for which VISICALC has been used by accountancy staff in one district council.

Such packages have limitations, particularly if it is difficult to include data directly extracted from the mainframe computer. It is obviously inefficient to double-handle data, but the developments in information technology are heading towards promoting the correlation of data from different sources and this should considerably expand the opportunities to create better planning and control information. As ever, the human element is the key factor in the efficient use (or any use) of such information.

Conclusion

It has been possible here only to touch on some of the most significant current issues in public sector financial planning and control. The tremendous diversity within the public sector of both principle and practice must be noted, but there are few areas where some further development is not possible, and some areas where considerable development is necessary.

7

Budget Making in Central and Local Government

STEN JÖNSSON

Making a budget in the public sector is one of the most difficult of human endeavours, at least if the budget is to meet conventional standards of rational choice. All kinds of human needs are processed through various agencies and translated into budgetary demands (sometimes called estimates). They are finally presented to elected decision makers. These decision makers are laymen trying to promote a better world through action based on their vision of the good society. Of course, they cannot analyse the activities and needs behind all the numbers in the budget documents presented to them; even if they could, there would not be sufficient time. Budgets are always made under time pressure and more often than not it is the printing office that sets the deadlines. The truth is that the task is impossible! There is no way Mr Jones' need for treatment of his ailing kidney can be compared to Mrs Smith's need for safe public transport when visiting her old mother. So why bother?

When the budget has been decided upon, further changes are invariably needed. All the long-term plans and forcefully argued activities of the agencies cannot be carried out because now there are to be cuts! Although the agency in question has said repeatedly to its superiors that its activities are planned as a package — one part of which cannot be taken away without catastrophic consequences — there have been some last minute cuts that take some money away but say nothing about which activities have to go. Why bother indeed?

But the difficulties do not stop there! At the University of Gothenburg we start every new budget year desperately trying to find out what actually happened. Our planning office quite readily gets hold of the total allocation to our University but soon finds out that there seems to have been a number of 'mistakes'. In our estimates we had stated very clearly that, according to the rules and regulations signed by the State as employer, a number of professors would get salary increases in the next year. But this unavoidable cost increase is not covered by the allocation. Consequently, our Chief Clerk places a telephone call with the University Chancellory which, in turn, refers him to the Ministry of Education. In the Ministry of Education some mathematically uneducated budget secretary says 'Yes, they have considered everything!' It is called stonewalling in the West. So we start out every year by redoing our budget. Faculties and institutes are forced to make cuts and no priority is ever stated. Hence, a little is taken away here and a little there. Those with foresight have padded their estimates anyway, so most of the time none of the catastrophies forecast materialize. But the question remains; why all this annual bother?

The reason is fairly obvious; resources are allocated to activities via the budget in the public sector. It is a fundamental difference between private and public sector organisations that the public organisation is related to its sources of finance by a budget, while the finances of the private organisation are moderated by market forces. Therefore a great deal of attention is paid to budgeting in the public sector, while performance in the market place provides the equivalent focus for the private sector organisation. So, if you want to have resources in the public sector to carry out all the good things you want to do, you had better be good at budgeting!

In the public sector it is also necessary to have formal decisions that authorise the expenditure of public funds (and fix the tax rate). It is therefore considered rational to take all the decisions on finance at the same time. Although private sector organisations have annual budgets that function in much the same way, they have more of the flavour of a forecast than a formal decision. When you deal with a market you do not have an exclusive right to decide about revenue; the customers will have their say too. However, in the public sector the budget decision is built on the exclusive right to tax citizens which, in turn, makes it necessary to make visible the decisions on both the tax rate and the appropriation of funds. If you are responsible for the tax rate you must be seen not to be extravagant with expenditure. The urgency of the needs satisfied by expenditure is the most important argument for taxation. This must be shown and the budget decision is a good opportunity to do so.

Finally, the budget decision is an important political occasion. In connection with it the different parties involved have an opportunity to present their policies. Publicity is assured due to the general interest and it would be foolish not to take advantage of the opportunity.

A budget, therefore, is many things and budgeting is a very complex process in spite of the fact that in practice you often merely take last year's budget and add a little here and there. Indeed, Wildavsky (1975) describes budgeting as 'attempts to allocate financial resources through political processes to serve differing human purposes' (p. 5). Moreover, the budget is also an increasingly important document because it is becoming more and more difficult to make ends meet. Most countries now have serious problems balancing their budgets and many local governments seem to be unable to solve the problems they face with the resources available to them. When central governments have deficits in their budgets one of the areas where cuts will be considered is in transfers to local governments. Austerity, therefore, makes local and central budgeting more interdependent.

The Budgetary Problem

Most new ideas in public sector budgeting are promoted on the basis of criticisms of the traditional budgetary process. PPBS, Zero Based Budgeting and other reforming mechanisms have all been advocated in that way (Novick (1965) Cheek (1977)). The irrationality of taking last year's budget as the base for the current year's, and arguing only for and against increments, has been repeatedly pointed out. Nevertheless, the old ways seem to survive (Olsen, 1970). The question to be dealt with here is: why? Since irrationality seems to be functional, there must be some rational (*sic!*) explanation why all intelligent people with both power and immense resources stick to it.

Let us first consider the basic structure of the budgeting process.

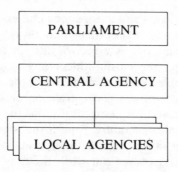

Figure 7.1 The Institutional Structure of Budgeting

A number of local agencies, often specialised in function (e.g. education, transport), present their estimates for expenditure in the forthcoming year to a central agency. The central agency not only consolidates these estimates into a total budget, but also calculates the revenue implications. The total budget is then presented to representatives of the parliament who order the central agency to make cuts and/or increase revenue to achieve a better balance between income and outgoings. The negotiations that follow, between the local and central agencies, go on until the deadline is reached. At this point the formal decision, which has to be made if services are to go on uninterrupted, is taken. That formal decision is made by an assembly of elected representatives in a very visible way that is preceded by a politically significant debate. Of course, there are variations on this structure depending on the size of the organisation, the nature of the activities and the political rules of the game; there may, for example, be several levels in the structure, or separate budgets for capital investment and operations. Be that as it may, the structure of budgeting generally may be described in terms of the interaction between local agencies, central agencies and a political decision maker. Together they face a very complex task and this has to be simplified. (See Figure 7.1.)

This is accomplished in two ways; by division of labour and by using rules of thumb. Probably the most important aspect of public sector budgeting is the division of labour laid down in the roles assumed by local agencies (who act as advocates), and central agencies (who act as guardians) (Wildavsky, 1975). Advocates argue as forcefully as they can for better services in 'their' area of responsibility (and as a consequence for more expenditure), while guardians play the role of the villain who always says 'there is no money'. The guardian role is a prerequisite for the legitimacy of taxation. Only after the most ruthless cuts in proposed expenditures is it acceptable to ask for an increased (or even maintained) tax rate. The advocates can concentrate on producing the most convincing arguments for expenditure in their area without worrying about total expenditure. That is the responsibility of the guardian, who can say 'no' (both the first and the second time) confident that the advocates will work tirelessly to promote the most urgent needs of their clients. In this way, the two roles together constitute a very sophisticated mechanism of calculation; provided, that is, that both sides stick to the rules of the game, which is essential if trust is to be maintained.

Within such a budgetary game it is quite natural for the guardian to use across-the-board cuts of, say, 2 per cent, to sound out the claims of the advocates. Their outcries will indicate what activities are essential and which can be reduced. It is also natural that advocates 'pad' their estimates to make room for the expected cuts. These are some of the rules of thumb. It might be said that the view presented here is too simple. Of course it is! There are differences in power and influence, long-term plans, commitments and political platforms, but it is still useful to structure our understanding of budgeting in terms of these general concepts.

If there is a breach of trust, the process easily degenerates. The guardian will impose strict control, and advocates will erect bulwarks of padding and secrecy. To avoid this, guardians will have to allow advocates some victories; and advocates, in turn, will have to accept the idea of cuts, without resorting to evasive tactics.

The Importance of the Environment

The budgetary process is a sensitive one. How it changes depends to a large extent on the characteristics of its environment. Wildavsky (1975) has pointed out the important of wealth and certainty. In a wealthy environment new activities can be financed by extra allocations — if they are urgent enough. In a poor environment there have to be reallocations and these give rise to an entirely different budgetary process. With certainty in the forecasts and estimates, the discussion can deal with the pros and cons of proposed activities. However, if there is uncertainty about whether or not stated figures will hold, those involved will use much energy to protect their reserves and avoid showing their hand. When the environment is rich and certain, budgetary behaviour will, typically, be incremental.

When the environment becomes increasingly poor and/or uncertain, which is often the case nowadays, behaviour will change. Austerity programmes at the level of the state will affect transfers to local government and others, and create uncertainty about a source of finance that was previously the most reliable. The local agencies will try to improve the protection of their base by mobilising the support of the their clients and the media and, if they are not able to avoid the cuts, by reluctantly pointing out other areas where cuts could be made with less harm. Sometimes it might be good politics to limit your losses by quietly accepting the cuts. To sum up; when resources become more scarce and uncertain, behaviour in agencies will become more 'political' in the sense that protection of particular interests will be more pronounced. The elected representatives of the people will feel a lack of control of the situation, and find difficulty in carrying out the promised changes of policy on which they may have won the last election (Brunsson and Jönsson, 1977). However, before we look at the budgetary process in conditions of austerity in more detail, it will be useful to compare the nature of political organisation with that of hierarchical modes of organisation.

The Political Organisation

The problem that the politically elected decision makers face is that they are supposed to promote democracy as well as efficiency. It is good for democracy if differences of opinion between groups of politicians are exposed openly. Therefore, political decision-making bodies are organised on the principle of conflict. An individual is recruited to a political assembly if he/she is good at arguing against the ideas of the other side. If several ideologies are competing it is assumed that good policy will result. Certainly the need for change will be on the agenda constantly. A political body is supposed also to be open to influence from the public. The strength of an idea is based on the following it can gather in open debate with other points of view. The majority bases its decision-making power on the voluntary association of interested citizens with its programmes. Such is the basis of the democratic tradition.

By contrast, the organisational hierarchy, which is designed to carry out decisions, is based on unity as its organising principle. In extreme cases (e.g. an army at war) dissent is punished severely. More usually, although the boss might not always be right, he is always the boss. Such an organisation is well suited to efficient organised action.

In the budgetary process these two types of organisation join in a common effort to solve an impossible task. Moreover, we demand that the politicians should control and direct the bureaucracy. However, the chances are that it will be the other way around; time constraints, expertise and specialisation all work in favour of the hierarchy and against an open, conflictual, part time, elected body where members are not experts on any of the items on the agenda. In an information business, like decision making in the public sector, expertise and time to concentrate on one area will normally have more influence over outcome than ideology. It is difficult for politicians to control large bureaucracies inhabited by experts on almost everything. But, even if the experts have an information advantage, politicians have the final decision. They can veto proposals put forward by the bureaucracy.

Normally there is no antagonism between the elected representatives and the bureaucrats and planners. However, it is important to be aware of the limited possibilities for implementing policies that are against the interests and convictions of leading bureaucrats. What politicians normally do is to scrutinise proposals in a defensive way to see that actions will not be too much out of line with the party platform. Most of the time the cooperation between the two types of organisations works excellently, particularly when great new programmes are implemented. Both politicians and bureaucrats are expansion prone; they both want to do more for their constituencies. But, when austerity demands that cuts shall be made—cuts that will decrease the capacity to do good—there will be differences of opinion, and the elected representatives will feel that the hierarchy has a considerable power to resist actions that threaten its survival. In stagnation, politics (party as well as departmental) intensifies and new patterns of behaviour emerge in budgeting.

Budgeting in Stagnation

One important consequence of cuts is the uncertainty they create. It is not only that cuts often come too late for a proper understanding of what was decided (due to the complicated process of negotiating in the final phase of budgeting), it is also the fact that an awareness of the likelihood of shortfall creates its own sense of uncertainty.

When facing uncertainty it is a normal human response to create reserves to be used as buffers when surprises occur. The feeling of lack of control is possibly the most important driving force in budgetary behaviour in austerity. It gives prominence to a new, or more accurately, to the revival of an old, role in newly poor environments. Advocates and guardians are joined by the hamster, a character that tries to create a surplus to be tucked away for a rainy day. Such a person works hard to implement austerity programmes and is an expert on painting the future in dark colours. But, on the other hand, he does not mind raising taxes or fees, nor even taking new loans.

If a surplus is created, it will be invested in current assets which can be liquidated in cases of emergency; for example, when the controller of our institute left, it was discovered that we had more than five years stock of overhead film in the cellar. It is also quite natural to be a little pessimistic about budgeted revenue (i.e. interest on bank accounts). In local government the hamster is probably the treasurer and in state agencies he can be found in central positions on almost every level.

Of course, the hamster behaves in much the same way in all seasons even though he might be quite starved these days! In expansionary periods his role may be quite functional. His reserves will serve as oil in the machinery by evening out miscalculations and making 'fire brigade' actions possible. In early stagnation, on the other hand, the reserves of the hamster can have a devastating effect on morale. In order to legitimate austerity programmes, central agencies (and central politicians) have to show that there is no money in the Treasury and that things will not get better soon. If it is discovered that there are hamsters in the system with 'undeclared' assets, then cheating will be regarded as *comme il faut* and austerity programmes will falter. However, if a central agency finds that local agencies can manage to save money without visible effect on services, it will probably be more ruthless the next time around (though by then there may really be no reserves left). For instance, when the Swedish Government cut a fairly large sum of money from the state grants to local government in 1981, there was an outcry over the lack of consideration for those who would suffer the consequences. Local politicians joined ranks in condemning the unilateral decision of the Government. That year almost every municipality in the land showed a surplus. This was the result of the joint efforts of numerous hamsters!

Budgetary Behaviour in a Newly Poor Environment

It is no simple task to describe the complexity of the changes in budgetary behaviour that occurs when stagnation sets in. Perhaps it is best to try to tell a short story about what happened in one particular organisation, the city of Gothenburg, and then draw out some general observations (Jönsson, 1982).

By most standards Gothenburg is a very rich city. It has enjoyed a steady growth in resources since the great take off in the early 1960s, when the present 'modern' administration was erected. Then, in 1975, there was a very expensive wage settlement for local governments and, on top of that, the effects of the oil crisis. The work on the budget estimates for 1976 had started under the presumption of continued steady growth. Moreover, a large number of long-term and medium-term plans provided a basis for a sustained growth in expenditure. However, when the City Office compiled the estimates there was a difference of about 10 per cent between the total expenditures and revenues projected for the first year of the five-year plan. Even so, not much happened during the summer except that the commissioner in charge of finance wrote his memo on how he proposed to balance the budget (which is required by law). He proposed a tough line; local agencies should cut their proposals down to the expenditure limits set forth in the five-year plan and then by a further 2 per cent. He managed to get a firm decision on that approach from the Executive Committee (which is the 15 person power centre of the city), with the exception that some programmes (care for the sick, the aged and children) were only required to come down to the expenditure limit. The next year was an election year!

The Subcommittee on the Budget set out in confrontational style when it implemented the cuts decision. However, the local agencies (education, medical care, welfare, transport, libraries, etc.) which are led by political committees with the same majority as the City Council were shocked by the unwillingness of the Subcommittee to discuss what activities should be eliminated to meet the cuts. Heated discussions as to who was responsible for the consequences of the cuts occurred. Local representatives would try to entice the Subcommittee to make concrete statements as to which activities should be cut, while the Subcommittee would refuse, maintaining that the question of priorities was the responsibility of the local committees.

Examples of successful strategies used by local agencies included: 'the media ploy', used by the Recreation Committee when it was about to report to the Subcommittee for the second time on how it planned to meet the cuts; and the 'sensitive cuts' approach, used by the Medical Care Committee.

The 'media ploy' involved the agency informing the press, one or two days in advance of the meeting with the Subcommittee, of what cuts are going to be proposed. In this way reporters had time to interview personnel who were shocked because the information was new to them as well. The Recreation Committee informed the press that five youth clubs had to be closed and, as a result, the headlines that appeared on the day of the meeting with the Subcommittee declared how young children were going to be thrown onto the streets, no doubt becoming drug addicts in the process. Youth clubs were also occupied. The result was a change in policy; the city decided to put *more* money into its own youth clubs and to *increase* its support to voluntary youth associations. The Recreation Committee got an increased expenditure limit!

The Medical Care Office proposed to meet its cuts by taking away politically sensitive programmes. The cuts were provocative even to an outside observer, but the Committee accepted them and presented them to the Subcommittee. The Subcommittee was outraged and forced the chairman of the Medical Care Committee to withdraw the proposals. This was done, but as a result the Subcommittee, lacking time to order alternative cuts, had to leave the Medical Care budget unbalanced (giving the deficit the title of 'general deduction for vacancies') and made a deal with the Medical Care Committee to save the corresponding sum of money during the year. The chairman of the Medical Care Committee went into national politics the next year.

When the deadline for the final budget decision approached, there was still a considerable imbalance in the budget. The Subcommittee ordered investment projects to be eliminated (without prior consultation), managed to negotiate a foreign loan and raised the tax rate, all in a hurry. The final difficult decisions on priorities and cuts could thus be avoided. The budget negotiations had started with confrontations but the climax — when the really painful sacrifices are made and justice is done to those who have tried to use stalling tactics — did not materialise.

The dissatisfaction with the outcome of the budgeting for 1976 spilled over into the estimates for 1977. Almost everyone talked about the inadequacy of the budget in compensating for inflation. The 6 per cent allowed was totally inadequate to cover increases on salaries and wages that amounted to close to 15 per cent. However, the directives for the preparation of the 1977 estimates again only allowed for 6 per cent increases in wages and prices — a strategy which was called 'unrealistic' by local agencies. Furthermore, local agencies were instructed to include in their estimates an interval of plus or minus 3 per cent, where items were to be ranked according to priority. It was thought that this would facilitate the final budget negotiations.

But the local agencies devoted much energy to pointing out the lack of realism in the directives. Inflation in 1976 had proved to be higher than 6 per cent, and to apply a 6 per cent adjustment to a base that was wrong in the first place was said to be unrealistic. Some agencies refused to work out a minus 3 per cent alternative. Justifications varied, but usually emphasis was placed on the worries of personnel. Most of these justifications were very naive and it is hard to believe that they were anything other than attempts to gain time.

The difference between revenues and expenditures in May was as large as the year before. About 10 per cent remained to be pruned from the estimates. As before, however, nothing much happened during the summer, with the political parties preparing for the election campaign in August–September. The official memorandum on how to balance the budget said that things were worse than ever and that a whole battery of measures would be needed in addition to cuts in the estimates. Among other things, a large tax increase was proposed.

The election campaign that was in progress during the summer months proved to be a close race. Polls showed a 50:50 situation between the two political groups. Not surprisingly, the main theme of the campaign turned out to be whether the city economy was well managed. In such a situation the ruling majority could not admit that there had been bad management. They even said that things were not as bad as they looked, and blamed the national government for the problems which made a large increase of taxes necessary.

The Subcommittee on the Budget, which had to deal with the local agencies before the election, refused to discuss any priorities; it merely ordered the cuts, telling agencies to be back with their final proposals after the election. Most of the agencies had prepared themselves thoroughly in order to convince the Subcommittee that last year's cuts were a mistake and that this year they would be a catastrophy. But the Subcommittee would not listen. The disillusioned representatives had to return home to make the ordered cuts.

In the meantime, the election resulted in a new political majority which would take control from the beginning of the following year. This new majority would manage the budget that was being worked on. However, the margin of victory was very narrow and soon after the election the political situation grew sour because of disagreement over election pledges and about reorganisation of the Executive Committee and its staff. Against this background the final budget decisions were taken in a hurry, as usual, but this time without the undivided attention that was customary. The budget was balanced through still higher taxes and more loans.

It was recognised that the budgeting procedure was now out of control. The confrontation of 1976 had been followed by the disillusionment of 1977. Something new had to be done by the new majority to establish a procedure that would result in local agencies viewing the budget as a commitment, even when cuts had to be made.

The new majority thought differently on these matters to the old one, which had consisted of a coalition of three parties. A coalition has to have a formal decision-making unit where the compromises between the partners can be arranged. However, when there is a one-party majority and that party has a tradition of party discipline, things are different. The new majority thought that there should be no negotiations between central and local agencies on budget priorities since it is the same political leadership on both levels. The political debate should be between parties, and not between central and local representatives of the same party. They decided that, under a new procedure, policies should be decided in the party organisation and then carried out in the municipal apparatus. Local politicians should see to it that policies were carried out within the expenditure limits laid down in the budget. In response to these proposals, the new opposition stated that they considered the negotiations essential since they gave the central agencies information on what marginal effects changes in the expenditure levels of different programmes would have. How can you set these levels if you do not have that information?

The new procedure was to start early in the spring with definite expenditure limits for every agency and more detailed directives on priorities than before. In addition, there would be no negotiations in the autumn; merely technical adjustments. Another consequence of the new majority was that members of the central Executive Committee would also serve as chairmen for local agency committees (for example, the school board). The idea was that they would act as guardians and keep the agencies within their expenditure limits. This was against the principles of the previous majority, which had maintained a strict separation between central and local assignments. They contended that if members of the Executive Committee assumed chairmanships in local agency committees, they would soon become advocates for the policies of local agencies within the Executive Committee.

The new majority implemented the new procedure however, and as a consequence there were virtually no negotiations in the autumn. Due to the change of procedure the whole process came under increased time pressure, but there was no drama. Balancing the budget was achieved partly through cuts, but mainly through the largest tax increase in the history of the city. It was justified by referring to the financial situation and alleged mismanagement by the old majority.

Discussion

So ends the story about budgeting in a city. The story illustrates that the process of budgeting is very fluid; there is constant change in both procedures and preconditions. There are never any set solutions. The process is always under way. One consequence of this is that there are very few fixed points to which technically rational behaviour can be anchored.

The case deals with a city administration, but similar studies in other kinds of public sector organisations have yielded similar features (Heclo and Wildavsky (1974) Anton (1964) Olsen (1970)). The distance between actors will be greater in central government budgeting and formalism maybe a little more pronounced. In principle, however, the story above illustrates an inside view of budgeting. Indeed, the essence of budgeting in the public sector can be said to be the squeezing of disorderly claims into the orderly format of the budget.

The description above concentrated on the procedural logic and saw things largely from the viewpoint of the central agency. But there is always the other logic present—the world of action. How are we going to get things done without the necessary money? If there are plans for action behind the estimates that are cut, these plans will be shattered. Agencies will then have to rely on the logic laid down in their habitual day-to-day operations. What can and cannot be done has to be determined on the basis of that practical experience. The two types of logic meet in the budget procedure and there are frequent misunderstandings. When pressure increases, central agencies will have to retreat to the logic of the guardian, balancing total sums, procedures and deadlines. The other logic, used by the advocates, draws its strength from the concrete production situations—describing what has to be done to achieve the desired results and getting outsiders to understand the problems and dilemmas. If the advocate succeeds in ensnaring the guardian with such concrete descriptions, he is likely to do better than when the guardian manages to keep his distance from the everyday activities, talking only about the general financial situation and the specific expenditure limits.

The budgetary process has been portrayed as something like a game, which it obviously is not. All the actors are dedicated men or women trying to do a good job. The aims are noble ones. However, the problem is impossible to solve satisfactorily. The process is also notoriously difficult to observe and describe, chiefly because there are so many rationalities involved, but also because much happens that is not easily visible. When the process defies description according to our cherished rational models of management, one easy way out is to charge the process with being irrational or a mere ritual, thus reverting instead to the language of prescription rather than description. If nothing else, the example outlined above points to the inadequacies of such views. Rationalities are at work in the budgetary process. They may seem perverse or subtle, depending on the point of view applied, but they are important for an understanding of what is going on. The case study demonstrates a number of important aspects of budgeting that are worthy of further comment.

Problem Solving by Confrontation

Problem solving by confrontation is the essence of this case, as well as of the model of budgeting advanced by Wildavsky (1975). The advocates and guardians confront each other every year in order to solve the allocation problem. There is, however, mutual dependence between these roles. Accordingly, the confrontation must be between friends or, if you will, only apparent. Trust in, and obedience to, ethical rules are necessary preconditions for budgeting of this nature. When either side violates the rules of the game, there is a risk that the process as a whole will degenerate into real confrontation. Indeed, this is what happened in this case. The first year was characterised by confrontation and the second by disillusionment and a procedural and motivational break down. During the third year, the procedure was reorganised and new rules of the game instituted. The learning acquired in the process was not so much concerned with activities as with procedure. Agencies may learn better budgeting without making better budgets. Indeed, it might even be ventured that central agencies might be able to exert a certain amount of control by changing the procedure at the point when local agencies seem to 'catch up' and master the procedural possibilities to their own advantage.

Budgeting for Control

Budgeting always seems to be conducted under extreme time pressure. There is scant evidence that central agencies ever exert any control over local activities except through the total amount of expenditure. What should be done, and how the money should be used, have to be controlled through means other than the budget. The ambitious vision of PPBS, where all kinds of control are integrated into one system, remains a vision. There is virtually no evidence that PPBS has anywhere achieved what it promised (Gunsteren (1976), Crecine and Fisher (1971), Wildavsky (1975), Jablonsky and Dirsmith (1978), Merewitz and Sosnick (1971)). The explanation is probably that it does not allow for the multiplicity of rationalities that are necessary for democracy to survive. This is a precondition for politics. After all, the agencies that are financed via the budget are just means for the implementation of policies, and policies and goals are supposed to change and shift according to the process of politics and the will of the people. The ambition to achieve efficient goal-directed control over the activities of a large number of diverse agencies is misdirected. Instead, budgeting in the public sector should be looked upon as a continuous struggle to achieve some measure of control without losing too much responsiveness to democratic forces. It is clear that the reins have to be tightened when resources become more scarce and that consequently the room for democratic discourse will be smaller. In such cases procedures are likely to be overthrown if they are not upheld by responsible actors willing to make unpleasant decisions. Thus, in stagnation, budgeting becomes more dependent than ever on individuals' attitudes towards responsibility.

Budgeting and Accountability

When you commit yourself to an act you feel responsible for the consequences of that act. You have agreed to cause things to happen and are ready to suffer the consequences, for better or for worse. This act of commitment is an act of will which presupposes that you were free to choose not to commit yourself.

In the budgeting context, having committed yourself to a budget, you have chosen to let it direct your activities for a period of time. To achieve this commitment is the crux of budgeting. A first condition to this end is that what the budget prescribes is viewed as 'realistic' (i.e. possible to achieve under present circumstances). In the case given above, some of the agencies rebelled against

Draconian cuts. Especially damaging to morale was the cut in investment that was done without consultation. If cuts are made without discussion, there is no opportunity for commitment to occur and the local agency will not feel accountable for the consequences.

Such a precondition for commitment is something like a discussion between free men ending in some kind of agreement. However, this type of situation is not easy to create in a hierarchial structure. When resources are scarce, power probably has to be exerted from the top. But local agencies will not feel accountable to their clients since the reductions in the resources available have been imposed from above. Therefore 'the top' might have to make the agencies accountable to itself by applying strict expenditure control (for a while). After a period of adaptation, agencies might again feel accountable to clients and act as advocates in budgeting.

Learning Over Time in Budgeting

When budgeting, agencies will try to persuade central decision makers to allocate an appropriate sum of money to their activity. However, local agencies are not very well informed about the activities of other local agencies. Consequently, they cannot make credible comparisons with the usefulness of expenditure on activities other than their own. Instead, they concentrate on putting forward arguments for the allocation of money to themselves, leaving it to the central agency to make the comparisons. When a local agency discovers that a certain line of argument results in them having extra resources it will be used again. Similarly if a certain kind of behaviour is conducive to its budgetary aims it will tend to reoccur. In these ways agencies will learn how to exploit the procedure to further the interests of their clients. But it is highly unlikely that agencies will discover better ways of dealing with these clients during the hectic weeks of budgeting. Learning how to serve clients better must be done outside of the budgetary context.

When the procedure runs out of control, the centre can regain a measure of control by redesigning the procedure. This is a principal way of adapting to new conditions. Local agencies will have to unlearn the old ways and learn new ones before they can 'catch up'. In the process they will scan the new situation to find solutions and bases for budget arguments.

What Kind of Improvement is Possible?

There is always a need to improve the budgetary process. Efforts to implement new techniques are often justified by reference to the irrationalities of traditional budgeting. It is clearly not very rational to take last year's budget as the base and discuss only incremental changes. Still, it is done everywhere and new techniques like PPBS or Zero Based Budgeting are declared failures by independent evaluators (Gunsteren, 1976). Just how is it that irrational procedures like those of traditional budgeting have survived and rational ones like PPBS have not?

The explanation can, perhaps, be found in the fact that budgeting is situated at the crossroads of processes for the rational analysis of input–output relations and processes for generating commitment to causes. It will be guided by goals and objectives as well as by responsibility and bonds of conscience. At the same time, there is not enough knowledge of the relation between causes and effects (Hofstede, 1981). Improvements will be hard to come by. In fact, in many cases it is even difficult to define what should be meant by improvement!

As far as the efficiency of the budgetary process itself is concerned, it seems safe to state that such a complicated process will benefit from improved communication. Trust and trustworthiness are the key factors in such an improvement. It can be promoted by the participants in the budgetary process being aware of each others' roles and of the great cost to the common effort of the loss of mutual trust.

References

Anton, T. (1964) *Budgeting in Three Illinois Cities*, Urbana, University of Illinois.

Brunsson, N. and Jönsson, S. (1977) *Beslut och handling — Om politikers inflytande pä politiken (Decision and Action — on the Influence of Politicians on Policy)*, Liber.

Cheek, L. M. (1977) *Zero-Base Budgeting comes of Age*, Americon, New York.

Crecine, J. P. and Fischer, G. (1975) *On Resource Allocation Processes in the US Department of Defense*, Discussion paper, University of Michigan.

Gunsteren, H. V. (1976) *The Quest for Control: A Critique of the Rational Central-Rule Approach in Public Affairs*, Wiley.

Heclo, H. and Wildavsky, A. (1974) *The Private Government of Public Money: Community and Policy Inside British Political Administration*, Macmillan.

Hofstede, G. (1981) 'Management control of public and not-for-profit activities', *Accounting, Organizations and Society*, pp. 193–211.

Jablonsky, S. F. and Dirsmith, M. W. (1978) 'The pattern of PPB rejection: something about organizations, something about PPB', *Accounting Organizations and Society, pp. 215–25.*

Jönsson, S., (1982) *A City Administration Facing Stagnation: Political Organization and Action in Gothenburg*, Studenlitteratur, Lund.

Merewitz, L. and Sosnick, S. H. (1971) *The Budgets' New Clothes*, Markham.

Novick, D. (ed.) (1965) *Program Budgeting: Program Analysis and The Federal Budget*, Harvard University Press.

Olsen, Johan P. (1970) 'Local budgeting—decision making or ritual act?, *Scandinavian Political Studies*, pp. 85–118.

Wildavsky, A. (1975) *Budgeting: Comparative Theory of Budgetary Processes*, Little Brown.

8
Planning and Control – Developments in Central Government

ANDREW LIKIERMAN

Introduction

The range of current issues in the field of financial planning and control for central government illustrates how accounting debate cannot easily be separated from economic and political developments. Some of these issues arise as a direct consequence of changing political priorities, for example as a result of the pressure to reduce the overall level of government expenditure. But in most cases they are a reflection of pressures and changing priorities of a more general kind. The traumatic effect on control systems of high and variable rates of inflation in the 1970s is one example. The general pressure for greater disclosure of financial information is another. There has also been a major resurgence of interest by the House of Commons in exercising detailed financial control over the executive.

This chapter deals with developments and issues in four main areas. First, the replacement of a financial planning system based on volume by one based on cash is discussed. Second, consideration is given to the use and effects of the cash limits control system. Third, some aspects of the increasing emphasis being placed on internal management control systems are reviewed. Finally, the role of the House of Commons as the focus for changing practices in external reporting, monitoring and control is examined.

Cash Planning

The most important single development of recent years has been the abandonment of planning in volume terms based on the public expenditure survey (PESC) system, and its replacement by a system for planning in cash.

The PESC system was the basis of public expenditure during the 1960s and 1970s, and used a constant price basis for the planning of expenditure from one year to another. However, pride seems to have clouded judgement in some of the claims made for it, even as late as the mid-1970s. As Lord Diamond said in 1975:

> No dramatic reforms can be anticipated in the near future. Nor is that a surprising conclusion to reach having regard to the major improvements achieved in the past decade and to the fact that this country is, as a result, in the lead among the governments of the world — 'well in the lead' in the words of one Treasury spokesman. (Diamond, 1975)

A former senior official from the Treasury made a similar claim: 'after many vicissitudes we have evolved a system for managing the public sector which, despite many continuing deficiencies, is probably superior to that found anywhere else in the world' (Goldman, 1973).

However, the problems of dealing with inflation were clearly apparent to Sir Richard Clarke, who exercised considerable influence in the development of the PESC system. He wrote in the mid 1970s

> looking ahead, however, the most critical problem for PESC may be that of working in conditions of inflation . . . when the fall in the value of money exceeds 10 per cent a year, and when it reaches say 20 per cent a year, the credibility of the numbers in the programmes and their monitoring against 'actuals' raises immense problems. (Clarke, 1978)

These comments are important in providing the background to the change to cash planning since many of the issues surrounding the new system are related to whether it can replace a volume-planning system based on PESC. The reasons why PESC fell from grace are clear enough, though there are different views on the relative importance of different factors. Certainly with the arrival of high rates of inflation, and also major variations in the rate of inflation between one year and another, the system came under increasing strain. The amount which had to be set aside to finance public expenditure became more and more difficult to plan. In analysing the reasons for the change, Pliatsky (1982b) picked out the difficulties of volume planning in figures so far removed from the actual cash to be spent, and the fact that many transfer payments, such as Social Security and debt interest, could not really be planned in volume terms. He also pointed to the new political climate resulting from the change in government in 1979 adding that, with the prospect of falling inflation, there was a reasonable chance the system might survive.

Heclo and Wildavsky (1981) isolated political irresponsibility in not facing up to the impact on public expenditure of external shocks to the economy. But PESC itself was held responsible for public expenditure being out of control, at least on a narrow definition of 'control'. 'PESC grew into a procedure that contributed to all the other troubles by making it difficult to know what was happening' since 'PESC has never provided a way of translating numbers from planning to detailed control figures within departmental programmes'.

In setting out the basis for the change (HM Treasury, 1981b) the Government provided the emphasis of its own concerns. 'The volume system did not supply any pressure to reduce the costs, since the volume of programmes was protected against rising costs' and pointed to 'the need to assess what is being achieved, preferably quantitatively. In the past, a volume series has too often been accepted by itself as a satisfactory measure of the output of a programme'.

Against this background the decision was taken to plan in cash terms from the financial year 1982-3 based on total amount to be spent, not the volume of goods or services to be provided. In the explanation of the new system (HM Treasury, 1981b) the advantages of cash planning were given as:

> Ministers discuss the cash that will actually be spent, and therefore what will have to be financed by taxation or borrowing, instead of talking about 'funny money' – the numbers which could be misleadingly different from the resultant cash spent . . .
>
> Expenditure figures can be related more readily to the revenue projections . . .

Changes in public sector costs are brought into the discussion . . .

Previously the volume plans — that is, plans in constant price — were regarded by spending managers as entitlements, carried forward from year to year regardless of what was happening to costs . . . the assumption now shifts in favour of maintaining planned cash expenditure, rather than a given volume of provision regardless of cost . . .

The decisions in the annual survey . . . can be translated directly into the cash limits and estimates presented to Parliament.

The improvement in the management of public expenditure was also emphasised in that managers would have to 'think more about what level of service they can provide with any given amount of money'.

While these changes have been welcomed by some as giving a system better attuned to the needs of planning government expenditure, there have also been critics of the new system and it should not be assumed that volume planning is dead and buried. Pliatsky (1982b) suggests that at a time of variable inflation rates (rather than falling inflation, as has been the case in the first few years of cash planning), a combination of cash and volume planning may be required. Otherwise the squeeze of resources would be too great.

My assessment is that the move away from planning in terms of historic constant prices is to be welcomed, and the experiment in cash projection should be given a fair wind but that, unless and until we can assume low inflation rates with confidence that they will actually happen, there will probably have to be some compromise between cash planning and programming in real terms over the medium term — meaning any period longer than a single year ahead. (Pliatsky, 1982b)

There is, in any case, something inherently implausible about the idea that volume planning can be abandoned altogether. At the start of the planning process some assumptions have to be made about the goods and services to be purchased in order to build up the planning figure for the coming year. The Government has not shown the slightest enthusiasm for disclosing what the volume assumptions are, or indeed that volume plays any significant part in planning (Treasury and Civil Service Select Committee, 1981b, 1982b, 1983), emphasising the message that the new system is a radical break with PESC. But it is doubtful whether MPs and others will allow so little disclosure about volume trends. They need to have such information in order to question the Government's relative spending priorities.

The fact that this issue simply will not go away is well illustrated in a sequence of increasingly acrimonious memoranda to the Treasury and Civil Service Select Committee (1982b, Appendices 1–3). Doubts about whether the new system represents a brave new world have also been expressed by Heclo and Wildavsky (1981) who are concerned that one numbers game has been replaced by another and that the end of PESC will mean that 'the real loss will be, not of a planning function that never existed, but an opportunity that once existed to improve policy analysis in ways that go beyond the routine of annual budgeting'.

The experience of increased economic uncertainty has also resulted in the number of future years for which plans are made being reduced from five to three. However, doubts must remain about the Government's ability either to plan or to decide its policy priorities for more than one year. In Sir Geoffrey Howe's graphic phrase, there is still 'something strangely unrealistic about those solemn lines of detailed figures marching across the pages into the middle distance' (Treasury and Civil Service Select Committee, 1980). Cash planning will make more difficult a careful assessment of the implications of decisions in future years. 'Many of the figures in the White Papers, particularly those for later years, simply represent the sort of levels of expenditure the government would like to aim at . . . rather than figures arrived at after consideration of their implications for the level of service provided' (Else and Marshall, 1981). And yet more starkly; 'Firm ministerial decisions are made only for the following year. Everything beyond that becomes mere projection; in practice it often has little to do with decisions' (Heclo and Wildavsky, 1981).

A number of issues arise from the arrival of cash planning, though it is still too early to assess how effective the system is likely to be. The freedom for departments to make trade-offs between volume and price effects if assumptions turn out to be incorrect may mean a worthwhile increase in administrative flexibility and therefore efficiency. On the other hand, it will make both planning and control much more difficult if the Government's assertion that volume is not being used in planning is really true.

The administrative pressures on the new system will start to build up if inflation starts to rise and if the relative price effect—the

phenomenon of wages and prices paid by the public sector changing at different rates to the rate of general price increase in the
economy as a whole — is unfavourable to public expenditure. There
will certainly be continued political pressure from MPs to disclose
more information to allow them to assess plans and monitor
results. Of course it will be *possible* to hold total expenditure
down, even if price assumptions are unrealistically low and even if
events force increased volumes of expenditure in certain areas. The
issue is whether the price for doing so by cutting expenditure
elsewhere will be too high in political terms. If the Government is
forced away from the present system, a combination of volume and
cash planning may be a logical successor.

Cash Limits

Since cash limits were introduced (HM Government, 1976), there
has been a good deal of debate on the way they have operated.
Probably the most publicly contentious issue is whether what was
intended as a control system is being used instead as a means of
controlling public sector pay. It is clear that at times when there has
been no incomes policy in operation, governments have used them
to influence at least the tone of wage negotiations (Bevan, 1980;
Bevan *et al.*, 1981). One ex-Permanent Secretary has implied a
stronger connection and has claimed that 'cash limits lead inextricably to a pay policy for the public services, whether imposed or
agreed' (Pliatsky, 1982a), but has also warned of the dangers of 'a
medium-term public service pay policy . . . to be enforced solely by
cash limits without the support of either consensus or powers, but
with the safety valve of special treatment for groups of workers
who can apply enough pressure'. It is, of course, impossible to
prove that cash limits are being used in this way since governments
are unlikely to admit to a pay policy when this is a direct contradiction to their policy commitments. However, there seems to be at
least enough circumstantial evidence of the connection, despite the
claims of successive governments emphasising that it is open to
those who manage individual cash blocks to offset higher
expenditure on one item (including pay) against lower expenditure
elsewhere in the block.

Another issue — one only marginally less contentious than that of pay—is whether or not the cash limits system has resulted in decisions which have made disproportionate cuts in capital expenditure in order to preserve jobs and to accommodate wage settlements which have been higher than those allowed for at the beginning of the year. 'There is the danger that the achievement of the Government's public expenditure targets will continue to demand the kind of short-run *ad hoc* cuts which have been a recurring feature of public expenditure crises over the past decade and which have, in the event, fallen predominately on capital expenditure' (Else and Marshall, 1981). Certainly, there has long been scepticism about cuts in numbers of civil servants. 'At the end of the day, the quickest and easiest cuts remain those achieved by delaying or reducing capital spending, not cutting 'chaps' in the Civil Service' (Heclo and Wildavsky, 1981), though there is evidence (HM Government, 1983) that manpower is indeed being reduced.

In response to the allegation that capital expenditure is suffering unduly as a result of attempts to maintain current expenditure, there have been a number of vigorous ministerial defences of the present régime and words of caution about treating the terms 'capital' and 'current' in public expenditure terms in the same way as they are used in the private sector. 'Investment in prisons and unemployment benefit offices . . . however beneficial or necessary . . . can hardly be regarded as adding to the nation's productive capacity although it is classified as capital' (HM Treasury, 1981a). Nevertheless, the construction industry in particular has been deeply concerned about the fact that capital programmes have in general suffered very considerably as a result of the Conservative Government's attempts to cut public expenditure (Treasury and Civil Service Select Committee, 1983).

The Government's response (HM Government, 1983) was to point to plans for increased capital expenditure and to blame local authorities and nationalised industries for failing to spend the amounts allowed. This was certainly a neat way of turning back the criticisms by both local authorities and nationalised industries that they were being starved of cash. It also needs to be seen as another round in a continuing battle to decide priorities within an overall government expenditure total which cannot meet the calls upon it.

An issue which has caused less public concern but a good deal of acrimony among spending departments is whether the cash limits are too rigid and whether there should be more flexibility to accommodate unexpected variations from the assumptions made when the limits were set, to allow more carry-forward from one year to another. The arguments on both these topics closely reflect similar issues in the private sector (Likierman, 1981).

In practice, however, it is clear that there is a great deal more flexibility within the system than is apparent — both through overspending of some limits, but also through a significant number of revisions from one year to another (Likierman, 1983). As Wright (1977) pointed out just after the system was introduced, there are dangers here too; 'For whatever good reason, the more cash limits are breached or revised, the harder it will become to make them credible and binding in the future'. In any case, in response to requests for carry-forward from one year to another, some limited concessions have been made on overseas aid and on the external financing limits of nationalised industries. There have also been concessions on flexibility within the National Health Service cash blocks. But attempts to allow more systematic carry-forward for departments involved in major capital programmes, such as the Ministry of Defence have only partially succeeded. It has been alleged (Public Accounts Committee 1980) that the failure to allow carry-forward gives rise to distortions in programmes in order to meet an annual spending limit. But the Treasury rejected these arguments because of the problems of public expenditure planning and control and the consequent need to set aside a sufficiently large contingency to meet any carry-forward (Public Accounts Committee 1981). Although these are issues familiar to the private sector, it is unlikely that the departments will let the matter rest. In addition, the stream of angry comments to Select Committees and the press will certainly continue to act as a source of pressure on the Treasury.

A separate set of issues on the operation of the cash limits system has been their application, through external financing limits (EFLs), to nationalised industries. The same questions about the impact on pay, on the balance between capital and current expenditure and on flexibility have been raised and debated since the limits were applied to nationalised industries (Henley et al., 1983). Nevertheless, there have also been issues on the specific application of EFLs to nationalised industries. These include a concern about whether control through cash is suitable for trading entities of this kind and whether such control is compatible with the requirement to meet financial targets, non-financial performance aims and to achieve a required rate of return on investment. The issues have certainly received a good deal of attention (Treasury and Civil Service Select Committee, 1981c), not least because the nationalised industries have evidently felt it necessary to have the debate in public as a means of exerting pressure on the Government. A related public debate about whether the consumers of an industry's goods or services are being asked to bear an unfair burden—financing current investment which benefits future consumers—also needs to be seen in the context of public jousting. Many of the issues concerning the nationalised industries' EFLs have almost certainly become so important only because of the generally poor relations between the industries and the Government and because of the overall cash constraints within which the industries feel themselves to be confined.

The future of the cash limits system in general is by no means assured. Pliatsky (1982b) has commented on the dangers of cash limits being associated with Conservative policies:

> It would be a great pity if present controversies about policy were to undermine the principle of cash limits, which in essence simply puts a figure on the rate of inflation that the government will finance in the coming year, but which at the same time have proved a uniquely effective instrument of good housekeeping. Criticisms of the Conservative Government's cash limits policies are largely misdirected, since cash limits are an instrument or method of carrying out policies themselves.

Barnett (1982) argues the same point in relation to the experience of the Labour Government of 1974–9:

> Because it [the introduction of cash limits] unfortunately coincided with the need to cut the volume of public expenditure, it was taken as another means of cutting public expenditure. The fact is that even if total public expenditure was as high as anyone could wish, it would still be important to have a system of cash limits. Without such a policy, priorities in public expenditure would not be those democratically chosen by Cabinet, but determined by the vagaries of what in the jargon is called relative price effect (RPE).

But according to Pliatsky the Conservative Government must also carry some of the blame for the connection between their policies and the cash limit system:

It will, however, give some colour to the criticisms if too much weight is put on cash limits to carry out policies, especially incomes policies, without a sufficient degree of acceptance for the policies themselves, or if the idea of cash budgeting as a medium-term rather than a short-term instrument is taken too far.

And Barnett comments 'regrettably, it seems that, at the moment, cash limits are seen as a kind of sham incomes policy, and much worse an unfair one, for the public sector only'.

The system was helped to survive in its early years by a pay norm, more recently by falling inflation and throughout by considerable flexibility. The combination of rising inflation, no control over incomes, underbudgeting for pay, lack of sanctions and substantial revisions and/or overspending could put the whole system of cash control under intolerable strain.

Internal Control

There have been two important stimulae to improve the Government's internal control mechanisms. The first has been the influence of the private sector through pressure from a Government which has clearly believed that the private sector has a great deal to teach the public sector and has, as a result, provoked a growing interest in applying private sector techniques. The second has been the need to make economies in the use of resources in the light of continuing demands on the public sector linked to a rate of national economic growth too low to finance them.

The major response to these pressures has been focused on the financial management initiative. The main objective of this 'is to promote in each department an organisation and a system in which managers at all levels have:

- a clear view of their objectives; and assess and, where possible, measure outputs or performance in relation to these objectives;
- well defined responsibility for making the best use of their resources, including a critical scrutiny of output and value for money;
- the information (particularly about costs), training and access to expert advice which they need to exercise their responsibilities effectively. (HM Treasury, 1982)

The initiative has come about as a result of efforts not only from the Government but also from the House of Commons. The

Government's effort was spearheaded by Sir Derek (now Lord) Rayner. Rayner, one of the managing directors of Marks and Spencer, was brought in by the incoming administration in 1979 to look at ways of improving efficiency in central government. He is perhaps best known for his 'scrutinies' of individual government departments – investigations into ways in which specific economies might be made. But Rayner was also concerned with what he called 'lasting reforms' of the way in which civil servants thought about management of the resources under their control (Rayner (1981), Allen (1981)).

The work on efficiency was given additional stimulus by the work of the Treasury and Civil Service Committee in their report on Efficiency and Effectiveness in the Civil Service (Treasury and Civil Service Service Select Committee 1982a). The Committee examined systems currently in operation in the civil service and picked out one in particular, the MINIS system in the Department of Environment, introduced by Michael Heseltine when he was Secretary of State (Likierman, 1982) as a result of a Rayner scrutiny. The Committee recommended that 'as far as practical, other departments should follow the example of the Department of Environment'. What appealed to the Committee was the idea that ministers and senior officials would act more as managers of the resources under their control through the close monitoring of expenditure which the MINIS system offered. By providing a systematic analysis of activities, it gave the opportunity to link costs more precisely to activities and to question priorities, including whether activities should be undertaken at all. It also gave, in most cases for the first time, criteria for measuring the performance of activities. For the financial year 1983-4 MINIS was supplemented for the first time by a computerised management information system called MAXIS (Management of Administration Expenditure Information System) which gives line managers regular updating on progress against a phased budget to help them reduce over-and-under spending. MINIS was in operation before the financial management initiative and is being developed further in ways compatible with other developments in central government.

The Committee also recommended a number of other measures which were very much in the spirit of the Government's ideas about improving systems and borrowing from private sector practice; so much in the same spirit that in their reply to the Committee (HM Government, 1982) the Government accepted most of the recommendations and announced that departments would be expected 'to follow MINIS or its nearest equivalent'.

This brief summary gives the background to a number of issues in the area of internal control. A linking issue debated over a long period is whether private sector experience is really applicable to the Civil Service. In the light of the experience of the previous 20 years, the faith of the incoming 1979 Government might be counted as surprising, since a number of attempts to introduce private sector techniques into the Civil Service have been notably unsuccessful. Within the Civil Service there has therefore been a distrust of those who have simply tried to apply business techniques to what they consider to be quite different types of organisations. In the context of the future of the Civil Service Department, evidence to a Select Committee (Treasury and Civil Service Select Committee, 1981a) showed the strength of feeling based on diametrically opposite, if predictable views. Sir Derek Rayner drew on experience of practice in industry and commerce to support his case for a merger, while former civil servants stated 'There is a seductive but false analogy with business that suggests that the Treasury should be seen as a sort of head office of the Civil Service' (Sir Anthony Part) and 'analogies drawn from experience in the private sector may be misleading' (Sir Samuel Goldman).

How far the reaction of these (among many) civil servants was a manifestation of the 'not invented here' resentment against the attempts to impose new systems (Kellner and Crowther-Hunt, 1980) is as difficult as ever to establish. MacRea and Pitt have argued (1980) 'public servants, as highly intelligent people, do not simply allow themselves to act the role of victim; they do not sit idly by and agree without question to changes introduced by politicians and the relative 'outsiders' who regularly sit on committees of enquiry into their work and organisation'. Certainly there have been those who have argued that it has been techniques being inappropriately applied which has given such transferability a bad name, and that there was no reason why techniques which held good in one type of organisation should not be applied to another (Steiss, 1982). This issue has provoked debate in other areas of financial control (Henley et al., 1983) and the results of the debate may well be useful for both public and private sector management practice.

A second major set of issues relates to the role of central management in the Civil Service and whether the same techniques can be applied in different government departments. These two linked questions cannot really be separated since the role of the central department in encouraging or directing individual departments to adopt certain techniques presupposes that there is sufficient similarity for a central department to be able to make these kinds of recommendations.

There have been those who have argued (Plowden (1980), Treasury and Civil Service Select Committee (1982a)) for a much stronger role for central departments, while many civil servants argue (Treasury and Civil Service Select Committee, 1981a) that the differences between departments are more important than the similarities. In many respects the debate parallels that in the private sector about the role of central departments in large, divisionalised private sector organisations, but the issue has been made more complex by recent organisational changes. The Civil Service Department was broken into two parts in 1981. The sections concerned with Civil Service pay were merged with the Treasury, while those whose functions included Civil Service efficiency were put under the Cabinet Office as the Management and Personnel Office (MPO). These changes have left the MPO with a difficult and ambiguous role and it remains to be seen how effective it will be able to be.

The Parliamentary Context of Financial Reporting, Monitoring and Control

The major regular financial reports—the Supply Estimates, Appropriation Accounts, Chief Secretary's Memorandum, Financial Statement and Budget Report and the Public Expenditure White Paper—are all presented to Parliament. A wider readership is of course assumed, but developments in financial reporting have been very much bound up with parliamentary developments in recent years. By far the most important of these has been a new structure of House of Commons Select Committees. Since 1979 there have been Committees 'shadowing' individual government departments, and this has provided a more specific focus for parliamentary monitoring through financial reports than the pre-1979 subject-based Select Committees were able to achieve. The wide-ranging nature of the new Committees' role is already evident (Liaison Committee, 1983).

Amid those changes, the Public Accounts Committee (PAC) has continued to play its key audit role, though there has been some uncertainty about the boundaries with other Select Committees. Two manifestations of this uncertainty have been the dividing line between the subjects to be covered by the Treasury and Civil Service Select Committee and the PAC, and the role of the PAC in monitoring nationalised industries (see Chapter 11).

Financial issues have very often been at the forefront of issues arising from these developments. This is because debate about the quantity and quality of the financial of the financial information available has been a focus for wider debate about the nature of the constitutional role and influence of the new Committees. The linking of accounting and constitutional issues is most evident in the presentation and role of the Supply Estimates. Opportunity was, until recently, given to the House of Commons as a whole to debate this detailed analysis of the plans for government expenditure on special Supply Days. But these days were used instead to debate general aspects of government policy. A special Select Committee set up to look at treatment of the Estimates recommended (Procedure (Supply) Select Committee, 1981) a monitoring role for the new Select Committees in examining the Estimates and Supplementary Estimates each year.

The procedure recommended by the Committee has, with modifications, been implemented (HM Treasury, 1983), but a number of important issues remain and it is unclear how far the Committees will go in exercising their rights to examine the figures in detail. Under the new rules they are not obliged to do so and it is up to each Committee to decide whether it wishes to call for further evidence, hold public hearings and make recommendations. It is then up to the Liaison Committee to decide which subjects will be debated on the floor of the House of Commons on special 'Estimates Days'.

Two reasons why they may choose not to delve in detail into the Estimates are the way the figures are presented and the limited power of the Committees. Taking each of these in turn, the difficulties of understanding the Estimates have long been a source of disaffection among MPs and the concerns already expressed about the absence of volume information as a result of the move to cash planning have particular importance for the Estimates which give little information on the breakdown between the price and volume components of expenditure. The need for this kind of information for control purposes was highlighted even before cash planning came into operation (Treasury and Civil Service Select Committee, 1981b) since it was clear that without the breakdown it would not be possible to know whether an increase in total cash allowed meant an increase in the volume of resources, an increase in the price level or a combination of the two.

The second reason that Select Committees may not choose to delve deeply into the Estimates figures is that they have very little effective power to alter the amounts disclosed. Committees cannot vote to increase expenditure and any reductions must be voted on by the House of Commons as a whole if items are referred to them by the Liaison Committee. This procedure does not go as far as many MPs had hoped in giving effective control of public expenditure to the House of Commons, and there is likely to be a continuing constitutional debate with financial information as the symbol of the power of Parliament. It is worth noting that this is the continuation of a wider debate about the power of the purse which has been at the heart of British constitutional history for many centuries.

As part of this same debate, and in parallel to the pressure for improved financial information, an attempt has been made to give Parliament a greater opportunity for consultation on the basis of the annual Budget. The Armstrong report (Institute of Fiscal Studies, 1980) set out the case for budgetary reform, including a draft Budget which could be the subject of discussion by Parliament and in the country. These ideas were the subject of a Select Committee enquiry (Treasury and Civil Service Select Committee, 1982c) and this particular recommendation was endorsed by the Committee. The Government, while promising greater disclosure in future years (Treasury and Civil Service Select Committee, 1982d), was unwilling to concede a full draft Budget. No doubt the idea of giving full opportunity for discussion has seemed to be too restrictive on the present freedom of economic manoeuvre.

While the Estimates have been the focus for much Parliamentary attention, other financial documents presented to Parliament have also been under review and the pressures for greater financial disclosure have mirrored many of those in the private sector. In particular there has been an improvement in the presentation of, and greater disclosure in, the Public Expenditure White Paper. There has also been some improvement in the general presentation of the other financial reports. These changes have not gone as far in providing either financial or non-financial information as a variety of reports had recommended (Treasury and Civil Service Select Committee 1981b, 1982a, 1983, Public Accounts Committee 1982), and there will undoubtedly be continuing pressure to make the figures more accessible to MPs and the informed general public.

Conclusion

Many of the issues mentioned in this chapter are not new to the area of public sector accounting. What is new is perhaps the sharp focus into which they have been put by a government concerned to reduce the overall size of the public sector and to bring in techniques from the private sector where possible.

The combination of important departures from previous practice in a number of areas and increasingly self-confident Parliamentary Select Committees will ensure that the issues outlined in this chapter (and indeed in several others) will be the subject of a continuing and vigorous debate.

References

Allen, D. (1981) 'Raynerism: strengthening civil service management'. *RIPA Report*, Winter, Vol. 2, No. 4.

Barnett, J. (1982) *Inside the Treasury*, Andre Deutsch.

Bevan, R. G. (1980) 'Cash limits', *Fiscal Studies*, Vol. 1, No. 4.

Bevan, R. G., Sisson, K. and Way, P. (1981) 'Cash limits and public sector pay', *Public Administration*, Vol. 59.

Clarke, R. W. B. (1978) *Public Expenditure Management and Control*, (ed. Sir A. Cairncross), Macmillan.

Diamond, Lord J. (1975) *Public Expenditure in Practice*, Allen and Unwin.

Else, P. K., and Marshall, G. P. (1981) 'The unplanning of public expenditure: recent problems in expenditure planning and the consequences of cash limits', *Public Administration*, Autumn, Vol. 59.

Goldman, Sir S. (1973) *Public Expenditure Management and Control*, HMSO.

Heclo, H., and Wildavsky, A. (1981) *The Private Government of Public Money*, Macmillan.

Henley, D., Holtham, C., Likierman, J. A., and Perrin, J. R. (1983) *Public Sector Accounting and Financial Control*, Van Nostrand Reinhold.

Kellner, P. and Crowther-Hunt, Lord (1980) *The Civil Servants*, Macdonald.

Likierman, J. A. (1981) *Cash Limits and External Financing Limits*, Civil Service College Handbook, No. 22, HMSO.

Likierman, J. A. (1982) 'Management information systems for ministers: the MINIS system in the Department of the Environment', *Public Administration*, Summer, Vol. 60.

Likierman, J. A. (1983) 'Maintaining the credibility of cash limits', *Fiscal Studies*, Spring, Vol 4., No 1.

MacRea, S., and Pitt, D. (1980) *Public Administration*, Pitman.

Pliatsky, Sir L. (1982a) 'Cash limits and pay policy', *Political Quarterly*, Vol. 53, No. 1.

Pliatsky, Sir L. (1982b) *Getting and Spending*, Basil Blackwell.

Plowden, W. (1980) in *The Future of the Civil Service Department*, Treasury and Civil Service Select Committee, 1st Report, Session 1980–81.

Rayner, Sir Derek (1981) 'Note on progress with Rayner exercises' and his evidence to the Treasury and Civil Service Select Committee, *Efficiency and Effectiveness in the Civil Service*, 3rd Report, Session 1981/2 Vol. 2.

Steiss, A. W. (1982) *Management Control in Government*, Heath.

HM Government (1976) *Cash Limits on Public Expenditure*, Cmnd 6440, HMSO.

HM Government (1982) *Efficiency and Effectiveness in the Civil Service*, Government Observations on the Third Report from the Treasury and Civil Service Committee, Cmnd 8616, HMSO.

HM Government (1983) *The Government's Expenditure Plans 1983–84 to 1985–86*, Public Expenditure White Paper, HMSO.

HM Treasury (1981a) *Capital and Current Public Expenditure*, Economic Progress Report No. 135., July.

HM Treasury (1981b) *Public Expenditure; Planning in Cash*, Economic Progress Report No. 139.

HM Treasury (1982) *Financial Management Initiative*, Economic Progress Report No. 150, October.

HM Treasury (1983) *Parliament's New 'Supply' Procedures*, Economic Progress Report No. 155, February.

Institute of Fiscal Studies (1980) *Budgetary Reform in the UK*, Oxford University Press.

Liaison Committee, House of Commons (1983) *The Select Committee System*, 1st Report Session 1982/3, HC 92.

Procedure (Supply) Select Committee (1981) 1st Report, Session 1980/1, HC 118.

Public Accounts Committee (1980) *Carry-Over of Cash Limits at the End of the Financial Year*, 27th Report, Session 1979–80.

Public Accounts Committee (1981) *Carry-Over of Cash Limits at the End of the Financial Year*, 14th Report, Session 1980–81.

Public Accounts Committee (1982) *Publication and Content of Appropriation Accounts*, 18th Report, Session 1981–82.

Treasury and Civil Service Select Committee (1980) *The Budget and the Government's Expenditure Plans 1980–81 to 1983–84*, 2nd Report, Session 1979–80, HC 584.

Treasury and Civil Service Select Committee (1981a) *The Future of the Civil Service Department*, 1st Report, Session 1980–81.

Treasury and Civil Service Select Committee (1981b) *The Form of the Estimates*, 6th Report, Session 1980–81, HC 325.

Treasury and Civil Service Select Committee (1981c) *The Financing of the Nationalised Industries*, 8th Report, Session 1980–81, HC 348.

Treasury and Civil Service Select Committee (1982a) *Efficiency and Effectiveness in the Civil Service*, 3rd Report, Session 1981–82, HC 236.

Treasury and Civil Service Select Committee (1982b) *The Government's Expenditure Plans 1982–83 to 1984–85*, 5th Report, Session 1981–82, HC 316.

Treasury and Civil Service Select Committee (1982c) *Budgetary Reform*, 6th Report, Session 1981–82, HC 137.

Treasury and Civil Service Select Committee (1982d) *Observations by HM Treasury on 6th Report on Budgetary Reform*, 2nd Special Report, Session 1981–82, HC 521.

Treasury and Civil Service Select Committee (1983) *The Government's Expenditure Plans 1983–84 to 1985–86*, 3rd Report Session 1982–83, HC 204.

Part 3
Value for Money and
Performance Review

9
Accounting and the Pursuit of Efficiency

ANTHONY HOPWOOD

'Every society keeps the records most relevant for its major values.'
(Lazarsfeld, 1959, p. 108)

Accounting for the public sector has become a major issue for both discussion and action. In the last few years both the language and the practices of accounting have entered much more frequently and forcefully into debates about the efficiency, accountability and even scope of public sector activities. Appeals are now being made to the apparent inefficiency, lack of cost effectiveness, unprofitability and waste associated with the public sector. Referring to the existing economic calculus, it is being said that we are now 'living beyond our means', supporting that which is not 'economically viable', and either unable or unwilling, to face 'the facts of economic reality'. Although there is a long history of investing in accounting mechanisms for recording, planning, controlling and making visible public sector activities, within a very short period of time indeed recent pressures for change have succeeded in challenging the adequacy of existing public accounts and management accounting practices. New demands are now being made for the practices of accounting to become even more implicated in public sector management.

Where have these pressures for change come from? What form do they take? And what are their implications? How, in other words, can we not only better understand the forces at work but also attempt to gain a more adequate appreciation of their consequences for both the technical practice of accounting and the conduct of business within the public sector?

Before focusing on these questions, however, it is useful to consider some of the ways in which existing accounting practices have become intertwined with quite substantive issues of public policy. For, like today, much of the power of the public accountings of the past derived from their ability to move beyond merely facilitating the operation of pregiven and relatively unproblematic forms of economic and financial management. Accounting has already been implicated in a more positive shaping and influencing of that which is regarded as problematic, the forms which public debates take and the options seemingly available for management and public action.

Accounting and Public Policy

Accounting records provide a way of freezing the decisions of the past (Bahmueller, 1981, p.193). What was problematic and debated can become lost within the accounting archive. 'Facts' can thereby be created out of dissent and disagreement. An aura of the obvious and the unchallengeable can and does emerge out of the residues of past actions which accounting presents.

The significance of the ability of accounting to forge a domain of the factual in this way can be seen in the patterns of both relative and absolute performance of many public sector bodies. Past subsidies, allowances and provisions, decisions on transfer prices and payments, and the specific means used for their financing, play a significant role now in determining where current costs are incurred, continuing subsidies required and profits and losses both generated and shown. The relationships between past policies in the areas of defence, industrial development and regional support, all have current impacts of this type. Examples abound in the interplay between taxation, economic and social policies. For the National Coal Board, British Rail, London Transport and the Central Electricity Generating Board the patterns of present financial performance emerge out of a complex array of decisions of a social and political, as well as purely economic, nature. But those decisions give rise to accounting residues which can be and are used independently of the contexts out of which they emerged. Being 'profitable' or 'unprofitable', 'subsidised' or 'a drain on the Exchequer', can have a powerful contemporary significance. In this way accounting seems to provide a means of judiciously selecting the time-scale for comment and debate. The compelling obviousness of the present can overwhelm the contingencies of the past.

The fact that accounting, as we know it, provides a partial record of organisational choices and actions has also been of enormous importance. Organisational accounts both reflect and, in turn, influence the emphases that are given in public debates. Consequently, the economic has undoubtedly been made more visible than the social and the political, in many spheres of public life. Now, however, the imperatives of those economic 'facts' can be contrasted with the more questionable dictates of political ideology and social preference, illustrating, in the process, the powerful influence that the recording tools of the public domain can have.

In fact, organisational accounts laid down to orientate management action to wider ends can themselves come to serve as statements of the ends to be achieved (Ridgeway, 1956). Much of the apparatus of national income accounting emerged to aid the management of a constrained wartime economy (Seers (1976), Tomlinson (1981, pp. 129–132)). In the postwar discussions on the desirability of economic growth, however, GNP started to take on many of the attributes of being an end in itself and, in the process, had a more widespread influence on other governmental policies. The imagery of profitability and self-sufficiency has been subject to the same transformation. And, in more recent times, we have seen how actions have come to be taken in the name of such indicators as the Public Sector Borrowing Requirement—a complex and ambiguous indicator that emerged in the context of attempts to manage a constrained economy.

Accounting has also become implicated in the development of the institutional structures and linkages which today characterise the public sector. Particular forms of accounts have been used to buffer certain organisations from the dictates of government policy and intervention. 'Losses', for instance, have served as a pretext for price increases which have provided subsequent investment autonomy, sometimes on a very large scale; profits, similarly, have been used as evidence of both the granting of greater autonomy and its positive achievements. More frequently, accountings have served to tighten the relationships between different parts of the public sector. They have been used as a means of restraint; to constrain expenditures, actions and policies. The selective visibility created by organisational accountings has served to further the salience of imposed patterns of standardisation and uniformity. The information which they produce is used to monitor and evaluate the actions of others, and more frequent plans, budgets and reports can facilitate centralised control at the expense of local discretion.

All told, accounting is already centrally implicated in the institutional frameworks, language and patterns of power and influence that characterise the public sector. As a means of collecting and reporting selective patterns of information it has played a not insignificant role in the construction of public organisations and policies as we now know them. There are, however, yet further pressures for public sector accounting not only to change but also to expand its sphere of influence.

Pressures for Public Sector Accounting to Change

The pressures for the expansion and reform of public sector accounting are numerous, diverse and even conflicting in nature. Moreover, the emphasis given to particular factors can change remarkably over time, as recent decades have illustrated. In what follows, an attempt is made to outline only some of the main forces at work in recent debates in the area.

Changing Conceptions of the State

One of the major factors behind the current interest in public sector accounting is the changing view of the State that has entered political discourse in recent times. The legitimacy and value of at least some State actions and prerogatives are now being questioned from the perspective of a very different ideological stance. Indeed, a new way of examining and managing the State is emerging, and accounting is being implicated in that process.

Agencies of the State are now being asked to account for their aims, actions and achievements. Many more of their activities are coming to be seen in quite explicit economic terms. Cost and efficiency rather than effectiveness are being highlighted and debated. Information on economic consequences is being demanded. 'Value for money' has now entered the vocabulary of government.

In a whole series of ways the practices of accounting are increasingly being used to infiltrate and change, rather than merely record, the activities of the State. A new economic visibility is being forged to emphasise what was previously ignored and to challenge what was previously taken for granted. Economic calculations are now being seen as a way not only of reforming the management of the State but also of influencing the priorities which are given in policy determination and decision making. Accounting is quite explicitly becoming implicated in the construction of different views of the problematic, the desirable and the possible.

Accounting and Economic Restraint

Organisations tend to increase their investment in economic calculation and visibility during periods of restraint. In what has become known as 'newly poor behaviour' (Olofsson and Svalander, 1975), the constrained organisation places a renewed emphasis on costs, financial information and the calculus of economic decision making. Mechanisms for enhancing economic visibility extend further into the organisation. Financial standards, budgets and plans become both more detailed and more subject to change. The organisation overall becomes more economically orientated, more influenced by economic calculation and, somewhat paradoxically (given that very frequently the economic difficulties emanate from without rather than from within), more orientated towards the seeming dictates of its own internal economic circumstances rather than the pressures of the world at large.

Accounting in the United Kingdom has tended to flourish during just such periods of economic difficulty. The auditing profession emerged during the great depression of the latter part of the nineteenth century, and was, in many senses, a product of attempts to reform the practice of bankruptcy administration. (Only later did the profession gain the legal requirement for an audit and the legal monopoly in its practice that together provide the basis for the auditing profession today.) At the same time, cost accounting and the elementary practices of financial control started to play a more important role in manufacturing organisations faced with a rising real cost of labour at a time of general deflation and recession. In the depression of the 1920s, cost accounting seems to have been used aggressively as a way of getting at the 'facts' of economic difficulty. Similarly, the slump of the 1930s saw a dramatic rise in the role and status of accountants in industry as members of the auditing profession started to enter the upper echelons of manufacturing industry. Accounting has also been called upon in other times of economic restraint. The practice of costing was much utilised and developed in the munitions factories of the First World War. The Second World War saw investment in an internal economic calculus for government that was to provide the basis for national income accounting as we now know it. And, in the post-war period of economic restraint, it was the government that attempted to further the practices of economic management in industry in the name of enhanced international competitiveness.

During periods of economic difficulty, accounting and accountants have consistently expanded their sphere of influence in the UK. However, the relatively large British investment in the profession remains quite localised in its influence, having, until recently, much less of a presence in the service, financial and governmental sectors than in the area of manufacturing industry. Now, it seems, the current recession is providing a pretext for that to change, at least for the public sector. As the economic receives more emphasis in government, and as economic decision making itself becomes more constrained, more and more demands are being made for the type of economic calculations that accounting provides.

The Search for Greater Efficiency

Continued economic restraint has given a new urgency to demands to improve the efficiency of management in the public sector. More and more accusations of waste, maladministration and inefficiency have been made. High staffing levels have been pointed out. The traditionalism and sluggishness of decision processes in the public sector is noted repeatedly. Although it is sometimes realised that the demands of public accountability and decision making in a political context can serve to limit the extent to which concepts of efficiency derived from the private sector can be applied uncritically in the public domain, there nevertheless remains a feeling that much could be done to improve resource utilisation. Efficiency remains a very real and persuasive dream.

To this end, there is a renewed interest in importing into the public sector management practices developed in the private sector. Reference is made to the valuable roles that might be served by more adequate instruments for management planning and control. Appeals are made to the potential offered by improved costing procedures, more specific criteria for resource allocation, improved management information systems, investigations of administrative efficiency and better audits (which compare actual accomplishments with both original intentions and experience elsewhere). Such improved management practices, including those related to accounting itself, are seen as being able to assist in locating the inefficiencies of the past and ensuring that better performance is achieved in the future, not least by making public sector management and employees accountable for their actions and decisions.

Accounting and the Demand for Accountability

Appeals to the concept of accountability pervade many discussions concerned with the advance of accounting practice in the public sector. Accounting is seen as a way of both making visible and disciplining performance so that accountability can be demanded, policed and enforced.

A major impetus to the development of financial accounting in the private sector occurred when a separate cadre of managers came to be recognised as being accountable for their actions and performance to shareholders, the legally recognised owners of business. Since then, periodic crises of confidence have resulted first, in more and more elaborate and detailed accountings of both organisational aims and achievements being demanded; and second, in the supply of such accountings by managers who have tried to maintain respect for their ability to manage the assets of others. Equally, in the public sector, accounting has been implicated with the development of notions of stewardship and accountability. Accounting information has flowed from agencies of the State to Parliament and the public at large in recognition of the emerging constitutional requirement for the former to provide an account to the latter.

In the 1960s and early 1970s there were, in many Western countries, quite major pressures to expand the concept of accountability. In the name of social performance, environmental impact and the quality of working life, attempts were made to redefine the basis of organisational accountability to include aspects of performance broader than the purely economic. Related efforts were orientated towards expanding the information provided by the organisation in order to enable assessments to be made of its performance in new areas of concern. Notions of social, environmental and energy accounting and auditing were discussed and experimented upon. In the public sphere not unrelated developments were underway. Wider audiences started to demand the right to question the actions of the State. Not only was the State increasingly being asked to account for its actions and achievements, but greater demands were also being made for the right to assess public information, attend public meetings and more generally observe and interrogate the machinery of the State so that others might construct their own accounts of its performance. Concepts such as 'freedom of information' and 'the right to information' started to enter the language of political negotiation and debate.

However, in retrospect, it is interesting to note that most of these developments were much less significant in the UK than elsewhere. Here they did not result in any appreciable questioning of, let alone change in, our concepts of either accountability or accounting. Ideas of wider accountings of the social remained peripheral to UK concerns. Nor was the traditional secrecy of the State effectively challenged in the name of wider rights to public information. Accounting maintained its emphasis on the economic, and disclosure, rather than access, remained the vehicle by which information flowed. The reasons for this relative lack of debate and change in the UK are little understood. However, it is possible to point to the continual dominance of the economic over the social in the UK, the emphasis that all sides of the political spectrum have put on the primacy of the ownership of assets (be they in private or public hands), rather than on other strategies for regulating their deployment and use, and the long history of constraints on the dissemination of information which still pervade our legal, administrative and constitutional systems.

From such a perspective perhaps we should not be surprised that recent discussions of the advance of public sector accounting in the UK continue to emphasise the narrowly economic. Efficiency and value for money, rather than effectiveness, are the focuses of attention. Equally, we can note how little attention continues to be given to strategies for the wider dissemination and use of information, accounting or otherwise. Although demands for more accounting are still permeated with the rhetoric of accountability, the latter continues to have quite a constrained meaning. Indeed, many recent discussions appear to emphasise the role that accounting can serve in advancing accountability within the machinery of the State, rather than between it and the public at large. Administrative rather than public accountability appears to be the problem at issue.

No doubt other factors have played a role in mobilising current concern with the state of public sector accounting in the UK. On the supply side, for instance, attention could have been drawn to the increasing interest of the accountancy profession in expanding its sphere of influence and activity in all areas of the public sector. However, hopefully, sufficient has been said to demonstrate that the interest in public sector accounting is not purely a technical one. Accounting is explicitly implicated in the development of quite strategic interests and concerns. Rather than emanating from the specifics of particular accountings, deficient or otherwise, current pressures for change have stemmed from views of the role which the particular might play in mobilising more general strategic arguments.

However, such strategic interests in accounting are now attempting to grapple with questions of the particular and the specific. A rhetoric of economy, efficiency and value for money is now being used to call for a detailed concern with the specific accounting innovations that can service these wider ends.

The direction of change, from the general to the specific, has important implications for those interested in understanding and directing the practical process of accounting reform in the public sector. The generality, and indeed ambiguity, of notions such as efficiency and value for money must be recognised. For, although the ideas appeal to the comparison of inputs and outputs, and financial resources with their consequences, the delineation of those inputs, outputs, resources and consequences remains both a practically and conceptually difficult endeavour, not least in organisations which are complex, have little tradition of financial administration and economic record keeping, and where outputs and consequences repeatedly arise in organisations different from those initiating the developments. In fact, very little is known about not only the practice of the new public accountings but also the wider impacts which might stem from such an intensification of economic visibility in the public domain. To date, accountings for efficiency and value for money have been advanced in the name of their presumed potential rather than their practical possibility or actual consequences.

On Examining the Practices of Accounting

In order to facilitate an examination of the practical consequences of public sector accounting developments, we now consider some of the ways of examining and questioning proposals for such accounting changes. Attention is directed towards the technical practices of accounting themselves, the ways in which they are embedded in organisations, and the wider issues to which extensions of accounting give prominence and significance.

Accounting as Technique

Given the ambiguity which pervades such notions as 'efficiency' and 'value for money' when used in public debate, it is always important to analyse proposals for the practical assessment of these concerns carefully and precisely. Only rarely can it be presumed that there will be a direct and unproblematic relationship between the issues of concern and their measurement in practice. More frequently, there will be a gap between the policies which mobilised interest and the specific accounting practices that result from them. Accounting, in practice, invariably requires a specification of detail and a reliance on other organisational practices and procedures that make the final assessments arrived at only partially dependent on the initial interest in them. When subsequently taken up and used in decision making and policy formulation, practical accountings can, and do, have the potential to result in consequences very different from those originally envisaged for them.

Discretion often exists as to what inputs are deemed to be relevant, the costs that are assigned to the resources used, the outputs that are seen to flow from them, and their assessment in both financial and other terms. Issues of organisational interdependency will invariably arise, questions of presumed patterns of causal relationships will need to be debated, and proposals for specific valuations, weightings and assignments of priority will rarely be straightforward and unproblematic. Indeed, the difficulties of accounting in practice are such that it is often easy to arrive at a whole array of costs, efficiencies and value-for-money assessments. Many of these never see the light of day, however. Some are buried as a result of seemingly technical accounting choices; others fail to be recognised because of the dominance of particular organisational emphases and favoured theories of the determination of outcomes and consequences; and still others never emerge from internal discussions of 'the message to be presented'.

The ambiguous relationship between the general and the specific in the accounting area is such that attention needs to be directed to the assumptions, choices and practices that enter into the process of making practical what was previously rhetorical. Proposals for accounting change should always be interrogated in the name of the technical; for if this is not done, the consequences that such accountings have may bear only a loose relationship to those which explicitly entered into their justification and development.

Accounting and the Process of Organising

Accounting has the potential to have organisational consequences beyond merely facilitating, in a technical manner, the processes of decision making and policy formulation. By making visible what was previously unknown, it can open up different areas of the organisation for examination and debate. That visibility can also transcend different levels of the organisational hierarchy. What is accounted for can thereby shape the patterns of power and influence both within the organisation and without. Those with the power to determine what enters into the organisational accounts have the means to articulate and diffuse their values and concerns, and subsequently to monitor, observe and regulate the actions of those that are now accounted for. An expanded flow of information on organisational resources, capabilities and achievements can enable the monitoring, control and planning of organisational actions to be more readily abstracted from their execution. Management, in other words, can become more centralised. New linkages can be drawn both within and between organisations. Different and more abstract criteria can be used for resource allocation. And opportunities can be created for new specialists to enter into the processes of decision making and policy formulation.

The process of organising is not invariant to the accounting of it. Different investments in accounting do have the potential to enable different decisions to be made by different people in different parts of the organisation. Only rarely, however, does an organisational questioning accompany proposals for accounting change. Without it though, an ambiguous rhetoric can enable a partially independent accounting to shape quite important features of organisational life in ways which might not have entered into its original justification.

Accounting and the Creation of the Significant

The selective visibility which accounting gives to organisational actions and outcomes can play an important role in influencing what comes to be seen as problematic, possible, desirable and significant. Neither organisational participants, nor interested parties outside, can ever know the whole extent of organisational life. Direct observation can play a vital role in determining what is seen and valued. However, in organisational hierarchies and in those circumstances where geographical distance and organisational boundaries restrict what is directly visible, observation is soon supplemented and often superseded by that which is recorded. 'Information', both accounting and otherwise, then comes to play a significant role in determining what is known of the organisation and what is expected of it.

In such circumstances, those who influence what enters into the organisational accounts have a powerful and influential role. Some organisational disturbances are more likely to be seen as problematic than others. Some organisational options for change will be able to appeal more readily to supportive information and facts than others. Some criteria for the evaluation of change will likewise find it easier to relate to the partial mappings of the organisation that are incorporated into the accounting system. In these and other ways, not only can the emphasis given to different aspects of the organisation be changed, but also different values can more readily enter into decision processes and appeals can be made to different legitimacies for action. The economic, for instance, can be given more attention than the social. The internal workings of the organisation can be emphasised rather than its external context. The immediate can be given priority rather than the longer term. Accounting, by shaping the realm of the visible, can have a major impact on the significance that is attached to both organisational life as it is and the directions of change which are considered desirable. Both the organisational landscapes of the present and the future are in part, at least, a creation of the accountings that are given of them.

A very conscious attempt has been made to emphasise the need to interrogate and understand proposals for accounting change in terms different and wider than those in which they are usually presented. The ambiguity and generality of the accounting desirable needs to be confronted by an insight into the specificity of actual accounting practice. This needs to be done in terms of its precise operationalisation, the impacts that it has on organisational functioning and the emphasis that it creates in discussions and debates. Just as accounting is called upon to serve more than the merely technical, so it needs to be evaluated in commensurate terms.

Accounting for Accounting

It is possible to examine developments in public sector accounting on numerous grounds and from a variety of different perspectives. In the discussion which follows, emphasis will be placed on just a few axes for questioning which, nevertheless, raise issues of quite widespread significance. Stemming from an appreciation of how the technical practice of accounting intermingles with the fabric of political and organisational life, the aim is to identify some issues which are worthy of consideration by a much wider audience than they attract at present.

Accounting, Technical Practice and the Realm of Politics

Accounting has the potential to create 'facts' out of the uncertain world of the past and even, in a planning context, the future. What was, and still is, debated and challenged can give rise to a residue of accounting calculations of what is costly, beneficial and of value. A world of the seemingly precise, specific and quantitative can, in this way, emerge out of that of the contentious and the uncertain.

A calculative priority can be given to the economic rather than the social. Costs, consequences and benefits can come to be divided into the defined and known, and the imprecise and intangible. In such ways accounting can create very different maps of organisational and social functioning. Particular emphases are given. Only certain chains of reaction are made visible. Only some consequences of actions enter into the world of the precise, the known and even the knowable. In part, at least, what comes to be known of organisational reality starts to be created by the accountings of it. A different view of what is central, and what is residual and peripheral, can start to be reinforced by the ways in which the calculations of accounting intertwine with the complex functionings of organisations as we know them.

Such changes in the visible are accompanied by other changes in organisational life. Expertise in the creation of particular organisational realities starts to emerge and be rewarded. Different legitimacies can come to be attached to arguments and viewpoints, depending on the extent to which they appeal to the domain of the newly factual. Quite specific calculative procedures for decision making and resource allocation can come to be used in contexts where underlying disagreements remain.

Accounting, in other words, can become implicated in the creation of a domain where technical expertise can come to dominate political debate. By appealing to the centrality of the newly visible, be it the economic or whatever, an imperative for technical action can more readily be justified. What were previously seen to be problems of political priority can now start to be seen as requiring management guidance and expertise. We must now face the facts of the newly emerged reality. Rather than debating and arguing, we must appeal to those with expertise in the technical. Politics must stay at the door of public organisations. Within them, so it is said, planning, decision making, resource allocation and the evaluation of performance must come to be seen in management terms. The emerging domain of the technically factual and necessary must be given priority over the domain of the political.

Such attempts to restructure the sphere of legitimate political debate and action have profound consequences for the nature of the society in which we live. Is it necessary, one wonders, for politics to be thus confronted by the domain of the technical? From what political strategies does this itself emerge? And what are the wider consequences for political and social life? Just what might be at stake in such a juxtaposition of the rhetoric of efficiency with that of democracy? Is it really necessary, one wonders, for the enhancement of the legitimacy of the technical to be gained at the expense of the legitimacy of politics?

Of course, not all changes in public sector accounting raise such fundamental questions. Indeed, accounting itself can be used to mobilise political arguments and debates. The ambiguity of technical accounting practice is such that it often has an uncertain relationship to political practice. Nevertheless, both some specific proposals for accounting change and the general emphasis which together they place on the managerial and the economic, suggest that, at times, accounting developments do need to be seen in such wider terms. Although often masked by the language of the technical and the procedural, accountings can have quite profound consequences in the political sphere.

Accounting, Organisational Visibility and the Centralisation of Authority

Accounting can also become implicated in the creation of very different patterns of organisational influence and control. The selective patterns of visibility which it creates can enable the local to become known to the centre. Institutional boundaries can be made less opaque. Different patterns of local behaviour can come to be seen, compared and more readily labelled as conforming to, or deviating from, the dictates of the centre. Equally, the preferences of the centre can more easily become known to the local. Procedures for planning, budgeting and performance assessment can serve to both disseminate and make real the demands of the centre. Constraints on local behaviour can be imposed on the basis of the calculative visibility created by accounting systems. Specific behaviours can be monitored and more readily restrained. The local can, in this way, come to be managed as a part of the centre. Organisational interrelationships can become tighter. Discretion can more readily be specified and monitored. Indeed, the local can start to enter into the plans, policies and strategies of the centre so that the meaning of the distinction between the local and the centre can be radically changed.

Yet again, accounting can become implicated in the attainment of a set of consequences which extend far beyond the merely technical. Questions, therefore, can be, and perhaps should be, asked of the organisational and wider consequences of accounting developments.

Just who is made visible to whom? Are the patterns of visibility symmetrical or otherwise? Can only the centre observe the local? Or can the local also observe the centre? Equally, what emphasis is placed on the forging of a visibility within the system of public administration, as compared with the creation of an external account? In other words, just what concepts of accountability (as distinct from accounting) are implicated in the process of accounting change?

Accounting and the Enhancement of Organisational Legitimacy

Accounting can also provide quite a direct basis for enhancing organisational legitimacy. Investments in rational organisational accounts and technical management procedures can be used to demonstrate to others that the organisation accepts the legitimacy of economic and technical bases for action and is seeking to further these ends. Accounts, plans, budgets and the practices of efficient management then become symbols of the organisation's commitment to efficiency both as an aim and a particular strategy of rational governance and management.

The manifestation of such accounting symbols need not result in their coupling to organisational action however (Meyer, (1979), Meyer and Rowan (1977)). The display of the rational accounts may be orientated to those who ask questions of the organisation and seek to probe into its affairs from without, rather than to those who determine from within the organisation's course of events. So, somewhat paradoxically, if the investment in accounting provides sufficient evidence of the organisation's commitment to the course of rational economic and technical action, the discretion so gained might be used to uncouple organisational actions from the accounts which are made of them. Accounting might, in such circumstances, provide the freedom for the organisation to be unaccountable. By successfully appealing to the symbols of legitimate action, accounting might enable the internal affairs of the organisation to have a looser relationship to the external accounts of them.

Accounting and the Routinisation of Concern

Thus, the practices of accounting can come to be valued independently of the precise ways in which they intermingle with other organisational practices to influence the course of practical events. In any event, accounting, often stemming from more wide-ranging and ambiguous concerns, can have difficulty reflecting the specificity of both particular mobilising concerns and particular organisational phenomena, not least in the public sector. In addition, accounting can also come to function as a specialist area of activity in its own right. Technical questions of accounting can arise independently of the contexts in which it functions; accounting can be changed in the name of its own organisational bases and management rather than the wider concerns of the organisations in which it operates.

Such tendencies serve to detach accounting from the organisations in which it functions and the concerns in the name of which it was mobilised. Efficiency, for instance, can lose its force as the basis for accounting changes, to be replaced by a more procedural concern for accounting for efficiency. Similarly, plans can become more important than planning; budgets than the process of budgeting; and costing than the ascertainment of costs. A routine emphasis on accounting as procedure and technique can, at times, supersede accounting's initial concern for the issues in the name of which it was introduced and reformed.

Such a displacement of concern does not always take place. There is no imperative in this direction. Care, diligence and continual attention can result in the routines of accounting maintaining their orientation towards the purposes which they were established to serve. Accounting can continue to penetrate the organisation and change it in the name of more strategic ends.

However, the tendency for accounting over time to emphasise the procedural and the routine, to the detriment of the managerial and the strategic, has recently been recognised as a problem in the industrial sector (Kaplan, 1983). There accounting's routine emphasis on the short-term economic has been seen to constrain the organisation's strategic vision and posture (Simmonds, 1983). Concerns have been expressed about the rigidity of the information and control practices which accounting has traditionally advanced. Accounting has been seen to emphasise the proliferation of routine techniques in the absence of a concern with the specific managerial consequences which they have. And quite active attempts are now being made in some parts of the private sector to reform accounting in the name of what it should be doing rather than what some now see as what it has done.

Accounting and Its Use

Accounting developments do not always lose contact with either the organisations or the missions which they seek to serve. Similarly, accounting does not have any automatic relationship to shifts in organisational legitimacy, the location of social power and influence, and what are seen to be legitimate or illegitimate bases for political action. Moreover, even when accountings of organisational actions and achievements do become intertwined with such substantive concerns, they do not necessarily have any automatic effects. Accountings can counter accountings: those provided by one organisation can confront those made by others. The routinisation of accounting can even limit the changes in organisational power that might stem from accounting developments. The legitimacy that a particular accounting helps to establish at the organisational boundary can protect rather than necessarily disrupt the internal political processes of decision making.

The consequences of accounting are multiple, often conflicting and far from automatic. There is no imperative intrinsic to the accounting mission (Burchell *et al.*, 1980). Although accounting can have very real consequences, those consequences are created in the specific contexts in which it is made to operate. The effects of accounting are determined by the uses that are made of it, the organisational and social roles which it is made to serve, the ways in which it intersects with other organisational and social processes and practices, and the resistances which its use engenders. Rather than being either a unitary or automatic phenomenon, accounting comes to function in a variety of very different ways in very different settings. And it is those ways and settings which influence the effects that it comes to have.

However, such a contingent view of accounting and its consequences does not deny that accounting can raise quite legitimate and significant questions at levels far beyond the purely technical. If for no other reason than this, accounting developments should be examined in a wider forum. Attempts should be made in this way to account even for accounting itself.

Accounting and That Which Happens in its Name

Throughout this discussion an attempt has been made to demonstrate that the consequences of accounting do not necessarily have a close and automatic relationship with the aims in the name of which it is introduced and changed. For one thing, the aims that are expressed on behalf of accounting are general and often ambiguous. Stemming from political and managerial rhetoric, they are rarely expressed in terms of the specific operational and pragmatic questions which accounting must address before it can give rise to its technical procedures and practices. However, that gap between the general and the specific can be a very large one. As a result, the precise operationalisation of accounting's aims can introduce quite significant elements of technical autonomy into the accounting process. These elements serve to distance the specific from the general to which it seeks to appeal. Equally significantly, accounting practices come to be enmeshed in wider organisational processes and concerns. The domain of the factual, that they create, gives rise to a visibility, emphasis and basis for governability that can enable the consequences of accounting to become both more pervasive and more independent of the original aims which might have been advanced on its behalf.

It is, therefore, always legitimate to seek to confront accounting with an analysis of the specific consequences which it has had. What has been changed in the name of accounting both within the organisation and without? What effects have attempts to increase efficiency actually had? What precisely has happened to costs, resources and outcomes? What organisational actions have been curtailed or expanded? What changes, if any, have been introduced into the power structure of the organisation and its processes of management and governance? And how do any such precise consequences of specific accountings relate to the missions and rationales which mobilised them in the first place?

Although such an examination should not be alien to the accounting perspective, accounting itself has only rarely been accounted for. The furtherance of accounting in the public sector could, however, provide an ideal context in which to ask questions of accounting; for its use in this sector can raise questions of a wider organisational, social and even political nature. Given this, perhaps we should use the current pressures for change as a basis for starting to account for accounting and to ask questions about what is actually achieved in the pursuit of efficiency.

References

Bahmueller, C. E. (1981) *The National Charity Company: Jeremy Bentham's Silent Revolution*, University of California Press.
Burchell, S., Clubb, C., Hopwood, A., Hughes, J. and Nahapiet, J. (1980) 'The roles of accounting in organisations and society', *Accounting, Organisations and Society*, pp. 5–27.
Kaplan, R. S. (1983) 'Measuring manufacturing performance: A new challenge for management accounting research', *The Accounting Review*, October.
Lazarsfeld, P. F. (1959) 'Sociological reflections on business: consumers and managers', in R. A. Dahl, M. Haire and P. F. Lazarsfeld (eds), *Social Science Research on Business: Product and Potential*, Columbia University Press.
Meyer, J. (1979) *Environmental and Internal Origins of Symbolic Structure*

in Organisations, Paper presented at the Seminar on Organisations as Ideological Systems, Stockholm.

Meyer, J. and Rowan, B. (1977) 'Institutionalised organisations: formal structure as myth and ceremony', *American Journal of Sociology,* September, pp. 340–363.

Olofsson, C. and Svalander, P. A. (1975) *The Medical Services Change Over to a Poor Environment,* Unpublished Working Paper, University of Linköping.

Ridgeway, V. F. (1956) 'Dysfunctional consequences of performance measurements', *Administrative Science Quarterly,* Vol. 1, pp. 240–247.

Seers, D. (1976) 'The political economy of national accounting', in A. Cairncross and M. Pur (eds), *Employment, Income Distribution and Development Strategy,* Macmillan.

Simmonds, K. (1983) 'Strategic management accounting', in D. Fanning (ed.), *Handbook of Management Accounting,* Gower Press.

Tomlinson, J. (1981) *Problems of British Economic Policy 1870–1945,* Methuen.

10
Raynerism and Efficiency in Government

LES METCALFE and
SUE RICHARDS

Introduction

Soon after the May 1979 General Election, the Prime Minister appointed Sir Derek Rayner as her Special Adviser on Efficiency. The appointment was unpaid and part-time. Sir Derek retained his management responsibilities with Marks and Spencer. A small unit, formally part of the Prime Minister's Office and physically located in the Cabinet Office, was created to assist Sir Derek in developing and managing a programme of work designed to improve efficiency in government. Helped by strong Prime Ministerial backing, the momentum of the Rayner programme or "Raynerism" as it is widely called, has been maintained ever since its inception. In itself this momentum merits comment. Previous ventures of this kind have faded away once the sharp edge of initial enthusiasm was dulled by the practical difficulties of implementation. For example, PAR, Programme Analysis and Review, which in some respects the Rayner Programme superseded, enjoyed only short-lived Prime Ministerial backing (Gray and Jenkins, 1982).

Efficiency in government is a political value and administrative virtue that has not achieved high priority in the past. This is not to suggest that nothing was being done by government departments before Sir Derek Rayner came on the scene. On the contrary, efficiency work conducted by management services functions such as O&M, operational research, audit and staff inspection units, is well established. However, it has generally lacked influence within departments and at the centre. As one practitioner responsible for management services in Customs and Excise observed, 'we tried before but without the clout' (Nash, 1981). The, now defunct, Civil Service Department did not succeed in overcoming strong traditions of departmental autonomy, or carve out an effective central role in implementing the management and efficiency recommendations of the Fulton Committee (Chapman, 1983).

It is worth enquiring, therefore, why Raynerism has succeeded in overcoming initial resistance and what are its prospects of establishing a more stable niche in the management of government. Is it, as some would argue, merely a 'quick and dirty' means of cutting back the size of the Civil Service? Or is it a means of strengthening the quality of management throughout government? If the latter, what does improving management in government entail? Does it mean applying proven techniques of management developed elsewhere or does it require the development of new methods to deal with distinctive public management problems? (Christie (1982), Allen (1981)).

These questions are important because widespread support for efficiency in principle has not meant automatic support for the Rayner programme. Raynerism has attracted criticism from both inside and outside the Civil Service. Some criticisms are well founded. Others are very wide of the mark. The term 'Raynerism' has itself contributed to the controversy. It has become a convenient, though often ambiguous, shorthand. Raynerism means significantly different things to different people. The purpose of this paper is to give a sharper focus to questions of efficiency in government based on current research into the Rayner programme.

In order to clarify the intentions, achievements, and challenges of Raynerism the paper is divided into four parts. The first analyses the concept of efficiency to bring out its political as well as technical dimensions. The second part attempts to dispel some prevalent misconceptions about the aims and methods of the Rayner programme. In the third part of the paper the role of the Rayner Unit and its *modus operandi* are examined. The final part discusses emerging issues associated with the development of the Rayner programme and its prospects now that Sir Derek Rayner, or Lord Rayner as he now is, has relinquished his position as executive head of the Rayner Unit. Sir Robin Ibbs has taken over as the Prime Minister's special adviser on efficiency. Like Lord Rayner, Sir Robin combines experience in the highest reaches of the business world with a knowledge of government — from his time as head of the Central Policy Review Staff. The Efficiency Unit, as it is now called, is headed by an Under Secretary who was promoted from within. These two appointments ensure a degree of continuity for central efficiency initiatives.

Efficiency as a Technical and Political Concept

Efforts to improve efficiency are often presented as if they were, by definition, politically neutral and uncontroversial. Improved efficiency appears to be an unqualified good and attacking efficiency is almost like attacking motherhood. There is a well-established tradition of portraying efficiency work in non-political terms as a technical process of making better use of resources, seeking least cost solutions and achieving better value for money. If inefficiencies occur, there is no justification for allowing them to persist. This technical concept of efficiency is found, for example, in the Third Report of the House of Commons Select Committee on the Treasury and Civil Service (1981–82) which drew a sharp distinction between *effectiveness* as 'the definition of objectives, the measurement of progress towards achieving those objectives and the consideration of alternative means of achieving objectives' and *efficiency* 'given the objectives and the means chosen to pursue the objectives, the minimising of inputs to the programme in relation to the outputs from it' (House of Commons, 1982a).

This restricted concept implies a purely instrumental definition of efficiency, concerned with means but not ends. Defining efficiency as the ratio of outputs to inputs presupposes the resolution of policy issues and the definition of a framework of policy aims and objectives. It also means that efficiency work cannot begin until objectives have been defined and criteria of effectiveness established. Once these conditions are met, efforts to improve efficiency can concentrate on ostensibly technical questions of achieving better results with given resources or the same results at the cost of lower resource inputs.

Putting on one side the difficulties of actually establishing a policy framework which eliminates ambiguity about objectives, to say nothing of risk and uncertainty, it is mistaken to represent efficiency in narrowly instrumental terms. The boundary between efficiency and effectiveness is a permeable one. Promoting efficiency requires the exercise of technical expertise and a variety of professional skills but political and technical considerations are always interwoven. Policy choices and political judgement are integral parts of the process of seeking improved efficiency. Technical considerations may define a feasible set of options, but they do not provide criteria for choosing among those options. Policy choices are involved in deciding whether to seek improvements by reducing resource inputs, by improving resource utilisation and hence outputs, or even by investing greater resources now in order to create conditions for substantially improved efficiency in the future. In addition, efficiency work may uncover unrecognised policy choices or lead to the revaluation of options. At a lower level, choices among specific alternatives need to take into account the costs and complexities of implementation associated with them as well as the potential benefits.

Political judgement enters the picture in another important way because efficiency has a dynamic, as well as a static, dimension. Judgement has to be exercised in determining the balance between organisations designed for operational efficiency and organisations designed for flexibility. If problems are expected to be stable, specialised structures and processes should be designed to deal with them. If changes in problems are anticipated, organisational adaptability, resourcefulness and capacity to manage change efficiently are desirable. The issue is a real one because organisations designed for given tasks and stable environmental conditions lack the in-built capacity to learn, innovate and generate new responses to cope with changing circumstances. Efficiency in operational terms may be bought at the price of inefficient, slow and costly adaptation to change (Landau (1973), (March 1974), Metcalfe (1982a)).

In practice, it is common to slur over some of these complexities. Not infrequently, as Mintzberg (1982) pointed out, efficiency gets a bad name because practitioners clutch at readily available indicators and efficiency comes to mean measurable efficiency. The only things that count are things that can be counted. Mintzberg identified three major ways in which premature quantification distorts efforts to improve efficiency. First, costs are more easily measured than benefits, and the pursuit of efficiency reduces to a search for economies. Second, economic costs are more easily quantified than social costs which are treated as externalities. Third, on the output side, proximate short-term results are more amenable to measurement, and performance criteria are distorted by giving them too much weight.

While these factors may operate anywhere, they are compounded in government by the well-known inefficiencies associated with the production of public, as distinct from private, goods (Olson (1968), Niskanen (1973)). To guard against these inefficiencies, measurement of costs and performance is important, but it is crucial that systems of measurement are appropriate to the task. For example, after the 1973–1974 secondary banking crisis, the Bank of England was given responsibility for developing a more effective bank supervision system. Rigid application of a common set of financial ratios across all banks and deposit-taking institutions would have been the simplest and quickest way of introducing a new system. In fact, the Bank evolved a more appropriate system to monitor and assess the behaviour of banks by using different measures and different ratios to suit the characteristics of different institutions (Metcalfe, 1982b). Promoting efficiency in government calls for similar care in devising relevant and reliable measures.

Raynerism: Common Misconceptions and Basic Themes

The foregoing discussion helps put the Rayner programme in perspective. The main thrust of Raynerism is consistent with a broad view of efficiency as closely linked with effectiveness. Raynerism, as a doctrine, is as much concerned with the quality of service provided by government as it is with tight control of costs. But, because there are persistent tendencies to portray it in more restrictive terms, it is useful to preface more detailed discussion by clearing away misconceptions which obscure basic themes.

One common misconception is to interpret Raynerism too broadly — as virtually equivalent to government policy on control of public spending and the size of the Civil Service. Clearly, the Rayner emphasis on efficiency is consonant with the Government's policy of moving towards a smaller and better run Civil Service. The policy aim of reducing the Civil Service to 630,000 by April 1984, together with the desire to reduce the costs of administration, are important parameters of the Rayner programme. They provide departments with incentives to take efficiency issues seriously. But Raynerism did not create the political context in which it operates.

The second error is the opposite of the first. Raynerism is defined too narrowly as merely a cost-cutting exercise (with scrutinies of specific areas of departmental activity the instrument used to secure cuts). Obviously, for reasons just mentioned, departments are interested in identifying where cuts can be made. The scrutiny programme has helped to define the scope for savings in particular areas. In addition, individual scrutinies have been widely publicised. The attention they have received from the media is hardly surprising. They have provided evidence of obvious bureaucratic failings, such as numerous, incomprehensible forms, or more picturesque illustrations of lack of cost consciousness, of which the £30 rat is a conspicuous example. Rats bred commercially for experimental purposes cost about £2. Those bred at a Ministry of Agriculture establishment were considerably more expensive once overheads and other hidden costs were included.

One function of scrutinies is to uncover the effects of past inefficiencies such as these and prescribe ways of eradicating them. At the very least, the scrutiny programme has shown that inefficiencies existed across a wide range of departments and created the pressure to eliminate bureaucratic deadwood, unnecessary procedures, overlapping and duplicated activities and misdirected effort. But the search for a leaner and fitter Civil Service does not imply that leaner necessarily means fitter. As well as concern with the *effects of past inefficiency* there has been a strong emphasis on identifying the *causes of future efficiency* – notably through the development of better management.

Major elements in the policy for management include: more explicit allocation of costs to functions; attribution of costs for common services; more delegation of authority to combat administrative defensiveness and over-centralisation; and clearer definition of managerial responsibilities at all levels. These themes underlie much of the work on specific scrutinies. Rather than being just a short-term cost-cutting exercise, the Rayner programme has sought to introduce lasting reforms in Civil Service management practice; changing the culture of Whitehall to give greater status to managerial functions and combat the traditional over-emphasis on the policy adviser role of the higher Civil Service. Whatever decisions are made about the size of the Civil Service, Raynerism prescribes better management as the key to improved performance.

A third misconception concerns process rather than aims. With a few honourable exceptions the press has presented the Rayner programme in personality terms. This runs contrary to the Rayner theme of initiating a process of departmental self-examination — reform from within. The way this process actually works and the issues raised by its development are discussed at length later. But, the central point is that managing change in the way government departments operate is a task well beyond the capabilities of any single individual.

A fourth misconception is related to the cult of personality. It is erroneous to represent Raynerism as the application of private sector principles and practices to government. At the most simplistic level, Raynerism is seen as the application of Marks and Spencer management practices to the Civil Service (Howells, 1981). More generally, being more business-like is equated with being more like business. No doubt, in terms of organisation and management, government has a great deal to learn from business. Scrutineers have shown themselves willing to go out and assess the utility of, for example, systems of financial control, and draw in outside expertise. But, a selective and discriminating approach is needed because of the diversity of private practice and the differences in context and purpose of business administration and public administration. It is not the case that the private sector has solutions to all public sector management problems. Nor has this been the Rayner approach. The main emphasis has been on asking searching questions rather than prejudging answers, on self-development rather than imitation. This is appropriate because, in many respects, problems of management in government are more complex than those of business; as Lord Rayner recently observed:

> There is no risk whatsoever of my assuming that running government is like running Marks and Spencer either in content or execution. Government has to provide services which no sane business would undertake and whether it is more or less of government that the nation needs, a government will have to deal with those issues which private enterprise and voluntary activities cannot handle. (Rayner, 1983, p. 3)

To summarise, Raynerism is a component of Government policy

and its direction and achievements are in part a function of political conditions. But it is more than a cost-cutting exercise. There are longer-term aims guiding what has been done. Journalistic licence has placed the emphasis on the man rather than the programme, but the important question is whether Raynerism in practice produces results that sustain its momentum.

Raynerism in Practice

Improving efficiency in government, as in any organisation, poses a dilemma – how best to balance external pressure and internal commitment. Each is necessary. External pressure is needed to ensure that organisations take the task of improving efficiency seriously. The absence of market constraints increases the need to establish other pressures towards improved performance. Internal commitment is also needed because lasting improvements depend on the willingness of people to co-operate in the process of making changes (Argyris, 1970). Some notable efforts to introduce changes in government have failed to get the balance right. For example, McNamara's reforms in the US Department of Defense were short-lived because the Programme Planning Budgeting System he introduced failed to win internal support.

> So long as Mr McNamara was able to overcome resistance to planning by force of his personality and enthusiastic support from Presidents Kennedy and Johnson, PPBS was used, albeit reluctantly, throughout the Department. As soon as Mr McNamara departed, the pent-up inertia and resistance began to transform planning into the previous political, incremental process. (Ansoff *et al.* (1976); see also Schick (1973)).

Without favourable attitudes and positive motivation the costs of managing change are high, and the effects of increased external pressure, temporary.

Both external pressure and internal commitment were evident in the Rayner formula. Sir Derek Rayner's appointment, his access to the Prime Minister and the formation of the Rayner Unit symbolised the high priority the Government gave to improved efficiency and constituted a very potent source of external pressure on departments. At the same time, the small size of the Rayner Unit ensured a substantial role for departments. Raynerism in practice sought to generate internal commitment as well as bringing political clout to bear on the process of improving efficiency.

Going with the Grain

In creating this process Sir Derek Rayner drew on his previous involvement in government, in the early 1970s, when he formed the Ministry of Defence's Procurement Executive and headed it, with the rank of Permanent Secretary. He concluded that improved management in government depended substantially on securing the commitment of the Civil Service to the task. And this meant working with, rather than against the grain of departmentalism. The *modus operandi* of the Rayner Unit was deliberately designed to give departments such as Industry, Environment, Defence and Inland Revenue a considerable role in examining and improving their own performance. Its aims are to provide a framework within which departments carry out their own investigations and to provide guidelines for individuals to work to.

This is illustrated by the opening paragraph of the 'Note of Guidance' Sir Derek Rayner wrote to explain his philosophy to departments and Examining Officers responsible for carrying out scrutinies.

> The reasoning behind the scrutiny programme is that Ministers and their officials are better equipped than anyone else to examine the use of the resources for which they are responsible. The scrutineers therefore rely heavily on self-examination; on applying a fresh mind to the policy or activity under scrutiny, unfettered by committees or hierarchy; on learning from those who are expert in it; on supervision by the Minister accountable for it; and on a contribution from my office and me. (Rayner, 1982)

Ministerial and departmental commitment is secured through the scrutiny programme in several ways;

(1) departmental choice of policies and functions to investigate;
(2) departmental selection of scrutineers;
(3) ministerial acceptance of scrutineers' recommendations; and
(4) departmental action to ensure implementation.

Of course, departmental choices and actions are not unfettered. In each respect, there is consultation with the Rayner Unit. But the onus to do the work rests on departments and especially on the selected scrutineers.

Importantly, scrutineers have been chosen, not for specific

technical competences, but for general ability. The choice of 'bright young Principals' has been criticised because relevant technical skills are required, especially in the management services area. In part, choices are a recognition of a need to make political as well as technical assessments of what is acceptable and feasible. But, as the scrutiny programme has evolved, individuals from a wider range of levels and experience have been chosen and, increasingly, small teams have been assembled to draw in needed skills.

Scrutineers have usually reported that the process of conducting their investigations is quite different from their normal work. Although they are usually 'insiders', the status of scrutineer detaches them not only from normal organisational constraints but also from normal sources of support. Perhaps because they are so clearly responsible for their diagnosis and the recommendations they make, scrutineers almost invariably feel a sense of isolation and loneliness. However, the scrutiny process, with its emphasis on asking basic questions about the need for activities, the costs of activities and the value they add to outputs, is designed to put scrutineers in a strong position to argue their case. This is reinforced by the insistence on seeing what is actually done, talking to the people involved (rather than relying on written reports) and, where necessary, bringing in outside expertise. There is also a cachet associated with being chosen to conduct a scrutiny. Scrutineers are expected to put forward definite proposals for action and often their reports are published.

Interdepartmental Comparisons

In addition to the political visibility of the scrutiny programme and the publicity individual scrutinies have attracted, the possibility of making comparisons across departments has put the Rayner Unit in a position to ensure that departments offer up significant problems. In contrast with the normal dynamics of interdepartmental relations, the scrutiny programme gives ministerial kudos for making savings rather than increasing expenditure. A department which proposed low level scrutinies, such as the streamlining of messenger services or the reorganisation of registries and filing systems, could be prevailed upon, subsequently, to tackle more managerially substantial areas of activity.

The scrutiny programme also offers the possibility of more

specific comparisons, or 'read across', where departments tackled similar problems. Comparisons of performance, whether in the production of outputs or use of inputs, are obviously simpler and more straightforward in a multiple retail store than in government. But there was some hope that the scrutiny programme would identify some common problems. In the event, 'read across' did not emerge spontaneously. An appraisal conducted in 1981 by CSD to evaluate the extent of 'read across' and the scope for extrapolation, uncovered only limited possibilities. This, in itself, indicated the degree of departmental discretion in choosing subjects of scrutiny. Even where cross-departmental exercises such as a scrutiny of departmental running costs were mounted, comparisons did not lead to simple league tables of departmental profligacy or parsimony. The differences which emerged reflected familiar differences between large and small departments, such as Defence and Energy, and between primarily executive departments like DHSS, Inland Revenue and Customs and Excise, and non-executive departments like Environment and the Treasury which operate mainly through other agencies. The real significance of this exercise was to underscore the need for better and more consistent management accounting; to ensure that costs are known and to provide a base for departmental comparison over time rather than comparisons between departments.

The scrutiny programme has been the most prominent feature of Raynerism in practice. From scrutinies conducted by individuals there has been a move towards small departmental and inter-departmental teams as well as service-wide scrutinies of, for example, Statistics, and multi-departmental scrutinies including Administrative Forms, Research and Development Support Services and Personnel Work.

By the end of 1982, when Sir Derek Rayner relinquished his position, over 133 scrutinies had been conducted. Once-for-all savings of £56 million can be attributed to them, together with potential recurrent savings of £400 million per annum and 21,000 posts. By March 1984 annual savings of £230 million had already been achieved, and firm decisions taken on measures which will realise a further £100 million. These, in themselves, are substantial achievements. There is no question that the scrutiny programme has been cost-effective; even if sceptics would want to revise the Rayner Unit's figures downwards, they are of the order of magnitude of the decisions made about public expenditure at the margin.

Lasting Reforms

Scrutinies are part of a larger concept of lasting reforms of management in government. Lasting reforms mean more than the introduction of new techniques. They depend upon substantial changes in the 'culture of Whitehall'. Perhaps even more than the scrutiny programme, lasting reforms depend on internal commitment in departments and on changing attitudes and assumptions about the role of management in government.

The basic premise of lasting reforms is that Ministers, as well as senior civil servants, acknowledge their management responsibilities. Ministerial responses have been varied. Some, like Mr Heseltine when Secretary of State at the Department of the Environment, embraced the concept of the 'Minister as manager' wholeheartedly. He introduced a Ministerial Information System (MINIS) and a structure of cost centres within the department to ensure tighter control over administrative costs. (A more detailed discussion of MINIS is included in Andrew Likierman's chapter in this volume.)

MINIS began as part of the Rayner programme and has subsequently figured prominently in public debate about the information ministers need to exercise effective control over departmental efficiency. The Treasury and Civil Service Select Committee recommended that other departments introduce MINIS or a 'clear equivalent'.

The Rayner doctrine includes a number of proposals for change in departmental organisation and management. This is significant in itself because management is a subject which has traditionally had low priority in the culture of Whitehall. Although changes have been introduced in the past, the usual assumption has been that 'tinkering with institutions' was unlikely to produce worthwhile results. The proposed changes are summarised under two headings.

First, changes are needed to achieve more accountable management through clear definitions of organisational objectives and management roles. This entails a redistribution of responsibilities designed to strengthen line management and unify the often fragmented control over resources at departmental level.

Second, specific prescriptions about administrative decentralisation and delegation of authority, better systems for attributing costs to activities and controlling the use of resources, improved management information as well as better arrangements for monitoring and measuring performance, are all required. All of these call for changes in the preparation of civil servants for senior management positions; more systematic planning of management succession and, as a corollary, more extensive and clearly targeted mid-career training. They also underscore the need to give higher priority to departmental management services. Indeed, a multi-departmental review of internal consultancy services is in progress.

Sometimes prescriptions have been made on a service-wide basis. For example, the current Financial Management Initiative is a large-scale attempt to introduce reforms of cost-control, management accounting and financial management throughout government. Other prescriptions have been embodied in particular scrutinies. For example, the scrutiny of the Regional Development Grants Administration, in the Department of Industry, led to the implementation of a more decentralised and streamlined system for dealing with applications. A scrutiny in the Ministry of Defence led to important changes in the status and organisation of management services and the creation of a Directorate of Management Audit (Mayne, 1982).

A Smirnoff Effect?

The concept of lasting reforms implies a continuing effort to improve performance rather than a short-lived push to introduce particular changes. In order to implement them, deeply ingrained beliefs and habits of thought have to change. The scrutiny programme has gone some way to achieving this. Some departments, including Health and Social Security and Customs and Excise, have initiated their own scrutinies and reinforced departmental management services.

At the individual level, carrying out scrutinies has had what might be termed, a 'Smirnoff effect' on attitudes. Scrutineers are never quite the same again. The experience of being held responsible for asking and answering 'zero-base' questions about the value added by activities and the costs associated with them produces changes of attitude and outlook which persist. But changes at the individual level are not enough to sustain an efficiency strategy. Lasting reforms depend on changing key elements of departmental cultures, and more complex changes in departmental organisations.

In particular, changes of attitude towards management and towards change are needed. The low esteem of management in government has already been mentioned. Although, surprisingly, there is virtually no systematic evidence about how senior civil servants view the management process and their role in relation to it, there is a widely held belief that it is regarded as of secondary importance. Actual and aspirant senior civil servants are motivated by and rewarded for the immediate services they provide to ministers, rather than the quality and cost effectiveness of the services they provide to the public. Writing a well-constructed ministerial brief on a topical subject or steering a Bill through Parliament has higher value in the culture of Whitehall than implementing a new policy or improving the administration of an existing policy.

The culture of Whitehall consists of the, often unspoken, set of assumptions about their role within which senior civil servants think and act. The upper echelons of the Civil Service retain an homogeneity of outlook fostered by recruitment and career development practices. Because its basic values are reinforced by many established practices, this culture is not easily changed. While efforts may be made, through training and other measures, to modify the attitudes and influence the behaviour of individuals, institutional arrangements and constitutional constraints continue to exert powerful pressures in pre-established directions.

For example, it remains the case that a minister's reputation at Westminster is a major factor in his or her political career. It is also an important influence on interdepartmental negotiations in Whitehall. Senior civil servants will therefore continue to see supporting their minister in Parliament as a top priority. A minister who neglects the everyday concerns of the House of Commons in order to take on a more active managerial role in his department may well find that, with his finger removed from the Parliamentary pulse, he fails to spot dissent among backbenchers which creates problems for his legislative programme. Once delays in the legislative process arise, serious consequences for related policies are inevitable.

Given the importance of parliamentary preoccupations, the

culture of Whitehall must in part reflect the culture of Westminster. Unfortunately, the political hall of mirrors distorts reality. Parliamentary interests magnify the importance of fleeting topics which are likely to cause political embarassment and diminish the importance of longer-term management questions. With very few exceptions, MPs are unconcerned with management in government. Even the new select committees, the aspect of Parliament most removed from the party battle, have concentrated almost exclusively on substantive policy issues and not on the management concerns which Rayner raises. The Treasury and Civil Service Select Committee has been the only Westminster forum where these issues have been addressed.

One hypothesis, based on more than casual observation, is that the low regard for management stems from a tendency to define it too narrowly. Indeed, on occasion, management is equated with an uncreative process of control of programmed, routine activities (Landau and Stout, 1979). This is much too restrictive to do justice to the management problems facing government. Even in the sphere of policy implementation it is often impossible to achieve good results without allowing managerial discretion to adapt and innovate in response to unforeseen circumstances. Equating management with control is more likely to increase bureaucratic rigidity than improve performance. Control of routine operations is only one facet of management. In any case, contemporary concepts of management are more general and flexible. Lasting reforms may well depend on enriching the culture of Whitehall by evolving new concepts of strategic management appropriate to the tasks and responsibilities of the higher Civil Service. But the ideas required are not all readily available. It is not just a matter of applying proven techniques or adapting existing best practice. Sustained development and innovation are also needed.

Thus, the implementation of lasting reforms is an important test case. There is a well entrenched 'culture of Whitehall' belief that central initiatives are not sustained. Instead, they fall into a cyclical pattern of criticism of administrative failings, political enthusiasm and commitment, a high initial level of reforming activity which gradually peters out in the implementation phase. At which point everyone agrees that an occasional 'shake up' is very desirable.

As William Plowden put it, civil servants have 'a well-developed sense of *déjà vu*' (Plowden, 1981). They have seen it all before and by implication they expect old patterns to repeat. Of course, if acted upon, these prophecies are self-fulfilling. The Rayner concept of lasting reforms is an attempt to replace pessimistic beliefs about administrative reform with the idea of progressive improvement.

Emerging Issues

Whether Raynerism, as a doctrine of self-sustaining improvement in management, takes root depends on responses to several issues which have emerged thus far. Some can be most conveniently discussed with reference to the scrutiny programme. Others are concerned, more broadly, with the direction of lasting reforms. Both raise questions about the role of the centre and how best to ensure departmental commitment.

Conduct and Implementation of Scrutinies

We begin with the scrutiny programme because it is the most prominent part of Raynerism and experience with scrutinies provides more general lessons. Since it was intended to secure departmental commitment, it is worth considering whether it has done enough in that direction.

It has become customary to refer to the 'scrutiny technique' as if scrutineers actually adopted a common approach. It is not the case that they have, and undesirable that they should. The danger in stereotyping the scrutiny technique is that it absolves departments from taking responsibility for improving performance while going through the motions of complying with expectations at the centre.

As a means of securing departmental commitment the Rayner guidelines are, in some respects, too prescriptive and, in other respects, not prescriptive enough. Rather than being a technique, the guidelines impose a procedure, a format and a timetable which shape the processes of investigation and the way recommendations are made. The minds of scrutineers are concentrated on defining manageable problems and recommending practicable proposals for change. The procedure also places an obligation on departments to make 'public' commitments to implementation. Criticism of the scrutiny procedure is not to be confused with the assertion that scrutinies are '90 day wonders'. It is often argued that the timetable of 90 working days is too rigidly enforced and, as a result, quality of data and depth of analysis cannot bear the weight of conclusions drawn from them. In fact, scrutineers have been able to renegotiate timetables, and the Rayner Unit has been flexible in responding to unforeseen difficulties or recognising in advance that some problems would require more time.

It is the conduct of scrutinies, rather than the timescale, that calls for scrutiny. The scrutiny format assumes the general applicability of a model of change, which works well in certain conditions and with certain types of problem but not with others. It is a model which works best when problems are amenable to independent analysis and lead to clear-cut recommendations to top management, followed by top-down implementation. This approach is most likely to work where problems are straightforward, possible solutions already exist and implementation is internal to a department. It has the advantage, in these circumstances, of producing workable recommendations quickly. But it is less well suited to problems and situations where these conditions do not hold.

In some instances scrutineers have used a different strategy. The scrutiny of the Department of Industry's Regional Development Grants Administration, mentioned earlier, utilised a more catalytic approach. The scrutiny investigation provided a vehicle for defining a set of problems of which people working in the system were well aware, but to which management had not responded. Hence, the scrutiny provided the occasion for initiating changes people were already prepared for. In this sense the process of investigation made an important contribution to implementation.

The Rayner guidelines are not prescriptive enough in that they do not indicate the range of strategies for managing change that are available or indicate the criteria for choosing among them and combining them. In addition to the strategies of direct recommendation and catalysis, there may be situations in which some mechanism for confronting and resolving conflicts is needed or else a process of joint discussion and analysis to accelerate adjustment to changes in roles and responsibilities (Blake and Mouton, 1978).

The joint Department of Employment/Department of Health and Social Security scrutiny of the unwieldy systems for 'Payment of Benefits to Unemployed People' illustrates the need for flexibility in choosing strategies. Implementing major recommendations depended on interdepartmental cooperation, not just between the departments directly concerned but on a wider basis. Bringing about the unification of originally separate, but increasingly inter-dependent and over-lapping systems for paying Unemployment Benefit and Supplementary Allowance, promised large savings and a more efficient service. However, implementing the main recom-mendations called for the redefinition of departmental responsibilities and a substantial initial commitment of resources in order to realise the savings. Putting the Rayner 'invest to save' principle into practice depended on confronting and resolving interdepartmental differences over division of responsibilities and provision of resources.

Given the nature of the proposals and the scale of the potential benefits in reduced costs and improved service, either more intensive efforts to resolve conflicts within the departments concerned were needed, or else a wider process of consultation to ensure the feasibility of recommendations in resource terms was required before recommendations were made. Probably both were necessary.

Several references have already been made to implementation. The assumption built into the guidelines is that there is a sequential relationship. Clearly, implementation cannot go ahead without authorisation. Nevertheless, whether intended or not, the manner in which scrutinies are conducted has important consequences for subsequent responses. These 'process' considerations cannot be dismissed simply by ascribing implementation problems to irrational resistance to rational recommendations. If internal commitment is important, it must reach down beyond the highest ministerial and official levels.

Not least among the reasons for increasing attention to imple-mentation is the fact that in many cases it is not possible to specify in advance exactly how to proceed. Sometimes a programmed approach to implementation is appropriate. More often, an adaptive approach is needed which takes more note of the spirit than the letters of original intentions (Berman, 1980). Willingness to assume responsibility for implementation in circumstances where plans have to be revised in response to an evolving situation requires greater commitment as well as greater managerial competence.

Interdepartmental Relations and the Role of the Centre

The problems discussed above arise within the framework of a 'one-off' scrutiny. Despite the exemplary function these scrutinies have had, it is arguable that in the evolution of the Rayner programme they will be superseded by scrutinies that cross departmental boundaries. Multi-departmental scrutinies and service-wide scrutinies have already been mentioned.

In so far as they make good use of comparisons between similar functions in different departmental contexts, multi-departmental scrutinies are potentially powerful tools for improving efficiency and effectiveness. In important respects they are breaking new ground. It is too simple to see them as providing 'read across', though this may be an outcome in the long-term. Multi-departmental scrutinies have more basic functions of building a useful comparative framework and inculcating habits of making and using comparisons across departments.

The benefits of this approach, which could be very considerable, can only be realised if their management requirements are acknowledged and met. The demands on both central and departmental team are substantial, and much of the value of the exercise is likely to be lost if opportunities for exchanging ideas and systematising comparisons are not built in.

This poses a problem; how best to define the role of the centre. Although the centre may develop expertise in managing multi-departmental scrutinies, its managerial role is more appropriately that of facilitator than director. Central programming would be unwise, even if it were possible. Indeed, the Rayner ethic of decentralisation and self-examination virtually defines the role of the centre as a facilitating role — aiding rather than directing. Any departures from this role create discrepancies which will undermine confidence; 'Don't do as I do . . . '.

Having said this, the centre does have an important and distinctive role that other departments cannot play, that is, as an agent of learning — assimilating experience from successive scrutinies as well as ensuring effective dissemination of ideas among departments involved in particular scrutinies. Since the substantive topics — administrative forms, support services, departmental costs, personnel work, financial management — vary widely, the purpose of central learning is to accumulate experience in managing these complex investigations.

Neither the importance nor the difficulty of this task should be underestimated. Multi-departmental scrutinies present novel and complex problems in the management of change. There is limited past experience, inside or outside government, to go on. Most private sector experience of managing change has focused on individual organisations or sub-units within organisations. The problems of managing change among organisations are virtually unexplored.

Upgrading or Breaking New Ground?

Much discussion of efficiency in government assumes that improvement is merely a matter of applying readily available 'modern management techniques'. While there is no denying the scope for upgrading, it is only part of the story. Past neglect of management means that there is room for improvement on many fronts — as the scrutiny programme has shown.

In some cases improvements can be achieved simply by levelling up. This requires that departments know about, and see the relevance to their own situation of, best practice in government. In other cases, more general upgrading is possible by adopting management methods developed outside government. Cost centres and more effective management accounting systems are means of ensuring budgetary responsibility and financial discipline.

If the most immediate gains are to be made in internal control of administrative costs and, more generally, tighter control of resource utilisation, some of the most important long-term challenges are in the area of programme expenditure in major policy areas. This is where the major part of public expenditure occurs — payment of grants and benefits and provision of services. This is where management in government presents new challenges for which there are no ready-made answers. Government must break new ground in the development of management concepts and techniques, and it must innovate rather than imitate.

There are two broad directions in which innovation and development are urgently needed in the future — organisation design and the management of relations between organisations.

Although government consists of a large number of organisations which vary widely in form and function, there is, paradoxically, a strongly held belief that organisation design does not matter.

Organisation design problems, or the choice between different forms of organisation and management structures, are trivialised and dismissed as mere 'tinkering with institutions'. Cosmetic political reasons, rather than contributions to effectiveness, are often given as the real explanation of structural changes. This underestimates the impact of design errors on performance. In reality, the effects of design errors are large and persistent. The wrong framework misdirects activity and fails to ensure accountability.

Government not only consists of a large number of organisations, but it also acts through networks of interrelated organisations. As attention turns to the control of programme expenditure, it becomes increasingly clear that questions of efficiency and effectiveness, no less than questions of control and accountability, hinge on the effective management of relations between organisations. In some cases this involves relations between departments; in others it concerns the network of relations between departments and non-departmental bodies, public and private. The development of appropriate tools of management for networks of organisations is still in its infancy, but it is certain that government will need to give much greater attention to this dimension of management in the future.

Conclusions

This paper has sought to describe and assess the Rayner programme as an attempt to improve efficiency in government, and correct some misconceptions about it. Raynerism has often been portrayed as a short-term cost-cutting exercise designed to reduce administrative expenditure and aid in scaling down the size of the Civil Service in line with the Government's overall policy objectives. It has also been presented in personalised terms as a campaign waged by an outsider with strong Prime Ministerial backing.

There is no denying that Raynerism in practice is concerned with the effects of past inefficiency. The scrutiny programme has achieved significant savings by identifying and eradicating inefficiences throughout government. Nevertheless, the real test of Raynerism will be whether this exemplary early work leads on to lasting reforms of Civil Service management. Implementation of policies for improved management is an essential means of securing efficiency and effectiveness in the future.

The importance Rayner attached to improving the quality of management is indicated by the way in which the scrutiny programme was designed. The approach adopted relied heavily on generating commitment in departments, rather than depending solely on outside intervention and political clout. Even so, more could be done to adapt the scrutiny method to different types of problems and give greater consideration to problems of implementation.

There is a view that Raynerism is simply introducing into government more up-to-date management techniques to control administrative costs and activities. There is no denying the scope or the need to do this. But, especially in multi-departmental investigations, Raynerism is, perhaps, beginning to move beyond tried and tested methods into much less familiar territory. Work in this area may well produce important innovations in management methods for dealing with very complex large-scale programmes of change. Making this happen puts a special responsibility on the central departments.

Continuation of this initiative depends, obviously, on sustained political backing. But its success depends on overcoming resistances built into the culture of Whitehall. As Sir Frank Cooper, the recently retired Ministry of Defence Permanent Secretary, observed in an RIPA lecture 'Government systems, practices and procedures are shaded towards politics and policies. Management comes well behind. There is still a gentlemen–players view, in which the former make policy and the latter implement it' (Cooper, 1983). The ultimate test of Raynerism will be whether it succeeds in introducing broader and more flexible concepts of management into government to displace these obsolete ideas.

References

Allen, David (1981) 'Raynerism: strengthening civil service management', *RIPA Report,* Winter, Vol. 24.

Ansoff, Igor, Declerck, Roger and Hayes, Robert (1976) *From Strategic Planning to Strategic Management*, Wiley.

Argyris, Chris (1970) *Intervention Theory and Method,* Addison-Wesley.

Berman, P. (1980) 'Thinking about programmes and adaptive implementation; matching strategies to situations', in Helen M. Ingram and Dean E. Mann (eds), *Why Policies Succeed or Fail,* Sage Publications.

Blake, Robert R. and Mouton, Jane S. (1978) 'Strategies of consulation', in Robert T. Golembiewski and William Keddy (eds), *Organisational Development in Public Administration,* Marcel Rekker.

Chapman, Richard A. (1983) 'The rise and fall of CSD', *Policy and Politics,* Vol. 11, No. 1, pp. 41–61.

Christie, Campbell (1982) 'The real Rayner targets', *RIPA Report,* Spring, Vol. 3, No. 1.

Cooper, Sir Frank (1983) *Freedom to Manage in Government,* RIPA Winter Lecture Series, March.

Gray, Andrew and Jenkins, Bill (1982) 'Policy analysis in British central government: the experience of PAR', *Public Administration,* Vol. 60, pp. 429–450.

Howells, David (1981) 'Marks and Spencer and the Civil Service: a comparison of culture and methods', *Public Administration,* Autumn, No. 59.

Landau, Martin (1973) 'On the concept of a self-correcting organisation', *Public Administration Review* No. 33, pp. 533–542.

Landau, Martin and Stout, Russell Jr. (1979) 'To manage not to control', *Public Administration Review,* pp. 148–156, March–April.

Likierman, Andrew (1982) 'Management information for ministers: the MINIS system in the Department of the Environment', *Public Administration,* Vol. 60, pp. 127–142.

March, James G. (1974) 'The technology of foolishness', in Harold Leavitt, Lawrence Pinfield and Eugene Webb (eds), *Organisations of the Future,* Praegar.

Mayne, John F. (1982) 'Management audit in the Ministry of Defence, *Management in Government,* Vol. 373, pp. 138–146.

Metcalfe, Les (1982a) 'Designing precarious partnerships', in Paul C. Nystron and William H. Starbuck (eds), *Handbook of Organisational Design,* Vol. 1.

Metcalfe, Les (1982b) 'Self-regulation, crisis management and preventive medicine: the evolution of UK bank supervision', *Journal of Management Studies,* 19.1, pp. 75–90.

Mintzberg, Henry (1982) 'A note on that dirty word "efficiency",' *Interfaces,* 12, pp. 101–105.

Nash, Philip (1981) 'We tried before but without the clout', *Management Services in Government,* Vol. 36, No. 3, pp. 137–144.

Niskanen, W. (1973) *Bureaucracy: Servant or Master?,* Institute of Economic Affairs.

Olson, Mancur (1968) *The Logic of Collective Action: Public Goods and the Theory of Groups,* Shocken Books.

Plowden, William (1981) 'Whate'er is best administered', *New Society,* 9 April, pp.53–54.

Rayner, Sir Derek (1982) *The Scrutiny Programme: A Note of Guidance by Sir Derek Rayner,* Management and Personnel Office.

Rayner, Lord (1983) 'The business of government', *The Administrator,* March, pp. 3–6.

Schick, Alan (1973) 'A death in the bureaucracy: the demise of federal PPG', *Public Administration Review,* March–April.

House of Commons (1982a) *Efficiency and Effectiveness in the Civil Service*, Third Report of the Treasury and Civil Service Select Committee, HC 236, 8 March.
House of Commons (1982b) *Efficiency and Effectiveness in the Civil Service,* Government comments on the Third Report from the Treasury and Civil Service Select Committee, 1981–82, Cmnd 8616, September.

11
Pressures for Change in Public Sector Audit

JOHN FIELDEN

The early 1980s are seeing unusual flurries of debate about the role, structure and content of public sector audit. Within a period of two years there has been a Green Paper, a Public Accounts Committee (PAC) Special Report, a White Paper and a Private Member's Bill on the role of the Comptroller and Auditor General. Why all this concern? What are the issues behind this eruption of interest in topics that have lain peacefully for decades? In this chapter consideration is given to the pressures for change and the key questions being asked. Initially, however, the status quo and the participants in the auditing scheme are examined.

The Current Auditors

In the private sector a standard definition of an audit has been agreed. It is 'an independent examination and expression of opinion on the financial statements of an enterprise'. In the public sector, as we shall see, there is less common ground, though the general tendency is for an audit to cover a much wider scope than in the private sector. Table 11.1 illustrates the present position in the constituent parts of the public sector. In each case the style and content of the audit is as follows:

Table 11.1 External Auditors in the Public Sector (May 1983)

	Exchequer and Audit	Monopolies Commission	Audit Commission	DHSS statutory audit	Private sector firms
Central departments	All	—	—	—	—
Non-departmental public bodies	Most	—	—	—	A few
Nationalised industries	—	VFM	—	—	All
Universities	Rights of access and inspection	—	—	—	All
Water authorities	—	—	—	—	All
Local authorities	—	—	Most	—	Some
Health authorities	Rights of access and inspection	—	—	Most	14

The appropriation accounts of central government departments, and any trading accounts or trading funds undergo annual certification audits by the Exchequer and Audit Department (E & AD), and are given a 'properly presents' or 'true and fair' audit opinion as appropriate.

In addition, E & AD staff devote from 30 to 50 per cent of their audit effort to value-for-money work. Topics for review are selected by them on the basis of an analysis of major expenditure programmes and larger governmental projects. Examinations by line audit divisions are supplemented by 'special studies' of a more advanced or evaluative nature, using specialist staff in appropriate areas. In choosing areas for major investigation, the Comptroller and Auditor General (CAG) acts entirely independently, though he may listen to suggestions from the Public Accounts Committee. In most cases his reports go to Parliament and are considered in detail by the PAC, which reports its findings to the House of Commons.

Non-departmental public bodies (a diverse group of organisations recently catalogued in a helpful publication by the Management and Personnel Office) are audited either by the Exchequer and Audit Department (E & AD) or by private sector firms. Where a body derives a significant part of its income from public funds, E & AD either audits or, if the body is otherwise audited, has rights of access to and inspection of its books and records. The representatives of the body in question can still be summoned to attend the PAC.

Nationalised industries are audited by the private sector, and the CAG has no access to their records. In a later section we discuss the criticisms of this position. In 1980 external accountability was heightened by the inclusion, as Section 11 of the Competition Act 1980, of a slightly anomalous provision for the Monopolies and Mergers Commission (MMC) to review the efficiency of nationalised industries on a regular basis. This has since been clarified as implying a four-year cycle of review with the selection process being in the Commission's hands, though in practical terms it can be exercised by the minister.

Universities are, technically, private institutions, though they receive at least 70 per cent of their funding directly from public sources. They are all audited by private sector firms, but the Exchequer and Audit Department has powers to undertake 'inspection audits' of universities' books and records. In practice this involves a cyclical review of financial management and efficiency and of compliance with conditions of grants imposed on their use of public funds.

All water authorities are audited by private firms, though from 1974 to 1982 two were undertaken by the District Audit Service.

Local authority audits are allocated by the Audit Commission either to their own staff (formerly the District Audit Service) or to private firms. In 1974 local authorities were given powers to select private sector auditors if they wished. Until 1980 only a few (about 25 out of 400) exercised these powers. The Local Government Finance Act 1982 completely changed the organisational framework and introduced a requirement for a review of value-for-money arrangements.

Health authority audits in England and Wales are primarily undertaken by DHSS audit staff, who are thus statutory external auditors to the authorities. However, the CAG has 33 staff who audit the summarised accounts of the authorities as prepared by the Health Departments. He is also able to examine the accounts and records of individual authorities for both certification and, particularly, value-for-money purposes. In 1982 and 1983 a trial privatisation was launched with 14 district health authority audits allocated to private sector firms by the DHSS, but this did not affect the CAG's rights of access. At the same time, a number of authorities chose to contract out all, or part, of their internal audit functions to the private sector due to shortage of suitable staff.

In order to complete this review of the present position, brief consideration will be given to each of the groups performing audit functions in the public sector.

The office of Comptroller and Auditor General, as it exists in its present form, was established by the Exchequer and Audit Departments Act of 1866, which was slightly amended by a 1921 Act of the same title. The CAG currently has a professional staff of 682, of whom 66 have an accountancy qualification. His other staff have undertaken a three-year course in accounting, law and auditing and have wide experience in public sector accounts. In recent years the Department has moved over to graduate entry (in keeping with chartered accountancy practices), and all entrants are required to obtain the Chartered Institute of Public Finance and Accountancy qualification.

The Monopolies and Mergers Commission is not, strictly speaking, an auditing body. However, the Competition Act of 1980 gave it a role in reporting on the efficiency of nationalised industries to the ministers responsible. The Financial Secretary to the Treasury stated that the MMC 'in its strengthened form will remain the main instrument for the external scrutiny of these industries'. Since November 1981 the MMC has undertaken a wide range of references, including the Central Electricity Generating Board, the Severn-Trent Water Authority, the National Coal Board and the south-eastern commuter services of British Rail. The studies have been carried out by experienced professional staff, drawn both from the permanent establishment and from external consultancy firms. They have resulted in voluminous reports which, in the words of Professor Maurice Garner, have shown 'that an independent audit can make a valuable contribution to improving the efficiency of public enterprise' (Garner, 1982).

The Audit Commission was established by the Local Government Finance Act of 1982. It has, in practice, two separate but related functions: a regulatory and inspectorial audit role on the one hand, and an operational audit role on the other. Under section 12 of the Act, the Commission is responsible for the audit of all local authorities; it can either, in consultation with the authority concerned, allocate an audit to a private firm or it can undertake it with its own staff, who are inherited largely from the predecessor body, the District Audit Service (DAS). The District Audit Service employed some 650 people spread over 60 centres in England and Wales, but, since a significant proportion of local authority audits is likely to be carried out by the private sector, the Audit Commission staff will not reach these numbers. In Scotland the audits of authorities have, since 1973, been overseen by the Commission for Local Authority Accounts, a body not dissimilar to the Audit Commission. However, nearly 75 per cent of audits are performed by private firms appointed by the Commission, and there is as yet no statutory emphasis, as in England and Wales, on the value-for-money content of the audits.

The Audit Commission is accountable to the Secretary of State for the Environment and is independent from local authorities. It has acquired a role in undertaking comparative studies of local authority performance and in seeking to identify good management practices as an aid to achieving value for money.

The statutory auditors of regional and district health authorities are officials of the Health Departments who carry out external audits of the authorities. The CAG also examines and certifies the annual summarised accounts in the Departments and has powers to look at both the authorities' accounts and records and the auditors' reports on them. The style and content of audit in the health service has developed independently from the CAG and the DAS and it has involved less emphasis than either on value-for-money questioning. However, it is likely that political pressures for greater efficiency in the service will bring in more general audit practices and standards.

The private sector has been drawn into public sector audits to an increasing extent since 1979. Since that date private firms have gained the audit of 14 health authorities and about 40 local authorities (with a bias to counties and London boroughs). The two water authorities who chose to retain the District Audit Service after 1974 have, under 1982 legislation, moved into the private sector. Some of the larger firms have significant experience in universities, local authorities and water authorities. Most of them have a stake in nationalised industries, where the scale and spread of the enterprises require the large resources of the 'Big Eight' firms. It is not uncommon for audit fees in the larger nationalised industries to exceed a quarter of a million pounds, and several large firms with offices spread throughout the country have qualified professional staff in excess of 1,000.

Pressures for Change

The 1979 Thatcher administration has reflected in its programmes for reducing the size of the Civil Service and the Rayner scrutinies a broad public concern about the costs and efficiency of the public sector. The anxieties and doubts of the taxpayer have found support at the highest levels. The spread of criticism, ranging from the popular, but penetrating 'Yes, Minister' television series on the one hand, to the painstaking Treasury and Civil Service Select Committee on Efficiency and Effectiveness on the other, has allied itself with growing calls for change from inside the service.

External critics have made three allegations. First, that the growth of the public sector has led to vast bureaucracies which are inflexible to change and ineffective for reasons of organisational inertia. There is thought to be a direct link between size and inefficiency. Concerns about their lack of accountability have also been expressed. Second, that the Executive has paid too much attention to policy planning and formulation and has shown itself to be bad at execution. Did a continuing series of scandals over waste and incompetence imply that public bureaucrats were bad managers? A procession of external enquirers followed Fulton in questioning whether the Civil Service gave the right emphasis to managerial skills in its training programme and criteria for promotion. Third, that the government of Britain has been remarkably ineffective, since the end of World War II, at curing the nation's problems. Was it fair to blame the politicians who came and went when the bureaucracy stayed constant and had a major influence on the success of programmes?

These allegations, whether true or not, all favoured an extension of audit and evaluation. The huge scale of public expenditure in absolute terms, and as a proportion of GDP, and the general absence of commercial disciplines (because of the lack of the profit element or any simple indicator of success or achievement) are further factors cited as fuelling concern.

Traditional public sector audit comprised financial audit and regularity audit. These have been defined by the CAG as being concerned with the adequacy of departmental systems to ensure that transactions are properly controlled and recorded and that Treasury rules are being followed (financial audit), and with a consideration of whether expenditure has been properly incurred under the authority of legislation and whether Parliament's presumed intentions are being met (regularity audit) ('The role of the Comptroller and Auditor General', 1980). However, this style of audit did not seek to uncover waste and inefficiency, nor did it highlight whether programmes were effective. Throughout the world, national audit agencies have been developing new forms of examination and evaluation in order to answer the concerns of those they reported to. Indeed, Sir Douglas Henley claimed (Henley, 1982) 'that in some advanced countries, including the United States, Sweden and to a large extent Germany, the national audit office has ceased, or virtually ceased, to do any formal financial audit as customarily understood at all'.

In parallel with public concern there has been an upsurge of interest in Parliament itself. A significant gulf has appeared between the views of the backbencher, as exemplified by the PAC's Special Report ('The role of the Comptroller and Auditor General', 1981a), and the Government's response ('The role of the Comptroller and Auditor General', 1981b). Whereas the Committee felt that accountability to Parliament was inadequate and required strengthening, the Government was reluctant to rush into the new organisational solutions proposed; 'accountability to Parliament cannot be created simply by changing the auditing arrangements', their White Paper said. This speedy rebuff hardly did credit to the strength of Parliamentary concern which centred on three key questions:

(1) that the CAG ought to cover *all* public expenditure instead of only 60 per cent as at present, and that the legislation establishing the CAG has failed to keep up with the wide spread of public expenditure;

(2) that Parliament had lost control of the CAG who was appointed by the Queen as an 'office holder under the Crown' and was not wholly accountable to Parliament, and that the Treasury was able to limit his resources;

(3) that quality of public audit is not consistently high in all areas and that the 'form of public expenditure is often not sufficiently tested to see whether the same results could be obtained for less money or indeed better results for the same money'. ('The role of the Comptroller and Auditor General', 1981a).

One argument in favour of change has been that the UK which, as in so many things, pioneered the concepts and process of public sector audit, is among the last to review or amend them. Experience in Canada, Australia and the United States has been quoted in support of a constitutional change. 'The similarity between the issues discussed in other countries and those raised in the evidence we have received is striking', said the PAC ('The role of the Comptroller and Auditor General', (1981a) Vol. I).

It will be helpful to look in more detail at some of the issues behind the changes proposed by the PAC and others. The possible mechanisms for performing public sector audit are considered first.

The Structure of Public Sector Audit

Who should carry out public sector audit? Is there not a strong argument for one overall agency able to set consistent standards and placed in a position of complete impartiality? Is it not also reasonable to suggest that public audit should be a public matter and not an arena where private profit-making concerns can flourish? These are the main questions under debate.

At one extreme it has been suggested that the CAG and his staff are clearly the basis for a broad agency, labelled the National Audit Office (NAO), such as the PAC proposed. Such a body would be able to follow public money and would have access to the books of those large companies supported mainly by central government funding. Unlike the present E and AD, it would have access to nationalised industries and present 'gaps', such as British Leyland or British Aerospace, would not be out of bounds.

At the other extreme to a NAO carrying out all audit is the option of a fully privatised public sector audit. If the private sector is competent enough to audit nationalised industries and to carry out *ad hoc* efficiency studies for government departments (which are then laid before Parliament), could it not perform audits *throughout* the public sector?

Between these two extremes there are several compromise arrangements. The first, of course, is the status quo. Another model might be the universities' one, in which any part of the public sector not audited by the CAG would be subject to an 'inspection audit' by him on matters of management and efficiency. When the CAG was first given access to universities' books the outcry from the Vice-Chancellors (traditionally a vocal and powerful lobby) was enormous. Since then, the reality of the CAG's careful and sensitive investigations, which have focused on best practice recommendations and comparative studies, has calmed the initial misgivings. If he were to undertake an inspection audit throughout the public sector along these lines, would this satisfy Parliament? A third possibility is found in Sweden, where two agencies perform audit functions; one concentrating on audit regularity and certification standards and the other on effectiveness and managerial efficiency. (See Richardson (1982) for a full analysis of this somewhat uneasy compromise.)

There are some immediate practical difficulties in the National Audit Office solution. The first relates to the scale of the change required. The July 1981 White Paper was quick to point out that the CAG could not both extend his standards of audit *and* take on the vast amount of extra work, such as the nationalised industry audits would involve. His staff would need to be increased significantly. Second, how would such a change affect the position of the MMC? Is one to assume that its role under the Competition Act would disappear? If so, would ministers and sponsoring departments be entirely happy to rely only on the CAG's reports on the nationalised industries they looked after? Finally, the ability of the CAG to recruit and retain enough staff of the right calibre to fulfil the National Audit Office function could be in doubt. The private sector has built up considerable competence and expertise, and this has been recognised by the CAG who occasionally takes in secondees from the private sector. This could all be lost, as few staff would be expected to move across to the public sector. The PAC thought that this could be overcome by raising the status and grading of NAO staff, but there may be a limit to the cost of the total state audit function.

However, in the past the CAG and his staff have not been reluctant to shoulder extra responsibilities. They argue that their staff calibre matches that of the private sector, while their experience of public sector finance and of value-for-money questioning is unrivalled. A National Audit Office would be built up gradually, even though in the first few years it might be necessary to second in extra staff from external sources.

The Status and Accountability of the CAG

The concern of Parliament about the CAG's status is of recent origin. John Garrett has sugested that Parliament has lost the control over the CAG that it once possessed. (Garrett, 1983). He quotes the CAG in 1903 as saying 'I am a parliamentary officer . . . directed by the Act to report to Parliament'. Frequent parliamentary references between that date and 1946 also implied that he was responsible to Parliament alone. However, in recent years the CAG's status has been interpreted in a totally different way. Cmnd 7845 described him as 'not subject to control either by Parliament or by the Executive in the exercise of his functions'. Against this, the PAC voiced its fears that the Treasury, as ultimate paymaster, could limit the E & AD's staffing and functions as well as issuing formal directions under the E & AD Acts.

Predictably, the CAG welcomed clarification of his position and suggested to the PAC that:

> The CAG's independence will best be safeguarded if he remains an office holder under the Crown . . . it is fundamental that he must not be subject to any external direction as to the manner or subject of the audit examination which he is statutorily required to carry out. This does not mean that he would decline to examine suggestions by a Parliamentary Committee that he should enquire into particular matters, but it would give him the right to exercise his own judgement on the most effective use of his resources and on whether he should report to Parliament on the results of any enquiries which he decided to undertake. ('The role of the Comptroller and Auditor General', (1981a) Vol. III)

Until 1983 there were thus two totally irreconcilable positions: the view of the government and the CAG that he should remain an independent office holder under the Crown, and Parliament's view that he should be an officer of the House of Commons even though he would be appointed under letters patent by the Crown. In the latter model, a Public Accounts Commission could direct the head of the National Audit Office to undertake and audit or to carry out special studies, though they could not influence the manner and style of his work.

Practice overseas as regards the appointment of the supreme audit officer varies. In the USA the Comptroller General is appointed by the President for 15 years and the office is non-political and independent, though much of his office's workload is inspired by Congressional requests. The same degree of independence arising from appointment by the Head of State is to be found in Australia, Canada, France, Japan and the Netherlands. In Sweden, somewhat unusually, the government of the day plays a major role in the selection and control of the Auditor-General. The parliamentary solution has been adopted in Israel and Austria, where the Knesset and the National Assembly, respectively, appoint the heads of the national audit institutions.

The Nature and Quality of Public Sector Audit

There is a welcome unanimity among all the participants in the debate that public sector audit should focus to a greater extent than it has done to date on questions of value for money. The CAG can claim that examination of economy and efficiency of government expenditure has been a feature of the E & AD's work for about 100 years, even though there is no statutory backing for this role (as has, for example, been given to it in local authority audits by section 15(1)(c) of the Local Government Finance Act, 1982). Thus, more value-for-money audit is universally held to be a good thing. Yet, definitions vary and there is a wide range of practical interpretation.

For example, the Green Paper made a distinction between VFM audit on the one hand, which it said relates to economy and efficiency, and effectiveness audit on the other. The latter is defined by the CAG as being concerned with the assessment of whether programmes or projects meet established policy objectives, and he considers it part and parcel of VFM audit.

In the local authority environment the term 'value for money' has become familiar since 1974, as the auditor has had a role in tracking down losses due to waste, fraud or poor value for money. There has been an emphasis on it as a means of cost reduction or improving efficiency, and few studies of policy effectiveness use the VFM label.

In nationalised industries the term has not yet acquired any general interpretation. The influential study by Redwood and Hatch, 'Value for Money Audits' (1981), suggested that a VFM audit 'should be concerned with systems for: i) taking and implementing policy decisions, ii) monitoring and controlling resources'. Questioning of this sort has formed only part of the terms of reference of efficiency studies of nationalised industries undertaken by the MMC. Other topics in their brief have been purchasing and tendering procedures, investment appraisal and planning techniques.

Given the wide range of interpretation of what value for money (VFM) means, is it surprising that the VFM content of external audit varies throughout the public sector? Table 11.2 attempts to illustrate the present application of VFM audit in the different parts of the public sector and shows also where internal agencies and *ad hoc* external enquirers undertake VFM or efficiency enquiries. Taking the scope of external audit as an example, it will be seen that only in local authorities is there a statutory obligation to incorporate VFM in the audit. Traditionally, the DAS claims to have devoted some 20 per cent of total audit effort to VFM work (see the comments by Kimmance in this volume). Private sector firms starting local authority audits see the VFM area as one where they can contribute new expertise and are offering higher percentages of VFM effort.

Table 11.2   Extent of VEM or Efficiency Review in the Public Sector

	Within external audit	Carried out by internal agencies	Ad hoc external reviews
Central government	Statutory	Rayner scrutinies	–
Local government	Statutory	Internal audit studies	Sometimes
Nationalised industries	Depends on sponsoring department	Agency varies	MMC and consultants
Health authorities	Not statutory. Depends on region	Some internal audit studies	–
Non-departmental public bodies	Where EAD is auditor or has access and inspection rights	Some	Some by consultants

As regards nationalised industries, there is no general acceptance of the need for a VFM element in external audit and few sponsoring departments have yet extended the audit scope to include value-for-money considerations. This situation is very fluid however, and some private sector firms are seeking to provide value-for-money questioning within their audit.

It is clear from Table 11.2 that the public sector is at a transitional stage in its adoption of VFM. It seems a reasonable assumption, however, that within five years there will be a statutory framework for the incorporation of VFM within the scope of all external audit. Internally, a wider adoption of the approach also seems likely. The nature of the agency for such reviews will probably vary depending on the staff skills and organisational arrangements. Typically, in large organisations there are already internal audit, management services, work study, and staff inspection skills ensconced in the structure. Some industries may hesitate to follow the example of British Gas and set up a further independent unit to carry out efficiency studies.

Value-for-Money Audits – the Content

Having reviewed the present scale and application of VFM in public sector audit, let us briefly consider the content. What should VFM audits be aiming to achieve? How should they proceed? A useful starting base in the debate is the affirmation that the primary responsibility for achieving value for money must be that of managers themselves. Thus, in the course of their managerial actions they should question the value for money of the operations under their control and may well carry out VFM studies, in the broadest sense. They may also commission agencies within their own organisation to perform studies for them. At the highest level in the structure senior management will also wish to receive assurance from some internal source that managers' operations are economical, efficient and effective. In this manner the bulk of the topics for Rayner scrutinies to date have been identified within departments and the Permanent Secretary has responsibility for implementing the resulting action plan.

Given this internal role in achieving VFM, what is the function of the external auditor? As regards local authorities, Section 15(1)(c) of the Local Government Finance Act 1982 states that it is the auditor's task to satisfy himself that the authority 'has made proper arrangements for securing economy, efficiency and effectiveness in its use of resources'. One interpretation is that this wording limits the role of the auditor to one of checking managerial mechanisms and procedures; he would not himself be expected to say that there was inefficiency in a department, only that there *might* be, because the information, control and reporting systems were defective. It removes from the auditor the danger of second-guessing the decisions of professional or technical managers. However, it allows him to suggest that things *are* wrong if sound project management procedures are not being followed in, say, a highly technical nuclear research project. Another interpretation of the VFM auditors' role is that he should do more than just test systems, rather he should look at operations in practice and comment where he identifies poor management practices.

The narrower interpretation of a VFM audit brings us quite close to Redwood and Hatch's definition relating to nationalised industries, quoted above. Systems for monitoring and controlling resources, and systems for implementing policy decisions are essentially information systems. The focus of the enquiry is thus on whether improved management information is needed. In a sense the auditor's role is to encourage best management practice in terms of management information.

Is this the limit of the audit? How does an outsider tackle the question of effectiveness? Is there a role for the auditor to undertake VFM studies himself? The E & AD believe they have an obligation to review the effectiveness of some policy decisions themselves. Dewar (1982) has described some special studies of this kind; for example, grants paid to farmers or oil companies for investment projects which they would have gone ahead with in any event, and a current study of the effectiveness of the Housing Improvement Programme. External auditors in the rest of the public sector prefer to tread cautiously in questions of effectiveness. The danger is that the auditor will be thought to be challenging policy objectives, whereas he will aim to ask whether the decision to go ahead with a programme was based on good technical analysis and information, and whether the programme achieved the objectives set for it at the outset.

Where the activities being reviewed are hard to measure and

qualitative, it will be much harder for the auditor to risk any statements on effectiveness, since if he does so he is being forced to make value judgements. If he is in an area where professionals themselves cannot agree, why should his opinion carry any weight?

Britain, compared with America or Sweden, devotes very little effort to the evaluation of policy decisions and their effectiveness. While these countries may have given too great credence to 'a rationality ritual' (Richardson, 1982), one wonders whether we have erred too far in the opposite direction.

Agenda for Improvement

As stated at the outset, this topic is being reviewed at a time of considerable change. The legislative framework, the organisational structure and the scope and content of public sector audit will be very different in 1990. In the course of the next few years it is to be hoped that the following three points will be resolved.

First, attention should be given to the uneven application of external audit questioning throughout the sector. It is logically indefensible to have large tranches of public money subject to a less rigorous degree of audit scrutiny than others. Why, for example, should the health service, which employs over one million people, appear to have fewer resources devoted to its audit? As part of the extension of common standards of provision, there should be greater exploration and development of common standards of practice. Should there not be an even standard of performance of public sector audit? If these issues are to be faced, the private sector contribution should not be overlooked.

Second, there is a need to consider a joint approach to the development of thinking on VFM audit and policy evaluation. There is a real risk that the differing interpretations of what value-for-money audits mean will become formalised in different parts of the public sector. The man in the street cannot distinguish between a VFM report from the Audit Commission and one from the CAG. Private sector firms differ in their approach to the staffing and content of their VFM audits. Should all parties not seek to agree on a common understanding of what a VFM audit is expected to do? What mechanism can best achieve this? Should consideration be given to a forum, such as the Comprehensive Audit Foundation in

Canada, which would explore the problems of definition and methodology? Or are informal bilateral or multilateral discussions preferable?

Third, the development of a closer partnership between the public and private sector providers of audit services needs to be discussed. The following chapter covers this point more fully. While there have been no serious differences of opinion between the two sides, neither has there been much close liaison. Part of the reason for this must lie in the allegiances to two differing professional bodies; the Chartered Institute of Public Finance and Accountancy and the Institute of Chartered Accountants in England and Wales. Fortunately, these are now drawing closer together. The days are near when a joint approach can be developed to common problems.

The pressures for change in public sector audit are deep-seated. It is likely that the response will be substantial alterations to the status quo and, one hopes, a real gain in our understanding of how to assess the efficiency and performance of public sector organisations.

References

Dewar, D. (1982) 'Current practice in the UK: central government', in *Value for money audits: Proceedings of a seminar,* Royal Institute of Public Administration.

Garner, M. (1982) 'Auditing the efficiency of nationalised industries: enter the Monopolies and Mergers Commission', *Public Administration,* Vol. 60, No. 4, pp. 409–428.

Garrett, J. (1983) Letter to *The Times,* 1st February.

Hatch, J. and Redwood, J. (1981) *Value for Money Audits: New Thinking on the Nationalised Industries,* Centre for Policy Studies.

Henley, Sir D. (1982) 'Current issues in public sector auditing', in A. G. Hopwood, M. Bromwich and J. Shaw (eds), *Auditing Research: Issues and Opportunities,* Pitman Books.

Richardson, J. J. (1982) 'Programme evaluation in Britain and Sweden', *Parliamentary Affairs,* Spring, Vol. XXXV, No. 2, pp. 160–180.

'The role of the Comptroller and Auditor General' (1980), *Green Paper,* March, HMSO.

'The role of the Comptroller and Auditor General' (1981a) *First Special Report from the Committee of Public Accounts,* HC 115, Vol. I Report, Vol. III Appendices, February, HMSO.

'The role of the Comptroller and Auditor General', (1981b) *Government's Response to HC 115,* July HMSO.

12
The Widening Scope of Local Government Audit and Private Sector Participation

PETER KIMMANCE

General Features of Local Government Audit

Prior to the establishment in 1983 of the Audit Commission for Local Authorities in England and Wales there were two types of local government external auditors: district auditors who were public officials and who performed about four-fifths of the audit work, and approved auditors, from firms of private accountants, who performed the remainder. Both types of auditor were independent of government but there was a non-statutory official, the Chief Inspector of Audit, responsible to the Secretary of State for the Environment for the quality of the audits. Certain conventions ensured the Chief Inspector's professional independence. Over the years his office, the Audit Inspectorate, developed a central role in developing audit practice within the local government audit service, a duty now assumed by the Audit Commission. The district auditors' duties have passed virtually unchanged to the Commission's auditors.

The local authorities to be audited are self-governing bodies exercising powers contained in statutes passed by Parliament. In respect of certain functions, these powers may be defined or limited by statutory instrument or directions issued by central government under the provisions of the relevant statutes. In spite of these constraints, local authorities have a wide discretion as to the manner in which they discharge their functions.

Given this local government autonomy, there is an evident need to see that bodies act within the powers granted to them. Such a check could be left to the courts but this would be cumbersome. In the first half of the nineteenth century district auditors were established to exercise inspectorial functions (in a manner derived from the concepts of Jeremy Bentham[1]). They were given certain legal powers designed to ensure that spending was related only to authorised objects and to enable losses to funds to be recovered. For the exercise of these powers the auditor is answerable to the courts. The district auditor, in this context, may be seen as a simple constitutional device for limiting local government activities to those which Parliament wish bodies to engage in, and for ensuring that losses from fraud or near-fraud are recovered. Of course, the existence of district auditors does not preclude action against an authority by an aggrieved party and the GLC 'fares' case (Bromley LBC v GLC (1982) (1 AER 129)) is a recent example of this happening.

The district auditor's main powers enabling him to carry out these duties have remained virtually unchanged since his establishment in 1844. They comprise power to:

(1) call for evidence;
(2) 'surcharge', that is to recover illegal payments and losses from those responsible;
(3) report publicly to mobilise public opinion.

The district auditor also has a role in the provision of local accountability. An elector may inspect a local authority's accounts and question the auditor about them. If the elector is dissatisfied, he may object to any item in the accounts, requiring the auditor to consider whether he should exercise his power of 'surcharge'. If the auditor does not uphold the objection, the elector may require him to furnish reasons in writing as a preliminary to an appeal to the courts.

The interplay of auditors and the courts enabled the way in which

---

1. (1748–1831) utilitarian philosopher, economist and theoretical jurist whose attempts to solve social problems scientifically influenced nineteenth century reformers.

the auditors exercised their powers to develop in line with the growth (in size and sophistication) of local authorities. In particular, the courts found it necessary to develop guidelines for determining when a local authority was exercising reasonably a legal discretion to incur expenditure in contrast to moving beyond such discretion. Guidelines were developed over the years and now the circumstances under which a district auditor or the courts may interfere with the exercise of discretion have been strictly defined by the courts. (Associated Provincial Picturehouses Ltd v Wednesbury Corporation (1947) (2 AER 680), Giddens v The District Auditor for Harlow (1972) (70 LGR 485DC)). To establish that an authority has acted contrary to law and so incurred unlawful expenditure, it must be shown that the authority has taken into account matters it ought not to, or has refused or neglected to take into account matters which it ought to, or has come to a conclusion so unreasonable that no reasonable authority could have come to it. However, the effect of the guidelines is to leave authorities with a wide discretion, as has been confirmed in a recent case (Pickwell v Camden LBC (QBD 1982), *The Times* 30/4/1982).

Possibly more important has been the role of the courts in clarifying the nature and role of audit. Parallel to the development by the courts of the concept of 'reasonableness' in the exercise of discretion, but linked firmly to it, was the idea that the auditor was not only concerned with illegality and fraud but also with 'wise and prudent administration'. The concept was embodied in a Local Government Audit Code of Practice, issued by the Secretary of State as Annex II to Department of the Environment Circular 79/73. The code linked the search for 'loss' by the auditor with a review for value for money. It stated that the requirements for the audit of public funds financed by compulsory levy are wider than those applicable to the audit of private undertakings. Because of this, the auditor must be concerned 'not only with the form and regularity of the accounts but also with . . . the possibility of loss due to waste, inefficient financial administration, poor value for money, mistake or other cause'. The latest act, the Local Government Finance Act 1982, which came into force during 1983, develops these ideas. It requires auditors to satisfy themselves 'that the body whose accounts are being audited has made proper arrangements for securing economy, efficiency and effectiveness in the use of resources'. All these ideas need a good deal of exploration.

The Audit Role

What is audit? It is suggested that the auditor has only one proper role — that of monitoring: the comparison of the situation which exists with that which might exist. Such comparisons are easy to understand in his work of establishing the regularity of the accounts; there should be few occasions where the auditor cannot establish some sort of usable statements of the two situations which he is seeking to compare.

Things become much more difficult, however, when auditors have an extended role, as in the local government field. This has come to be loosely termed 'value-for-money' auditing. The term 'value for money' has been used a great deal lately and has been applied to auditing as if it were a fresh discovery. It is not: ways of doing things have changed, but the underlying principles of local government audit have not.

In simple terms, the auditor must examine what is going on in order that he may give assurance to the public. He is not, therefore, concerned only with what appears in the accounts, but also with the cost effectiveness of chosen policies. In carrying out this role there is the danger that the auditor will be tempted to 'second guess' the audited organisations' judgements. The 1973 Code of Practice is quite clear on this point; 'it is . . . not the function of the auditor to express his own opinion as to the wisdom of particular decisions taken by councils in the lawful exercise of their discretion'. It is for councillors and officers to manage, and this includes monitoring the results of their decisions. *It is for the auditor to simply monitor this process.* If management's monitoring is defective, the auditor must produce evidence to prove that this is so.

It will be observed that the auditor's role in such circumstances is the same as that found in narrower aspects of audit activity: testing the situation which exists against that which might be expected to exist. If the auditor compares declared policy intentions with results, he is not questioning the policy decision, but monitoring its effects. However, intentions (or policy aims) are often ill-defined. Audit enquiries may well bring pressure to bear on management and this may result in somewhat clearer statements of objectives. More generally, the auditor is faced with what may perhaps be described as implied aims. Councillors are concerned to 'run a good service', or 'provide a minimum service as cheaply as possible', or 'get the most they can from the budget available'. Objectives stated in this way do not cover the full range of possibilities, but give some idea of what councillors usually have in mind.

It is these sort of considerations which go into the making of councils' annual budgets. Councillors and their officers put views forward, options are considered and sums allocated for the various activities. It might seem from this that all the auditor is required to do is see that the various budget allocations are spent with due regard to economy, efficiency and effectiveness. This is, in fact, a good starting point for the auditor, though, by considering practices within an activity, he may find ways of enhancing the 'three Es' in such a way that calls for variations in the budget and then, indirectly, for changes in policy. How should the auditor tackle the task?

The so called 'systems audit' approach is well established for financial auditing – the auditor cannot examine every transaction in detail so he must depend on the internal systems and controls, and he must see that these are working effectively and that there are no significant gaps. Ideally, his approach to value-for-money matters should be exactly the same. It might be argued that he need look only at the internal monitoring systems and test their effectiveness. But the systems for internal monitoring in this area are often undeveloped. Even if the auditor confines himself to a review of the cost-effectiveness of funds allocated to particular activities, he is likely to find gaps in the monitoring processes and he will need to carry out sufficient work to demonstrate possible losses of value for money arising from such weaknesses. In order to understand how the auditor might do this work, it is necessary to understand how the methodology of 'broad scope auditing' developed.

The Development of 'Broad Scope Auditing'

In the early 1960s district auditors were finding increasing difficulty in performing the broad based audit required of them, mainly because of the growth and increasing sophistication of local government services. A much more structured approach to the audit was developed and, for want of a better description, this came to be called 'the structured form of audit'. The audit is arranged in three stages:

(1) overall review — a comprehensive analysis of the characteristics and problems of the authority;
(2) essential tasks — to verify the balance sheet and examine financial systems;
(3) cyclic work — in depth audit of selected areas of activity.

The three parts are not mutually exclusive. For example, work done for either of the first two stages may indicate lines of enquiry which may be followed fruitfully at the third stage. Similarly a third stage project may well include work normally covered at the second stage.

Over the last two decades this form of audit has been found to be capable of considerable development. The third stage quickly became what has been called, somewhat loosely, management auditing. There has been a strong bias towards the comparison of the practices of authorities for various activities. The more important studies have been reported serially in a standard form (Audit Inspectorate, 1970 to 1982) and circulated to all auditors under the title 'Efficiency and Management Exercises'. In 1976 the Report of the Layfield Committee on Local Government Finance recommended that such work deserved to be expanded and put on a more regular footing. The recent publication (CIPFA, 1982a) of a selection of such studies probably represents a final flowering of a line of development which depended largely on the field work of individuals. The pattern for such work in recent years is for it to be centrally directed by the Audit Inspectorate, thus implementing a suggestion made in the Layfield Report. This work, continued by the Audit Commission, has shown what can be done with a mixture of private and public sector experience and talents, and is described at length later in this chapter.

The second stage of the audit has also undergone change, the origins of which lie in the audit arrangements made under the Local Government Act 1972. The former unsatisfactory arrangements for 'professional audit' were replaced by 'approved audit', and both district auditors and approved auditors were required to work to common standards under the supervision of the Audit Inspectorate. This brought public and private sector auditors into close proximity and, incidentally, into competition, since local authorities could choose to have either district or approved auditors. So there was an opportunity and a spur for them to learn from each other. Approved auditors had to get to grips with broad based auditing.

For district auditors, the private sector's emphasis on giving a 'true and fair' view on financial statements gave a much clearer objective for essential task work.

Both these trends may be seen in a recent report by a working party of the Chartered Institute of Public Finance and the District Auditors' Society (1982b). The report was an attempt to formulate best practice on the basis of audit as currently developed, and to express findings in standards for auditors. The working party which produced the report comprised district auditors, local government officers and private and public sector accountants. As to the matter of an audit opinion on published financial statements, the working party recommended that this should be explicit rather than implicit as in the current legislation. Under s.157 of the Local Government Act 1972, the auditor had a duty to see that the accounts were lawfully prepared in accordance with proper accounting practices. He was also required to report, in the public interest, any matters arising from or in connection with the accounts.

The auditor was also required to enter a certificate on the accounts at the completion of the audit. The main purpose of this was to state that he had completed the audit in accordance with the statutes and, in particular, that he had discharged his duties in relation to any illegality or losses (it may be recalled that he has power to 'surcharge' such items). But, such procedures, especially if objectors or the courts are involved, are lengthy and there may be a considerable delay before a certificate can be entered. Thus the habit arose of publishing 'abstracts of accounts' 'subject to audit'. This was regarded as unsatisfactory in the light of the audit experience mentioned earlier, and a recent requirement on local authorities to publish an annual report (including accounts) led the working party to recommend that there should be an audit opinion on published financial statements, in addition to any statutory certificate or public report which may be required. The general effect of all this activity has been to place greater emphasis on the need to ensure compliance with accounting standards and for the publication of clearer and more informative accounts. An initiative by the Chartered Institute of Public Finance and Accountancy in the form of an annual competition for the best set of published accounts has also played its part in promoting a change of attitude towards published accounts and a demand for an opinion.

Another major contribution from the working party has been to produce a standard on the scope of the auditor's duties in relation to economy, efficiency and effectiveness — words which have appeared to describe the ingredients of value for money, particularly for public sector audits in the United States of America and Canada. The working party's report discusses whether effectiveness can usefully be considered by the auditor. It concluded that although the assessment of effectiveness is difficult, if not on many occasions impossible, to leave consideration of it entirely outside the auditor's remit would limit the range of auditing. This conclusion was based on the simple truism that an activity may be carried out efficiently without being effective in forwarding its purpose. The working party approved an extract from a discussion paper published by the Chartered Institute of Public Finance and Accountancy's Output Measurement Research Working Party, which is worth quoting for its clarity:

> Any organisation with limited resources facing a wide range of alternative courses of action must decide how to employ those resources to best achieve the objectives of the organisation. It must know whether its policies are in fact contributing to the solution of the problem with which it is concerned . . .
> It is not sufficient for the organisation to know that it is spending its money very efficiently or spending more or less on its activities than other similar organisations in the same management situation. It is not merely concerned to know, for instance, that it is building homes for the aged more cheaply than it has done before and, even, more cheaply than any other authority providing similar accommodation. What it needs to know is whether provision of the homes in fact contributes to problems facing the aged. Similarly, an organisation should not concern itself only with a cost per mile of highway constructed or the durability of road surfaces, but with the impact those activities have on the transportation requirements of the area. It needs, in other words, to be concerned with effectiveness as well as efficiency. An organisation which uses resources in a highly efficient manner in the pursuit of a policy which proves to be quite irrelevant to the problem it faces is taking fruitless action.

However, the standards working party issued a warning:

> We fully recognise that effectiveness is an important ingredient in the value-for-money concept, perhaps more important than economy or efficiency in the execution of programmes. But we think that much more information than we have is required about the practical application of this concept and the skills that are needed by auditors before a separate audit standard with satisfactory guidelines can be drafted . . .

Some clues as to how auditors might cope with the concept arise from a consideration later in this chapter of the work done on comparative studies.

The Development of Audit Tools

The central role established for the Audit Inspectorate gave the necessary impetus to the development of several audit tools which enabled the auditor, particularly at the overall review stage of the audit, to recognise problem areas and, in some circumstances, to enable him to suggest well-tried solutions. Three of the most important developments concern statistics, management practices and centrally directed studies.

Statistical Intelligence

Since the principal local authorities have, in each of their classes, similar powers, an obvious approach is to use comparisons. It is possible to carry out a comprehensive comparison of inputs using annual statistics published by the Chartered Institute of Public Finance and Accountancy. But for audit purposes a specialised statistical intelligence service has been developed with the assistance of staff seconded from the Government Statistical Service. The aim is to identify significant variations in the provision or performance of services in order to establish possible starting points for further investigations at the local authorities concerned. Data has been assembled by computer to provide ready access and facilities for analysis and manipulation.

Work in the field of statistical analysis has been discredited by simplistic attitudes to comparative costs – the assumption that if a service costs more than average, it must be less efficient than the average. In order to make such comparisons more creditable, it is necessary to take account of the differing characteristics, circumstances and objectives of individual authorities.

The Audit Inspectorate, in conjunction with the District Auditors' Society, commissioned a consultant to group authorities with socio-economic similarities. The consultant devised such a scheme based on 40 variables from the 1971 Population Census.

Authorities appear in one of 30 clusters. By comparing authorities appearing in the same group, some confidence is possible that like is being compared with like, though detailed investigation sometimes identifies further variations which affect cost.

Management Check Lists

The second tool is concerned with the identification of best practice. This ties in with the systems approach and the monitoring concept. Check lists which provide an indication whether management systems are satisfactory or are capable of improvement provide a useful audit tool. Although there are few situations where there is a single correct answer, there exist some statements which carry authority as 'good practice' and these may be used as a basis for management systems check lists. Obviously, this sort of development can take place only with the assistance of experts in each particular field. As might be expected, the major contributions to this work came from auditors and officers already working in the local government field. However, private sector consultants have been used particularly to ensure that no advantageous private practice has been overlooked.

The aim of the check lists is to help the auditor to form an opinion on an authority's management systems by suggesting key matters relating to objectives, organisation, procedures, information and controls which he could reasonably expect to find have been considered by an authority when establishing systems. Attention is also drawn to performance indicators which should be available. The check lists are prescriptive in style, being based on what is seen as accepted, sound practice. This enables the auditor to identify and consider, in the light of local circumstances, variations from a norm. Broadly, the check lists enable the auditor to consider:

(1) whether adequate consideration is given to the availability of and effect on resources when the authority decide on their policies and objectives;
(2) the adequacy of the organisation and procedures adopted to carry out those policies and achieve those objectives;
(3) the means available to measure the economy and efficiency with which the policies and objectives have been pursued and their effectiveness.

Each check list follows a standard form: an introduction indicating its scope and limitations followed by sections dealing with an organisation's objectives, organisation and procedures and management information. There is also a section on performance indicators derived from practical experience. Whether it is worthwhile to include within the check lists a section on objectives may well be open to question. Earlier the difficulty of defining objectives in relation to activities was mentioned. But definition is sometimes easier when the consideration is confined to a particular system. For example, that stocks should be maintained at a predetermined level, or all outstanding creditors should be paid in a monthly cycle, or all applicants for housing with an assessed need exceeding 'X points' shall be housed with three months of application.

Such objectives, or variations on them, or the entire absence of formulated objectives would come to light when the auditor reviewed procedures. In practice, however, it has been found that the 'top down' procedure – of searching first for the objectives of management systems – has brought into focus more clearly diseconomies arising from the choice of objectives. Again, it must be emphasised that the auditor, in exposing the effects of objectives which give rise to, say, costly procedures, is not questioning the right of the organisation to persist in doing things in the manner they have chosen. He is exerting influence on the organisation to induce a reconsideration of objectives. In particular, in circumstances where it appears to be justified, he can bring matters forward for wider debate by using his power of public reporting.

A similar commentary may be applied to the use of performance indicators. Certain of them may lead to a reconsideration of objectives. Of course, it is again necessary to reiterate the need to exercise caution in utilising such figures. They must be considered within the context of the procedures being examined. For example, the cost for the payment of each creditor may be low while the total cost of paying creditors may be high. Such a situation might arise where an organisation is attempting to pay all outstanding creditors on a weekly rather than a monthly basis. A change to monthly payments (spread throughout the period) would be more in line with accepted practice and reduce overall cost without significantly varying the unit cost per payment.

Comparative Studies

The Layfield Committee concluded that external auditors were best equipped to carry out comparative studies. Although experience since the time of that recommendation tends to support such a view, in fact, it seems of little importance who does the study, provided it is well done. What the auditor requires is appropriate information to help him with his work, and ability to persuade or help people to create changes. There are several organisations which carry out studies; for example, the Local Authorities Management Services and Computer Committee (LAMSAC) and the Local Government Operational Research Unit (LGORU). In commissioning studies in any particular field the Audit Inspectorate has been careful to ensure that no other body has work in hand which might be useful to auditors. Also, in arranging its own studies it has chosen subjects likely to be of greatest use to the audit function.

During 1978 and 1980 experiments were made in producing study reports on various local government activities and these are reported in my annual reports for these years. Several methods were employed for assembling information on which to base reports. For example, one on incentive bonusing was prepared by a district auditor, expert in this area of work, on the basis of evidence produced during the course of normal audits. Another on contract auditing was produced on the experience in one audit district. Several others (for example, reviews of computer audit, internal audit and management services) were based largely on questionnaires issued by the Audit Inspectorate. Others (for example, on polytechnic financing and targetting) were carried out by Audit Inspectorate staff.

In all these studies there emerged a common pattern. Most of the work was carried out by audit field staff in cooperation with appropriate local government officers. Certain studies (for example, that on polytechnics) impinged on, and called into question, central government policies. Above all else, the directing and coordinating role of the Inspectorate was found to be vital.

The problem at this time was that the studies made excessive demands on audit field staff and there was little hope of expanding the study programme without extra resources. Fortunately, money became available to engage staff on a contract basis. The Audit Inspectorate was then faced with a number of choices. It could set up multidisciplinary teams in the manner of the United States'

General Accounting Office. It might also establish for each study an advisory committee of appropriate professionals on the pattern set by the Canadian Auditor General.

It was decided to adopt formally neither of these arrangements, though the work pattern which finally emerged had recognisable similarities. The reasoning leading to this decision was based on the strong tradition of cooperation and participation by local government officers in the audit function. Since the objective of the studies was to promote change, and such change could be made only with the active participation of the local government, it seemed inevitable that we should seek to draw them into the studies. We were likely to have adequate experience of how things were done from district audit staff, and professional advice from local government officers in the field and, hopefully, relevant professional bodies. What appeared to be required from the outside were people with wide experience of management and organisational structures, especially in the private sector, to supplement existing public sector knowledge. Such people were likely to be found in firms of management consultants. Accordingly, major consultancy firms were circulated with specifications of proposed studies on which they were asked to comment and to suggest members of their staff who might be suitable for the work involved. Interviews followed and appointments were made on a judgement of the person most likely to contribute to the study, particularly with regard to a capacity to innovate and work with people in complex situations.

Simultaneously with this process, for each study a search for a cross-section of authorities was carried out. In each case the local district auditor consulted the appropriate local government officers, and the chief executive sought staff cooperation. Professional officers with particular interest in the study area were consulted informally and, more formally, the professional bodies concerned were invited to participate.

With the passage of time, a somewhat more formal structure began to emerge. The various local authorities' associations were consulted on the programme of work and much advice has tended to be channelled through them. Special mention should be made of the TUC's Local Government Committee which has been kept in the picture and which helped to create a positive attitude among trade unions to the various studies. Central government has also provided inputs.

Reports in draft are circulated to interested parties and the final version published. Sometimes the report is sufficient to assist auditors in their work, but often the issues are complicated so audit guidelines are produced. In some areas of work the guidelines have proved insufficient and some briefing and training of auditors has proved to be necessary. The full use of the studies has been hampered by lack of resources.

At the commencement of this work it was necessary to overcome local government's fears that the studies would degenerate into mere league tables of costs without regard to quality of service or local discretion. Of course, cost differences in themselves are fairly meaningless without explanation of the various reasons for them. Perhaps the most heartening feature of the whole exercise has been the virtual disappearance of this fear and the use made by local government officers of the various reports which have been produced.

In addition to the centrally controlled studies, several local studies at particular local authorities have been carried out under the direction of district auditors. The procedures adopted to appoint specialist assistance are similar to those for central studies. However, there has been a tendency to choose people with directly relevant qualifications and/or experience, no doubt because problems at a single authority can be more clearly delineated and the appropriate problem solver identified. A selection of such studies is listed in Annex A.

Example — Social Services   It may be helpful to look in some detail at one of the studies and to consider its genesis and the methods employed. For some time the Audit Inspectorate had been urged by professionals working in the social services field to make audit more relevant. After informal discussions it was decided to cover four aspects of the social services departments:

(1) the care of children;
(2) the care of the elderly;
(3) the care of the mentally handicapped, and;
(4) administration.

The first study undertaken was on the care of children and this will be described as an example of how work is undertaken. First, the costs of the various child care authorities were examined. There was a wide range of cost depending on the method chosen to care for children. For example, the direct cost of fostering children amounted to about £25 per week while the highest cost of keeping a child in a home (in a Community Home with Education) was £175 per week. The way in which authorities cared for children varied widely:

(1) fostering ranged from 20% to 60%;
(2) residential care ranged from 10% to 65%;
(3) children placed home on trial ranged from 5% to 50%.

Obviously the mix in the ways in which children are cared for affects the overall cost of the service.

After the initial review, eight authorities were selected for detailed examination. It must be emphasised that they were not a representative sample, but were selected to reveal the effects of different patterns of child care with particular regard to:

(1) the average cost per child week in care;
(2) the proportion of child population in care;
(3) the extent to which fostering was utilised.

There was no attempt to come to conclusions on the relative merits of the various methods of child care, which were regarded as a matter for judgement by appropriate professionals. Nevertheless, an analysis of data did appear to offer firm evidence that fostering gave rise to no more child breakdowns than did the use of residential homes. The general conclusions of the study were that there was scope for increasing fostering, but that there was also a need to plan and invest in appropriate staff to carry through a successful programme and save money. Further, adoption again merits investment which would produce savings. Observation and assessment centres and community homes with education were expensive and often not properly used, and some authorities had sought and found savings using alternative methods.

The foregoing summary does scant justice to a carefully constructed report, but it is sufficient to enable us to discuss certain questions about the role of the auditor. At its most basic the report is suggesting cheaper ways of looking after children. In other words, it is looking to economy and the efficient use of resources, and this relates back directly to the budget process in which councillors and officers are involved. Yet, it actually goes further in its analysis by putting forward the view that if changes were made in the care of children that were economical and efficient, the arrangements would be no less effective. Indeed, in the view of a majority of professional officers engaged in child care, the cost-effective ways of care, adoption and fostering, are more generally effective in caring for children. Such views may be incapable of being supported on the basis of measurement, but are founded instead on the observations of very experienced officers. Whether it is worthwhile to pursue the possibility of measuring effectiveness seems very doubtful. In the USA there has been a good deal of effort put into 'programme evaluation' but, as might be expected, there seem to be severe difficulties in evaluating anything other than the simplest of operations.

Although the use of definitions for the components of value for money — economy, efficiency and effectiveness — helps to promote thought and understanding of matters under analysis, it is suggested that, for practical consideration, we are faced with a direct question: 'is there a better way?' This comprises a review of all aspects of the matter subject to investigation: looking at what is done at this place, is the same thing being done elsewhere with the same or better results, is it cheaper, or in the view of a majority of professionals, better? We thus challenge policy through the effects of policy, that is 'bottom up'. However, to challenge policy is not to change it. Political values, however hazily perceived at the budget stage, pervade considerations. Analysis may show a certain course of action to be better than the existing line, but, in a complex and democratically based society, it may not be politically possible to promote change. Therefore, in such an environment, all the auditor (or the officer or manager) can do is to provide analysis and attempt to persuade. What is abundantly clear from the child care study is that change requires an investment of additional resources and savings and cannot be achieved quickly. Other studies are listed in Annex B.

The Future

The developments outlined in this chapter received statutory recognition in the Local Government Finance Act 1982 which provided for the establishment of an Audit Commission to

supervise local government external auditing. Possibly three of the
things required of the auditor merit comment:

(1) to give an opinion on the accounts. As mentioned earlier, this arises
directly from the interaction of private and public sector auditors;
(2) to satisfy himself that the body under audit has made proper arrangements for securing economy, efficiency and effectiveness in the use of
its resources. Although legislation in these terms is to be found in
other countries, the provision in the 1982 Act is based on
developments in the structured form of audit;
(3) to carry out audits in accordance with a code of audit practice which
is to be prepared by the Commission to 'embody what appears to the
Commission to be best professional practice with respect to
standards, procedures and techniques to be adopted by auditors'.
The report on draft standards mentioned earlier will provide a useful
starting point for the code.

The Commission has powers to support the field force with
the findings of comparative or across-the-board studies. An
interesting additional power given to the Commission enables it
to study the effects on local government of central government
policies and to supply reports to the Comptroller and Auditor
General. This provision arose from the efforts of those who favour a
national audit office under the aegis of Parliament and may be seen
as an interesting increase in the accountability of central government. Attention was drawn earlier in this chapter to the findings of
studies providing material which calls into question central government policies.

The Audit Commission also has the power to carry out audits
with either directly employed or contract staff or a mixture of both.
This will allow it to break away from the existing statutory mould of
district or approved audit and to use resources imaginatively.
However, local government audit will need more resources if it is to
develop further and garner fruits from the new establishment. At the
same time the Audit Commission will need to ensure that its audit
organisation retains cohesion, for it is this property which
strengthens the impact of the auditor in the field where his main
influence is required. The experience gained in the past few years by
the Audit Inspectorate and public and private auditors should
stand the Audit Commission in good stead.

Annex A

District Audit Reviews Using Other Professional Disciplines (Usually from Private Sector)

(1) Contract procedures — architect's department
(2) Contract works   — extensions to further education college
                         — modernisation
                         — conference centres
                         — shopping centre
(3) Computers   — management
                         — procedures
(4) Incentive bonus schemes
(5) Homes for elderly   — comparative review
(6) Highway stores   — organisation
(7) Housing repairs and maintenance — controls
(8) Management services
(9) Management review
(10) Payment procedures
(11) Planning and technical department
(12) Purchasing
(13) Supplies department
(14) Transport

Annex B

Comparative Studies by the Audit Inspectorate

(1) Borrowing — factors involved in the costs of borrowing.
(2) Conracts–review of pre- and post-contract procedures used for building works.
(3) Conveyancing — review of cost of alternative methods.
(4) Direct labour — review of building maintenance organisation and procedures.
(5) Further Education Colleges — staffing arrangements.
(6) Highways — the factors contributing to variations in maintenance costs.
(7) Housing–the factors contributing to variations in supervision of management costs.

(8) Leisure and sports centres — review of financing methods, management and charging policies.

(9) Police — review of use of civilians and overtime working.

(10) Polytechnics — review of factors contributing to variation in costs of financial systems following the issue by the Chartered Institute of Public Finance and Accountancy of a manual of guidance on 'Financial information systems for institutes of higher and further education in the maintained sector'.

(11) School meals — review of variations in ways of providing the service.

(12) Social services — (described in text).

(13) Town and country planning — scope and method of development control.

(14) Superannuation — management and investment performance.

References

Jones, R. (1981) *Local Government Audit Law*, HMSO.

Audit Commission (1983a) *Code of Local Government Audit Practice for England and Wales*.

Audit Commission (1983b) *Improving Economy, Efficiency and Effectiveness in Local Government in England and Wales*.

CIPFA (1982a) *Standards for the External Audit of Local Authorities and Other Public Bodies Subject to Audit Under Part III of the Local Government Finance Act, 1982*.

CIPFA (1982b) *Local Government Value for Money Handbook*.

Efficiency and Management Exercises: Series with restricted circulation 1970–1982: see index of most useful studies in CIPFA's *Local Government Value for Money Handbook* (1982).

Local Government Audit Service (Audit Inspectorate), Reports of the Chief Inspector of Audit for the years ended 31 March, 1978, 1979, 1980, 1981 and 1982.